# Wisconsin

Tracy Will
Photography by Zane Williams

COMPASS AMERICAN GUIDES
An Imprint of Fodor's Travel Publications, Inc.

## Wisconsin

Copyright © 1994 Fodor's Travel Publications, Inc.
Maps Copyright © 1994 Fodor's Travel Publications, Inc.

Library of Congress Cataloging-In-Publication Data
Will, Tracy 1954
Wisconsin/Tracy Will: photography by Zane Williams.
p. cm. —(Compass American Guides)
Includes bibliographical references and index
ISBN 1-878867-45-8 (hard) $24.95; ISBN 1-878867-44-X (paper) $16.95
1. Wisconsin—Guidebooks. I. Title II. Series: Compass American Guides (Series)
F579.3.W54 1994          93-50598
917.7504'43—dc20          CIP

Editors: Barry Parr, Kit Duane, Jessica Fisher          Designers: Christopher Burt, David Hurst
Managing Editor: Kit Duane          Map Design: Eureka Cartography
Photo Editor: Christopher Burt
Compass American Guides, Inc., 6051 Margarido Drive, Oakland, CA 94618
Production House: Twin Age Ltd., Hong Kong          Printed in China
10 9 8 7 6 5 4 3 2 1

The Publisher gratefully acknowledges the following institutions and individuals for the use of their photographs and/or illustrations on the following pages: **Mike Long**, pp. 244; **Jerry Stebbins**, pp. 86, 90, 252, 257; **Medford Taylor**, p. 256; Ashland Historical Society, pp. 258, 259; Chippewa Valley Museum, Eau Claire, p. 158; Collection of Dom DiMento, Oakland, p. 70; Fort Atkinson Historical Society, p. 109; Harley-Davidson Co., Milwaukee, p. 143; Marathon County Historical Museum, p. 266; Marquette University Archives, pp. 24, 28, 30; Milwaukee Public Museum, p. 227; Murphy Library, U. Wisconsin, La Crosse, p. 5; North Wood County Historical Society, Marshfield, p. 219; Oshkosh Public Museum, pp. 31, 76; Outagamie County Historical Society, p. 77; Sheboygan County Historical Research Center, pp. 92, 96, 97, 98, 99; State Historical Society of Wisconsin, pp. 15, 19, 22, 34-35, 39, 40, 43, 51, 55, 74, 80, 116, 152, 154, 162, 164, 174, 183, 187, 212, 223, 242, 243, 260; Underwood Photo Archives, pp. 129, 149; Usinger's, Millwaukee, p. 140; Watertown Historical Society, pp. 112, 115. Many thanks to reader Michael Derr; and artist /typesetter Candace Compton-Pappas.

*To Dap and Connie.*

## ACKNOWLEDGMENTS

This book would not have been possible without the help of my wonderful wife, Gay, who rode shotgun and took notes, and my two boys, Roland and Glenn. I changed the boys' diapers and popped in Glenn's pacifier over 14,000 miles of Wisconsin highways. Many thanks are due to my editors Barry Parr and Kit Duane and to Chris Burt for his unyielding love of Wisconsin. The folks at the State Historical Society Iconographic Collection and Archives provided vital assistance for which I owe them at least one beer. I apologize for being unable to pack all of Wisconsin into this book, and I guarantee any traveler will find something I missed in places unmentioned, and both the locals and travelers will be the better for it.

# C O N T E N T S

## Literary Extracts

## Topical Essays

# Maps

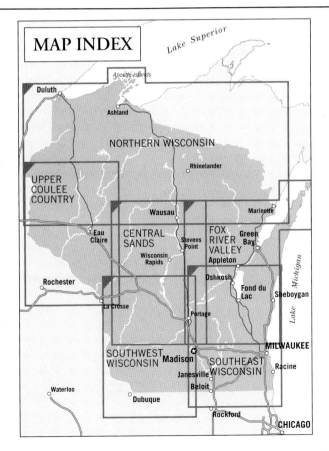

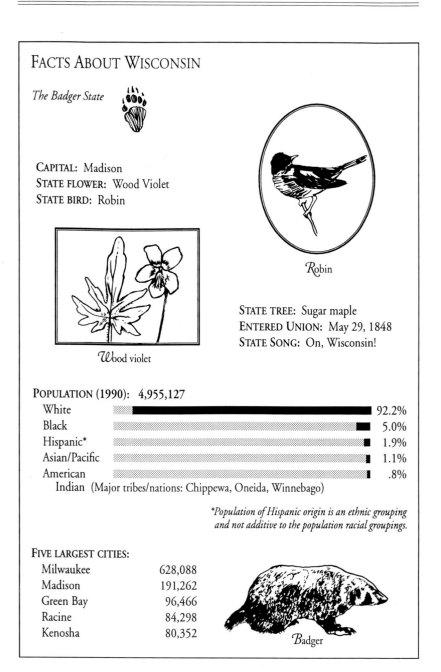

# FACTS ABOUT WISCONSIN

*The Badger State*

**CAPITAL:** Madison
**STATE FLOWER:** Wood Violet
**STATE BIRD:** Robin

*R*obin

**STATE TREE:** Sugar maple
**ENTERED UNION:** May 29, 1848
**STATE SONG:** On, Wisconsin!

*W*ood violet

**POPULATION (1990):** 4,955,127

| | |
|---|---|
| White | 92.2% |
| Black | 5.0% |
| Hispanic* | 1.9% |
| Asian/Pacific | 1.1% |
| American Indian | .8% |

American Indian (Major tribes/nations: Chippewa, Oneida, Winnebago)

*\*Population of Hispanic origin is an ethnic grouping and not additive to the population racial groupings.*

**FIVE LARGEST CITIES:**

| | |
|---|---|
| Milwaukee | 628,088 |
| Madison | 191,262 |
| Green Bay | 96,466 |
| Racine | 84,298 |
| Kenosha | 80,352 |

*B*adger

*S*ugar maple

**ECONOMY:**
Principal industries:
manufacturing, trade, agriculture, tourism
Principal manufactured goods:
machinery, foods, fabricated metals, transportation equipment, paper and wood products
Per capita income: $18,046

**GEOGRAPHY:**
Size: 65,503 sq. miles (169,653 sq. km)
Highest point: 1,951 feet (591 m) Timms Hill, Price County
Lowest point: 579 feet (175 m) Lake Michigan

**CLIMATE:**
Highest temperature recorded: 114°F (45°C) at Wisconsin Dells on July 13, 1936
Lowest temperature recorded: -54°F (-48°C) at Danbury on Jan. 24, 1922

Wettest place:
42.45" annual rainfall at P. K. Reservoir in Sawyer County

Driest place:
25.87" annual rainfall at Plum Island in Door County

**FAMOUS WISCONSINITES:**
Edna Ferber ◆ Harry Houdini ◆ Robert La Follette ◆ Orson Welles
Georgia O'Keeffe ◆ Spencer Tracy ◆ Hamlin Garland
Thornton Wilder ◆ Frank Lloyd Wright ◆ Sen. Joseph McCarthy

# H  I  S  T  O  R  Y

WISCONSIN BEGAN ABOUT ONE AND A HALF BILLION years ago, give or take a few hundred millennia, when cataclysmic pressures injected a thick lode of magma into the earth's crust. Cooling slowly, this lode became red granite flecked with black mica and quartz brilliants spread over thousands of square miles. Basalt intrusions rimmed its margins and quartzite mountains rose above this primordial land mass. Later, a shallow sea covered the landscape, building up layer upon layer of sand and shell. These in turn formed calcium-rich sediments laden with microscopic diatoms, sea anemones and jellyfish, flowery undersea chrinoids, scuttling trilobites, seven-foot-long swimming tusks called endoceri, great undersea reefs of coral, and whiskered ammonites. Eventually, these sediments solidified into limestone. Magma oozed up through crevasses and cracks, leaving mineral deposits that became hidden treasure in modern times. As the Mid-Atlantic rift spread, separating the North American and European plates, it slowly shifted Wisconsin to its present location, raising a towering mountain range in the north, and draining the Devonian seas.

## ■ ICE AGES

Wisconsin's present landscape owes much of its substance and beauty to the erosive power of flowing and frozen water. Beginning about one million years ago, glaciers hundreds of feet high swept over most of Wisconsin four different times, cracking and splitting the granite bedrock by sheer weight of ice, grinding down the mountains, scraping away the sedimentary layers, piling hills, and carving enormous depressions in the land. The deepest depressions filled with water and became the Great Lakes. The sedimentary sandstone, dolomite, and limestone layers from northern and eastern Wisconsin were pushed south, forming the moraines that mark the glacier's final reach.

Most of Canada and the northern United States lay beneath the icy floes, and four lobes of ice covered most of Wisconsin; but one part of the state stayed free of glaciers. This so-called Driftless area lies along the west and southwest section of Wisconsin.

Two thousand years after reaching their farthest extent, the glaciers melted and retreated north at a rate of about 1,000 feet (305 m) per year, leaving a changed land. Roughly 11,000 years ago, drumlins—large piles of sand and gravel—rose above an ice-scrubbed landscape. Eskers traced the sandy track of rivers that cut beneath the ice. The north was littered with granite gravels and lakes gouged into granite bedrock. Enormous glacial erratics—chunks of granite carried hundreds of miles from their places of origin—were left sitting incongruously and rather mysteriously atop small, rounded hills. Meltwater sculpted whimsical shapes in sandstone at the Wisconsin Dells and cut a deep groove to form the bluff-lined Mississippi Valley. In the Central Sands, towers of sandstone were cut by torrents of water from melting glaciers.

Plant and animal species that had survived in the Driftless area of southwestern Wisconsin began streaming into these pristine, fresh-scraped landscapes. Birds, mammals, insects, fish, reptiles, and amphibians gradually invaded the marshes, sloughs, creeks, streams, rivers, and lakes. Soon the landscape would receive its first human visitors.

## ■ ANCIENT INDIAN CULTURES

When the glaciers had melted away, the hills and dells of the Driftless area became a home and hunting ground for nomads. Their Stone-Age sophistication is astounding—exquisite stone implements, bone tools, and animal skins adorned with appliqué and sewn with sinew attest to their knowledge and demonstrate a mastery over a raw and evolving world. The earliest hunters used spears and bolos, but later groups used an atlatl, a throwing stick, to hurl stone-tipped spears at the mammoths, camels, giant beavers, and rhinoceroses.

These early nomads described their activities and recorded their beliefs in carved rock and cave paintings. More than 50 sites in Wisconsin have been discovered, depicting animals and armed hunters with spears and, later, with bow and arrow. These ancient graphics have been eroded by water, lichens, and vandalism, but most are protected by archaeologists, who study them for rare insights into a Stone-Age culture. No one yet knows for sure whether these early hunters are the direct ancestors of the native peoples who have lived in Wisconsin during the past 5,000 years—or whether they followed the big game out of Wisconsin, never to return.

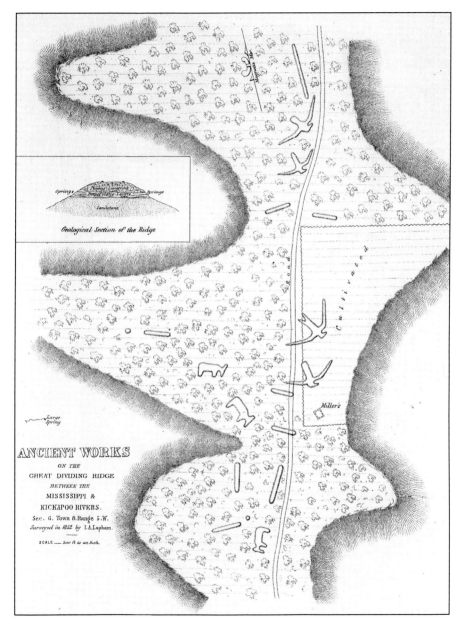

*Indian burial mounds are sprinkled all across southern Wisconsin and were often formed in the shape of animals—such as these surveyed by Increase Lapham in 1832. (State Historical Society of Wisconsin)*

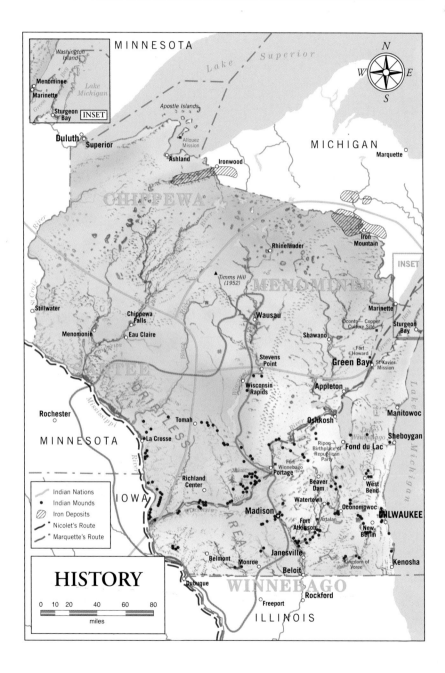

# HISTORY

| | Indian Nations |
|---|---|
| • | Indian Mounds |
| ⊘ | Iron Deposits |
| ╱ | Nicolet's Route |
| ═ | Marquette's Route |

0  10  20    40    60    80

miles

■ COPPER CULTURE AND MOUND BUILDERS

About 5,000 years ago, the best we can tell, a migratory people who fired clay pots, hunted, and practiced agriculture settled in Wisconsin. They built mounds of earth, mined, traded, and worked copper to make utensils. Wisconsin copper objects even found their way to Mexico, suggesting that an extensive trading network reached across North America, no doubt facilitated by extensive water travel throughout the Mississippi and Ohio valleys, and the Great Lakes.

After the copper culture waned, another culture, even more extraordinary, settled widely in Wisconsin. These Mound Builders, or Woodland People, were active in Wisconsin for about a thousand years. They constructed nearly 15,000 mounds in linear, conical, and round shapes, as well as effigies shaped like panthers, turtles, birds, snakes, buffalo, and even an enormous human form. Many of the effigies stretch for hundreds of feet. Round mounds served as burial sites for clan members; but the specific function of most mounds remains a mystery. Turtle and bird effigies may have served as ceremonial icons representing the clans or the objects of the hunt. Or, they may have served an astronomical purpose, perhaps predicting the seasons that govern agriculture, hunting, and fishing.

*Petroglyphs of unknown origin found among the sandstone bluffs of Wisconsin's Driftless area in the southwestern quarter of the state.*

When the French asked the Winnebago about the mounds, they were described as ancient and mysterious, predating the memory of the tribe, but the Winnebago also used and maintained the mounds for ceremonial purposes into the modern historical period.

Although many were plowed under or destroyed to make way for development, effigy mounds are still found at many sites in western, southern, central, and eastern Wisconsin: Indian Mounds park in Rice Lake, Barron County; the Copper Age site near Oconto, north of Green Bay; in the Milwaukee, Menominee, and Fox (Pishtaka) river valleys; in Madison and around adjacent lakes; and in the Rock River, Wisconsin, and Mississippi valleys. The most recently built mounds overlook northeastern Lake Winnebago at High Cliff State Park.

## ■ THE ONEOTA

The mound-building culture appears to have wound down about A.D. 1000, and no more mounds were built. Instead, gardens began to appear. Recent discoveries of garden plots and bits of pottery have helped us to distinguish another culture, falling between the Woodland Mound Builders and modern tribes, which we call the Oneota. No one can say whether their culture grew from the Woodland People or if they are the ancestors of Wisconsin's modern tribes—though their gardening methods appear to have been adopted by the Winnebago.

Oneota gardens were filled with exotic new vegetables like pumpkins, squash, corn, and beans. These were dried and saved for winter to augment stockpiles of berries, gathered fruits, and nuts that had previously supplemented the traditional diet of the Mound Builders. A stable food supply meant that groups of people could cease their nomadic wandering.

Little is known of the short-lived Oneota culture. Its surprising sophistication is only now being rediscovered, and promises many extraordinary revelations. At one site in Iowa County, the life-size effigy of a natural-looking human head was found near one of their gardens. Such realistic depictions of the human figure are rare in Native American culture and art.

## ■ MISSISSIPPIAN COLONY

About the same time as the Oneota culture appeared, a surprising group of immigrants established a village on the Crawfish River, which feeds the Rock River. The mysterious village of Aztalan, east of Lake Mills, was surrounded with a stockade of timbers covered with clay "brick." Two pyramids, built of clay and fill, dominate the riverbank, their construction intriguingly different from the earth effigies of the Mound Builders. Inside the stockade were gardens for corn and storage caches.

Aztalan was a trading village of Mississippian Indians, an outpost of the Cahokia mound culture of Southern Illinois, where the largest pyramids in North America outside of Mexico were built about 600 to 800 years ago. The Aztalan settlement lasted for about 200 years, and then was burned and abandoned—no one knows why.

# ■ MODERN INDIAN TRIBES

## ■ WINNEBAGO

The traditional domain of the Winnebago, or Hochungara, stretched from La Crosse to Green Bay, down the Fox River Valley to the highlands of southwestern Wisconsin. Before the arrival of the Europeans, the largest Winnebago villages were on Doty Island in the Fox River at Lake Winnebago, on the plains of La Crosse, in the Wisconsin Dells, at Madison, and at Lake Koshkonong. Like their Sioux cousins, who once lived in the woods of northwestern and western Wisconsin, the Winnebago speak a Siouan dialect.

*Winnebago mothers and babies photographed at Tomah, ca. 1910.*
*(State Historical Society of Wisconsin)*

The Winnebago fished with weirs and spears at their *ocooches* (fishing areas) in the rivers and streams of southern Wisconsin. They also practiced agriculture, planting gardens of corn, squash, beans, and pumpkins. Their diet was supplemented by berries, nuts, wild rice, meat, fish, and mushrooms that were dried and stored for winter use. Their basketry and other weaving skills were accomplished.

The Winnebago mined lead crystals from the hills of the Driftless area, and formed them into effigies for talismans and trade. To their neighbors, the Winnebago were known as the "People of the Stinking Water," probably because their summer fishing camps were ripe with the decay of scraps from their abundant catches of fish. When the French heard this, they thought that "stinking water" might refer to the ocean. Inspired, they traveled eagerly out to meet the Winnebago, hoping through them to find the Northwest Passage to Asia.

■ M E N O M I N E E

The Menominee were a woodland tribe of the upper peninsula of Michigan and parts of northeastern Wisconsin, where they had lived perhaps for several hundred

*Village of Folle-Avoines of the Menominee Indians, near Green Bay, as it appeared to an early French expedition. (State Historical Society of Wisconsin)*

*(previous pages) Aztalan Indian Mounds State Park.*

years. Their name comes from the word *mahnomin,* which means "wild rice," an allusion to their reliance on gathered wetland rice. The Menominee speak an Algonquian language, like the Chippewa, who adopted many of their customs and artistic design styles.

The Menominee were among the first tribes to meet the French as they traveled from their outpost at Sault Ste. Marie down Green Bay to the mouth of the Fox River. They maintained good relations with the Jesuit missionaries, and some converted to Christianity. Following negotiations with Territorial Governor Henry Dodge in 1836, the Menominee agreed to cede their lands between Lakes Michigan and Winnebago to settlers from the east, though they retained their land along the Wolf River—today one of the most prosperous reservations in the country. Because they managed their forest and never clear-cut their land, it is as productive and diverse as it is beautiful.

## ■ SIOUX (DAKOTA)

Although the Sioux are best known as the horseback-riding nomads of the northern Great Plains, the eastern part of the tribe lived for many centuries in the North Woods and upper Mississippi Valley of Wisconsin. The Santee (or eastern Dakota) hunted, gathered, and fished in the same lakes, rivers, and marshes that later were occupied by the Chippewa.

The arrival of the Chippewa, driven by their prophetic manifest destiny, meant an end to the North Woods paradise enjoyed by the Wisconsin Dakota. The Chippewa fought with the Dakota for years over wild-rice-growing areas in western and northern Wisconsin on which the Sioux depended. The two tribes took scalps and attacked each others' hunting parties, but eventually the Sioux were forced to leave their traditional lands; when the French introduced the Chippewa to the fur trade, it accelerated the rout. The Chippewa called the Dakota the "Naudowasewug," which the French rendered into Nadowessioux, or Sioux, a term that meant "like snakes" or "enemies."

The Sioux at first found refuge in the dense woods of the western coulee region, but were pushed off to Minnesota after another conflict with the Chippewa. The last Dakota camps in Wisconsin—situated along the Mississippi between the St. Croix and the Black rivers—were ceded to federal authorities at Washington in 1837, when the Sioux agreed to move west of the Mississippi.

In Minnesota, they again fought the Chippewa along the margins of the woods and prairie. Becoming increasingly intolerant of the steady influx of settlers, they massacred many of the Scandinavian and German farmers who had pushed into southwest Minnesota in the Minnesota Uprising of the 1860s, at New Ulm, Minnesota. The European refugees straggled to Eau Claire, Wisconsin, but returned soon after American troops settled the uprising in summary fashion.

## ■ CHIPPEWA

The Chippewa (or Ojibwa) first arrived in Wisconsin at Madeline Island in Lake Superior about 600 years ago. Originally, they lived on the Atlantic coast and shoreline forests of Maine, New Brunswick, and Nova Scotia. According to Ojibwa origin legends, seven prophets came out of the sea and told them they should journey upriver, away from the midden heaps of oyster, clam, and mussel shells piled over the generations, and search for Mahnomin, "The Place Where Food Grows On Water." Whether their legends are based on spirit visions or from contact with stray European fishermen—Portuguese, Irish, and Norse who had wandered ashore after fishing the Grand Banks—the Ojibwa packed up and headed upriver.

*Chippewa making maple sugar at the turn of the century.*
*(Marquette University Archives, Milwaukee)*

For more than four hundred years, the Chippewa people fought their way up to the Wisconsin headwaters of the St. Lawrence, emerging at the end of their travels as a full-fledged woodland culture, skilled in fishing, hunting, canoe-building, and quillwork. The Chippewa are famous for the design of their sewn and puckered moccasins, adorned with elaborately dyed porcupine quill emblems.

The Chippewa were most populous along the northern reaches of the Great Lakes, especially of Lake Huron, Georgian Bay, and Lake Superior. It is thought that they first headed south across Superior to the Apostle Islands, where they found marshes filled with wild rice—the food that grows on water. This fulfillment of their legendary quest proved too potent for even the Sioux to halt their forward advance. The war that followed drove the Sioux from their traditional range in the North Woods.

Bands of Chippewa lived in the Apostle Islands for a few hundred years, then abandoned the islands for the lakes, woods, and rivers of northern Wisconsin, where hunting, gathering, and wild rice were abundant.

■ THE FOX

The French called them "les Renards," the English, "the Fox"; to the Menominee they were the Outagami, "people who live on the other shore." The Fox came into Wisconsin from lower Michigan, an aggressive, clever tribe who carried their totem, the hawk, into battle. Considered arrogant, quarrelsome, and brash by those who first met them, the Fox refused to submit to any white man. Determined to follow their own way of life, they continually tried to disrupt the French fur trade in order to drive white settlers from the Fox Valley.

■ FRENCH ARRIVE

Exploration of the lower St. Lawrence River Valley by French sailor Jacques Cartier (and others) began in 1535. In 1608, Samuel de Champlain (1567–1635) built a fur trading post at what is now Quebec City, and officially claimed Quebec for France. Having established a permanent settlement at Montreal in 1642, the French were better situated than Britain, the other great European power in northeast America, to explore and exploit the vast Great Lakes region. On its way to Montreal, the St. Lawrence River drains all five of the Great Lakes —Superior, Michigan, Huron, Ontario and Erie—as well as a vast, forested hinterland of lesser lakes and rivers, including northern and eastern Wisconsin.

## VOYAGES OF PIERRE

*Pierre Esprit Radisson (1636–1710) was one of the first French explorers to make his way along the southern shoreline of Lake Superior. The tribes he encountered in Wisconsin were most likely Chippewa (then at war with the Sioux). Radisson visited the Apostle Islands and the mouths of the Montreal, Bad, and Brule Rivers before portaging across northern Wisconsin to the St. Croix River. Radisson writes in his journal about the narrows between Lake Huron and Lake Superior near what is today the city of Sault Ste. Marie, and later he makes reference to what is probably Devil's Lake in southwest Wisconsin.*

We come to the rapid that makes a separation of the lake of the Hurrons, that we calle Superior, or upper, for that the wildmen hold it to be longer and broader and befits a great many islands, which makes [it] appear in a bigge extent. This rapid was formerly the dwelling of those with whom we were with, and consequently we must not ask them if they knew where we laid. We made cottages at our advantages and found the truth of what those men had often [said], that if once we could come to that place we should make a good share of the fish they call the Assickmack, which means whitefish. The bear, the beaver, and the deer showed themselves to us often, but to their cost; indeed it was to us like a terrestrial paradise. After so long [a period of] fasting, after such great pains we had taken, [we] find ourselves so well to choose our diet, and resting when we had a mind to, it is here we must taste with pleasure a sweet bite. We do not ask for a good sauce, it is better to have it naturally; it is the way to distinguish the sweet from the bitter. . . .

❖ ❖ ❖

Some days after, we observed that there were some boats before us, but were uncertain who they were. We made haste to overtake them fearing the enemy no more. Indeed the faster we could go the better for us, because of the season of the year, that began to be cold and freeze. They were [from] a nation that lived in a land towards the South. This nation is very small, being not 100 in all, men and women together. As we came nearer them they were surprised at our safe return, and astonished to see us, admiring the merchandise that their confederates brought, the hatchets and knives and other utensils were very commodious, rare, precious, and necessary in those countries. They told us the news one to another while we made good cheer and great fires. Some days after we separated ourselves and presented gifts to those that were going another way, for we received a great store of meat which was put up in barrels, and grease of bears, and deer.

After this we came to a remarkable place. It's the bank of rocks that the wild men made a sacrifice to: they call it Nanitouckfinagoit, which means the likeness of the devil. They fling much tobacco at it and things in veneration. It is a thing most incredible that the lake should be so boisterous, that the waves should have the strength to do what I say in my discourse: first, that it's so high and deep that it is impossible to climb up to the point. . . .

—Pierre Esprit Radisson, *The Voyages of Pierre Esprit Radisson*,
describing events in the mid-1600s; published 1885.

Despite such difficulties as Niagara Falls, the river was a conspicuous highway right to the heart of the watery wilderness. The primary interest of the French in the region was fur, principally beaver, which enjoyed a great market in the courts of Europe. The French formed alliances with the Great Lakes Indian tribes, partly to supply the fur trade, and partly as a political counter-balance to the British and their allies, the tribes of the Iroquois confederation, who controlled much of the land south of the St. Lawrence and around the lower Great Lakes.

The first of the French to arrive in Wisconsin may have been Etienne Brulé (ca. 1592–1633), a fearless young lieutenant of Samuel de Champlain, commandant of New France. Brulé lived for many years among the Huron, and discovered a northern route to the west end of the Great Lakes that ran up the Ottawa River (which joins the St. Lawrence at Montreal) to Lake Nipissing, and west to Georgian Bay on Lake Huron. There, in the vast territory bordering the three northernmost Great Lakes, the French could search for hunting grounds and conduct their affairs with friendly tribes like the Huron and Chippewa. Brulé may have walked on the shores of Wisconsin in 1621 on his extensive tour of Lake Superior.

By disposition, he favored the native ways of his adopted Huron, not the French settlers of New France. Brulé joined the British in a conquest of Quebec in 1629, but returned to the Huron when the British withdrew in 1632. Three years later, his adopted Huron decided that the adventurous Frenchman was fit for only one thing, so they clubbed him to death and ate him.

It was with a related party of Huron that Jean Nicolet (1598–1642) arrived at Green Bay in 1634, a pistol in each hand and wearing Chinese silk robes. Having heard that the Winnebago tribe of that region were known as the People of the Stinking Water, Nicolet thought they might be the gatekeepers to the fabled Northwest Passage to Asia; hence, the Chinese costume. From his deathbed, Nicolet described the scene to an attendant priest, who recorded his words as follows:

They met him. They escorted him and carried all of his baggage. He wore a grand robe of China damask, all strewn with flowers and birds of many colors . . . the women and children fled at the sight of a man who carried thunder in both hands, for thus they called the two pistols that he held.

Nicolet and his group canoed up the Fox River to the rapids at Kaukauna, then walked to a flat island at the head of Lake Winnebago.

There assembled four or five thousand men. Each of the chiefs made a feast for him, and at one of these banquets, they served at least six score beavers.

When French explorer Jean Nicolet landed near Green Bay in 1634 he walked ashore in Chinese silk robes brandishing pistols in the mistaken belief that the Winnebago could show him a passage to Asia. (Marquette University Archives, Milwaukee)

The short dalliance between the French and the Winnebago was enough to seal the latter's fate. European diseases carried by Nicolet and company cut through the Winnebago like a sword, killing five of every six people. By the time the French returned, they were surprised by the lack of Indians in the Green Bay area, where thousands had lived before. In place of the Winnebago, the French found different tribes that seemed to have moved in from elsewhere, and who greeted the Europeans with suspicion.

The mid-seventeenth century brought more French explorers to Wisconsin. In 1656, Pierre Esprit Radisson (1636–1710) and his brother-in-law, Médard Chouart des Groseilliers (1625–1698), journeyed to the region on orders from Quebec. They made their second trip in 1659 without permission of the French governor, visiting the lands around Lake Superior. They canoed past the Apostle Islands and the great rock caves of Devil's Island, and made their way to the Lac Courte Oreilles (Lake Short Ears) camp of the Ottawa, where, surrounded by huts and birchbark canoes, "The women throw themselves backwards uppon the ground, thinking to give us tokens of friendship, and of wellcome." When they returned to Montreal in 1660, with a flotilla of Indian canoes loaded with furs, the French governor confiscated the furs and threw them both in jail for trading without a license. The pair defected to the British almost as soon as they were set loose from prison. Largely through the efforts of the brothers, the British established the Hudson's Bay Company in 1670, breaking the French monopoly on fur trade with the Great Lakes and Canadian Indian tribes.

Other French adventurers and Jesuit priests followed in the wilderness in quest of fur or souls. The first missionary in Wisconsin, Jesuit Father René Ménard, was traveling to visit an outpost of Huron Christians in 1660 when he stepped from a canoe so it could negotiate a patch of rapids on the Black River. Ménard was never found again, but his clothing was discovered years later among some religious artifacts in the possession of the Santee Sioux.

Jesuit Father Claude-Jean Allouez (1622–1689) fared better and, in 1665, founded a mission near the site of Radisson's fort, on Chequamegon Bay. From this outpost, Allouez explored and made contact and a few converts among the North Woods tribes. In 1669, he built the rustic mission of St. Francis Xavier above the mouth of the Fox River. This was the kernel of Wisconsin's first city, which the French called La Baye Verte; the site today is in the Green Bay suburb of De Pere.

Almost as an afterthought to the establishment of Green Bay, France officially claimed the Great Lakes hinterland, including Wisconsin, for New France in 1671. This greatly expanded New France, which already included the shores of the St. Lawrence River, Newfoundland, Acadia (Nova Scotia), and parts of the trans-Appalachian West.

The key to the heart of Wisconsin, and the interior of the continent, still lay undiscovered by the French. This was the Fox River portage, linking the Great Lakes (and ultimately Montreal) with the Mississippi Valley, also claimed by France. A mere mile of canoe portage separated the headwaters of the Fox River, flowing into Lake Michigan at Green Bay, from the Wisconsin River, which flows into the Mississippi.

Forty years after Nicolet arrived in Green Bay, Father Jacques Marquette (1637–1675) and Louis Jolliet (1645–1700) uncovered the secret of the Fox River portage for the *fleur de lis* of France. With the help of native guides, Marquette and Jolliet were the first Europeans to ascend the lower Fox rapids and pass the great Lake Winnebago in 1673. Picking their way through the wild rice marshes of the upper Fox River, they traversed the narrow portage and dropped their canoes into the Wisconsin River, floating from there down to the Mississippi, "the Father of Waters." To the French, this became an essential link between the St. Lawrence and the Mississippi, thus connecting the far-flung theaters of French colonial interests.

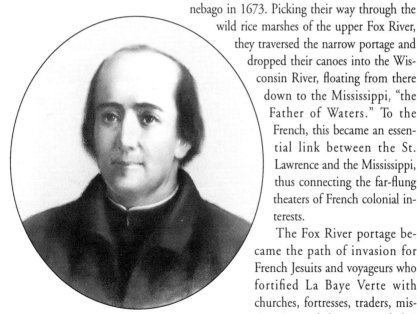

The Fox River portage became the path of invasion for French Jesuits and voyageurs who fortified La Baye Verte with churches, fortresses, traders, missionaries, and the *coureur de bois* ("wood rangers," or outlaw traders). A second permanent settlement

*Father Jacques Marquette discovered the Fox River portage linking the Great Lakes to the Mississippi River in 1673. (Marquette Univ. Archives, Milwaukee)*

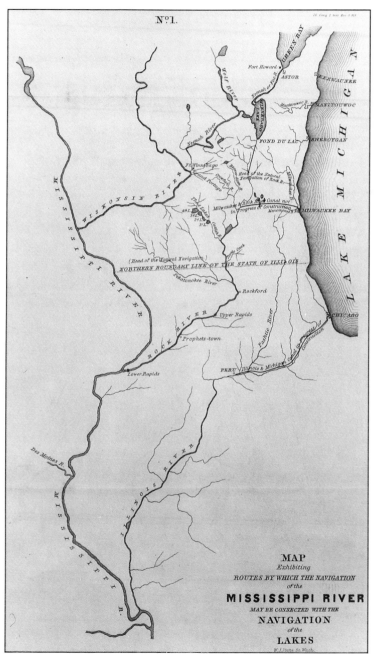

*The key to the rapid development of industry in Wisconsin and northern Illinois was the establishment of several canals and portages connecting the Great Lakes to the Mississippi River. (Oshkosh Public Museum)*

was built at Prairie du Chien, where the Wisconsin River meets the Mississippi, to protect the French kingdom of fur. Other river routes were explored and exploited —the Brule to the St. Croix, the Bad to the Chippewa, and the Montreal to the Flambeau.

Though popular legend touts the French as living in harmony with the natives, and often marrying into the tribes, the French exploited the Indians' hunting abilities, and played the tribes off against one another. They also brought disease, alcohol, and religion, which furthered the eventual fading of the traditional tribal cultures. Though wars and alliances were also a part of Native American heritage, French political ambitions, often violently at odds with British (and American) ambitions, forced the tribes into new alliances and exhausting new wars.

As the competition between the English and the French heated up, the tribes were forced to take sides, and the French used a confederation of Wisconsin tribes to fight the Iroquois. In a period of perceived French weakness, Fox tribes who controlled the upper Fox River Valley started charging tolls for passage over the Fox River. Complaints about the blockade filtered back to Montreal and a decision was made to break up the Fox control of the route. A military presence gradually crept into Green Bay. The French sent a boatload of armed soldiers upriver disguised as traders, to confront the Fox, who controlled the heights above the river. As a Fox and Sauk contingent walked down from their stockade to collect their tax, the French troops opened fire, ending the Fox stranglehold.

When the Indian allies of the French attacked a Fox camp (near what is now Detroit, Michigan) in 1710, retaliation against the French began. The Fox formed a loose confederation with other Wisconsin tribes; when that fell apart they sought to join with the Iroquois against the French, but were pursued by French forces south into what is now Illinois, and slaughtered. Though their chief surrendered, remnants continued to fight occasionally, until 1739, when (with French influence waning) both sides saw the mutual advantage of peace.

## ■ BRITISH INHERIT

One of the most remarkable residents of New France, a man often called the Father of Wisconsin, was Charles de Langlade (1729–ca 1801), of French/Ottawa stock. A seasoned warrior who fought in his first battle at the age of 10, he was a brilliant military tactician and inspiring leader of troops. His greatest triumphs, ironically, were in the war that brought the close of French influence in the New World.

In 1754, France, Britain, and their respective allies commenced a great war over their imperial holdings, primarily in North America. Known as the French and Indian War in the United States, the war lasted nine years, and was fought principally to determine which European civilization would control the North American hinterland, especially the Mississippi basin. Langlade was crucial in allying the Wisconsin tribes, who accompanied French troops in battle against the British, and he is personally credited with the devastating victory against British and American colonial troops in the Battle of Monongahela (Pennsylvania) in 1755, in which Gen. Edward Braddock was mortally wounded, and the British army spectacularly routed. Langlade and his troops triumphed repeatedly throughout much of the war, defeating Roger's Rangers on Lake Champlain and capturing Fort William Henry. However, Langlade met his match with General Wolfe at Quebec in 1759, when the British took the city, and French fortunes crumbled. Montreal fell in 1760, and Langlade and his troops retreated through Wisconsin to the Mississippi.

When the Treaty of Paris ended hostilities in 1763, Canada and all French holdings east of the Mississippi (including Wisconsin) were ceded to Britain by the French.

Langlade took up residence in Green Bay, though it should be noted that he couldn't resist a good fight when there was one to be had. He fought on the British side in the American Revolution.

As it turned out, the American Revolution precluded any strong British influence in Wisconsin. Though British forts remained in the region till after the War of 1812, and British fur traders continued to buy furs, the overriding British policy toward Wisconsin was to ignore it as "Indian country." The Fox Valley remained strongly French in character until far into the era of American dominance. For instance, the Grignon family, descendants of Charles de Langlade, controlled much of the fur trade during the later French and British eras from their base in Green Bay. During the American era, Charles Grignon built his family home in Kaukauna, near the Fox River—the first home built in Wisconsin of dimension lumber and machined trim molding, which he imported from Buffalo, New York. It has stood there since 1838.

*(following pages)* Braddock's Defeat *on July 9, 1755, as depicted by Edwin Willard Deming. Charles de Langlade, the Green Bay fur trapper on left, is directing the attack with Indians from Wisconsin and Michigan. Gen. Edward Braddock is just falling from his horse, the bridle of which is being caught by Maj. George Washington. (State Historical Society of Wisconsin)*

## ■ YANKEES IN WISCONSIN

When the Yankees took over the region, the Winnebago, Sauk, and Fox still reigned supreme, though not for long. Wisconsin was organized as Indiana Territory in 1800, and recast as part of Michigan Territory in 1818. The American government sent Indian agents to negotiate with them, backed up by the army, which established outposts at Green Bay, Prairie du Chien, and at the Fox River portage. A young army lieutenant named Jefferson Davis supervised construction of the latter, Fort Winnebago, which still stands on a small rise above the marshes east of Portage. The Indian Agency House at Portage served as the social center for the frontier, with John Harris Kinzie and his wife, Juliette, performing as the host and hostess with the mostest for the rough-and-tumble collection of traders, vagabonds, soldiers, and farmers who passed through on their way to push back the edges of the wilderness.

As with so many states of the Far West, the discovery of valuable minerals heralded a huge jump in immigration to Wisconsin. Instead of a gold rush or silver boom, however, the lure in Wisconsin was lead, a metal most useful for producing bullets and lead-based paint. As hunting was the way to survive in rural America (and as war is never long out of fashion), there was an avid market for the heavy gray metal, once it was processed and smelted.

These heavy metal deposits spilled from clefts in the rock outcroppings in the southwest part of Wisconsin. The Winnebago had guarded the secret for hundreds of years, but they shared it with the French. Only after the arrival of American traffic on the Mississippi did an interest in the lead and zinc deposits start to grow. Jesse W. Shull and two other men with ties to the Fox tribe began to mine lead in 1822. In the same year, a mining lease was granted which led to a rush of miners and rough souls prepared to enter the Indian territory illegally and start extracting lead ore.

It took seven years for the trickle of miners to become a flood, and by 1830 more than 5,000 miners tore out nearly 14 million tons of lead ore. The miners were called "badgers" because they dug underground pits for homes and covered them with logs to protect their claims and tough out the severe Wisconsin winters. The Mississippi River and the Illinois town of Galena thrived on the badgers' industry, with steamboats carrying lead downriver and returning with more pairs of hands and stout backs to work the deadly mineral from the subsurface veins. Although the mining was taking place on Indian land, there was a coarse and well-armed disregard for the rights of the soon-to-be-displaced natives. The present-day town of Dodgeville began as a dug-out pit, covered with timber, surrounded by a timber stockade and bristling with the guns of 230 miners under the "command" of Henry Dodge, who in 1836 would become the territorial governor of Wisconsin. (Dodge also argued for opening up to mining, lands secured from the Winnebago under the Treaty of 1827.)

Treaties signed with Wisconsin Indians between 1836 and 1848 established several reservations scattered across the North Woods, granting the tribes the right to hunt, fish, and gather materials on public lands. In return, the Menominee, Chippewa, Sioux, and Winnebago ceded much of their land to the government. Many of the tribes ultimately had to move on, like the Kickapoo, who ended up down near the Mexican border in Texas, and the Sioux, who moved on to the western plains. Some eastern tribes, like the Munsee, and the formerly dreaded Oneida of the Iroquois confederation, moved to lands purchased in Wisconsin.

There were two brief clashes between the Indians and the Americans in Wisconsin. The first came when Red Bird, a chief of the Winnebagos, killed the half-black, half-French Gagnier family on its homestead in the southwest lead-mining region in 1827. He turned himself in to the troops at Fort Winnebago, in Portage, and died in prison awaiting trial. Things quieted down until the so-called Black Hawk War of 1831 and 1832, when a group of U.S. Army and irregular militia chased the band of Sauk Indians led by Black Hawk (1767–1838) up the Rock River Valley, past the lakes of Madison, to the Wisconsin River at Sauk City, before turning west to the Mississippi. There, most of the Indians were slaughtered trying to cross the river and escape to Iowa.

## ■ GROWING STATE

Whatever else can be said of the Black Hawk War, it did introduce Wisconsin to the rest of the country. Immigrants from other parts of the United States and Canada started to stream into the region. Wisconsin Territory was established in 1836, and statehood declared in 1848.

From the state capital in Belmont, the heart of the lead-mining region, the Territorial Legislature agreed to move to a new capital in Madison. This was largely because of land speculation and bribery on the part of James Doty, a Green Bay attorney (and later governor) whose floating land titles allowed him to cherry pick the finest parcels.

# BLACK HAWK'S RETREAT

When a branch of the Sauk tribe, exiled west of the Mississippi in the 1830s, sought to return to their homelands in Illinois, the resulting debacle was known as the Black Hawk War. Black Hawk was an older Sauk chief who refused to accept the land treaties with the United States, and who wanted his people to remain on the land where their families had been buried for centuries. Rejecting claims of new settlers on the site of their former village, Black Hawk crossed the Mississippi with a few clans.

The confrontation scared up a posse of irregular militia of several hundred Illinois settlers, including Abraham Lincoln. Instead of retreating west, Black Hawk led his followers north to Wisconsin through the Rock River Valley, cutting through marshes and forest to escape the militia. Native men in the rear guard fought skirmishes near Lake Koshkonong to protect their women and children. The U.S. Army, with Capt. Jefferson Davis and Jeb Stuart in tow, were dispatched in pursuit of Black Hawk, in part to keep the militia in check. The militia chased Black Hawk west, where Black Hawk escaped through the marshes of Madison. Finally, on the heights of the Wisconsin River overlooking what is now Sauk City, a large battle took place where the Sauk stood and fought a costly battle, but enabled many Indians to escape across the river.

Many Sauk men were wounded or killed, and were left to the militia, who treated the dead callously and the wounded with cruelty. Lincoln recalls that the Indians didn't draw near as much blood as did the mosquitoes in the Wisconsin swamps, a wry reference to the Indian's defensive posture during the "war."

Black Hawk tried to surrender several times, but the militia refused to bargain with his emissaries. The chase led west to the Mississippi near the Bad Axe River. Beaten and starving, the remaining party of 300 Sauk tried to make their escape to a camp across the Mississippi in Iowa. They nearly succeeded, but suddenly a gunboat heading south from Fort Snelling (St. Paul) surprised the Indians as they were crossing the Mississippi. Some women and children made it to safety in Iowa, but the remaining native men were mowed down like a scythe through grass, according to one eye-witness. Black Hawk was captured and sent to prison in St. Louis. He traveled to the East Coast in the following year, and was reported as saying that he only returned to the lands of his forebearers so that his people, the Sauk, could raise corn and honor their ancestors. Although he became a celebrity of sorts, he died a few years later, far away from the burial grounds of the Sauk.

On his way back from the massacre, Abraham Lincoln rode through Jefferson county and stopped for the night at a farm for some food and rest. When he awoke the next day, his horse had been stolen. Lincoln had to walk the 250 miles back to the city of Springfield, Illinois.

*Chief Black Hawk.
(State Historical Society
of Wisconsin)*

One of Doty's goals was to improve transport through Wisconsin with canals. The first was built in 1853, soon after the completion of the Erie Canal, bypassing two stretches of rapids near Kaukauna between the Fox River and Lake Winnebago. The limestone walls and wooden sluice gates are remarkable, especially when considering that all the stone was hand-worked and placed using oxen, and that all the excavation was done with hand shovels. Dams and locks at Little Kaukauna and the Kaukauna Rapids allowed boat and barge traffic to move between Lake Winnebago and Green Bay, connecting the fledgling city with the Fox River portage.

Travel by road was possible, but no treat in these early days. The military roads connecting the American forts at Green Bay (Fort Howard), Portage (Fort Winnebago), and Prairie du Chien (Fort Crawford) traced Indian trails, serving scarce commercial value. The best roads were made of rough-hewn planks or corduroy (felled trees), like the Watertown Plank Road, a toll road laid on sand that carried traffic, jostling and bouncing, between Milwaukee and Madison. Teamsters hauled settlers—mostly Yankees and New Yorkers, and later, European immigrants—inland on the westward journey, returning to Milwaukee with loads of whatever frontier goods might sell in a growing port town.

*The construction of rail lines in the mid-nineteenth century enabled the lumber industry to become a major economic force in Wisconsin. (State Historical Society of Wisconsin)*

In the mid-1850s, the railroad followed the same track across the glacial basin, cutting through long, low sand eskers and drumlins, and skirting the marshes from Milwaukee west to the wood and water stations of Watertown, Waterloo, Marshall, and Sun Prairie, and on to Madison. Railroads were later extended to the Mississippi River, making a new and much more convenient portage across the state.

To harvest the enormous tracts of timber sprawling over the north, a lumber industry evolved around Lake Winnebago. Oshkosh, Appleton, Neenah, Kaukauna, and Green Bay flourished, and the wealth extended to Fond du Lac at the south of the lake. The rivers were pressed into service to float logs down to the mills. The mansions of the lumber barons still stand as testimony to the early wealth generated by this water- and steam-powered industry.

When big timber was exhausted, paper-making took over the boom. The river cities of the southeast increasingly became industrial centers, providing brick and lumber for homes, and manufactured goods for settlers. Along Lake Michigan's shoreline, the port cities of Kenosha, Racine, Milwaukee, Port Washington, Sheboygan, and Manitowoc received immigrants to Wisconsin and exported the manufactured goods from Wisconsin's mills and factories.

Discovery of iron in Dodge and Sauk counties in 1850 accelerated the industrialization of Milwaukee, where the production of iron rails and farm implements soon led to more sophisticated iron and steel tools. Discovery of iron in 1886, in Iron County and the Gogebic Range, meant pumps were needed to drain groundwater from the deep, hard-rock mines. These challenges turned Milwaukee and other cities toward specialty manufacturing. Reflecting Wisconsin's changing economy, many heavy machinery and durable goods manufacturers started to take their places besides timber, paper, fishing, agriculture, and meat-packing industries. A prominent example of this expansion of Wisconsin's economy is Milwaukee's E. P. Allis Company, later to become Allis-Chalmers. After starting business as an iron foundry in 1845, the company turned to manufacturing flour-milling equipment in 1878, and soon diversified into steam engines, pumps, pipe, water heating equipment, gauges, gears, shafts, foundry equipment, and heavy machinery. After hitting its peak around the turn of the century, it was one of the largest heavy machinery manufacturers in the world. Sadly, Allis-Chalmers continues to reflect the state of much Midwestern heavy industry in the late twentieth century: today, the company is a mere shadow of its former self.

# ■ CHANGING POPULATION

The immigration of Germans to Wisconsin was probably the most important ingredient in the development of the state's manufacturing base. Many of the early German immigrants came to Wisconsin to avoid army conscription, and were mechanics and craftsmen. They settled into the growing city of Milwaukee to create a "German Athens," where German beer and music, sauerkraut and sausage, opera and Teutonic language thrived in a decidedly German community, influencing others throughout the state. German brewers also found ideal conditions for their trade in Wisconsin, and turned the state into a formidable force in the beer brewing business. German was taught in many schools, where English was a second language until World War I. Then anti-German sentiment quickly diminished the public's tolerance of overt German culture. German sauerkraut became Victory Cabbage; German culture went underground.

The Germans were only the first part of a flood of immigrants that flocked to Wisconsin between 1850 and 1920. Norwegians, Danes, Swedes, and Finns found the available farmland of Wisconsin to be a welcome relief from the rigid inheritance rules in their homelands. Families were able to buy Yankee land, given up when their intensive wheat farming burned out the prairie soils. The development of dairy farming, with tobacco plots on the side, provided the raw materials for the manufacture of cheese and cigars. Much of Wisconsin's tobacco country still has a large Norwegian population.

The Swiss also founded several enclaves in Wisconsin, most notably New Glarus and Monroe, where their distinctive architecture and cheese-making skills are as alive today as when they first scouted the state for a new place to settle in the 1860s.

Most Italian emigration occurred in the late 1800s and early 1900s. As with each new wave of immigrants, Italians tended to work as skilled artisans in the building trades and laborers in the factories. Italian communities developed in Milwaukee, Racine, and Kenosha, as well as in Madison, where stoneworkers helped built the magnificent State Capitol.

Eastern Europeans, fleeing ethnic unrest in their home countries of Czechoslovakia, Serbia, Croatia, Poland, and Romania, found niches in the bustling communities of Milwaukee and the southeast. Russian, German, and Eastern European Jews also arrived in Milwaukee, fleeing persecution in Europe. One young Ukranian

*German immigrants helped establish a beer industry in Wisconsin with the introduction of hops necessary for the brewing process. (State Historical Society of Wisconsin)*

Jewish immigrant who arrived in Milwaukee with her parents in 1906, Goldie Mabovitch, never gave up the dream of a Jewish homeland. She later moved to Palestine and was elected to the Israeli parliament in 1949, adopting the Hebrew name of Golda Meir (1898–1978). She became Israel's fourth prime minister in 1969.

Wisconsin's progressive movement was born on the flood of immigration. Its champion was Robert La Follette (1855–1925), and its mission was to break the power of the rail bosses, lumber barons, and utilities chiefs who controlled Wisconsin economics and politics. La Follette's aim was to give due process to government, which too often could not enforce taxes or laws on powerful interests who were aided by their cronies in the legislature. His reform-minded programs struck a responsive chord in the hearts of German and Norwegian immigrants, who believed that bosses corporate interests, and corruption were rife in Wisconsin. La Follette barnstormed the state, giving 15 speeches a day, and became governor in 1901. In 1904 he championed an open presidential primary, which lets voters select candidates without revealing their party preference. He became a U.S. Senator in 1905, thanks largely to his appeal to the Protestant ethnic groups of Wisconsin, and his persuasive and entertaining speechifying. In 1924 he ran for

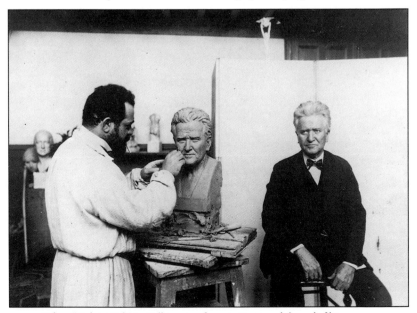

*Robert "Fightin' Bob" La Follette poses for posterity toward the end of his career as a senator who championed reforms in labor laws. (Underwood Photo Archives)*

U.S. President as the candidate of the League for Progressive Political Action, thinking himself a natural successor to Teddy Roosevelt. Like most third-party candidates, La Follette came in third, but he and his family remained a powerful influence on Wisconsin politics until after World War II.

With the rise of industrialism in Wisconsin, organized labor became a vibrant political force, so much so that Socialism became the official party of the city of Milwaukee by the turn of the century, and it stayed in power for many decades thereafter by avoiding scandal and paying uncompromising attention to the rules. Socialist Party member Victor Berger was the mayor of Milwaukee until World War I, when he ran for the U.S. Congress, and won.

## ■ MODERN TIMES

With the 1920s came Prohibition. Hundreds of breweries were shut down, temperance police broke up illegal stills and home brewing, and the organized crime moguls of Chicago used Wisconsin as a conduit and cache for Canadian, European, and bootleg booze.

The Ku Klux Klan enjoyed a short heyday during the 1920s, when it claimed nearly 75,000 members opposed to Roman Catholics, blacks, Jews, and foreigners. Their popularity was short-lived, however, and by 1927 membership had dwindled to a few hundred.

With the stock market crash of 1929 and the onset of the Depression, industry went idle, reducing its output by two-thirds. In 1930, Phillip La Follette, son of Fightin' Bob, deposed plumbing magnate Walter J. Kohler, a one-term Republican governor. He extended progressive reforms to the banking industry and the electric utilities and forged the state labor code. During his second term he implemented many important projects that remain a hallmark of Wisconsin today: the reforestation of the North Woods by the Civilian Conservation Corps; hundreds of public works projects; and the establishment of parks, roads, and schools.

World War II did for Wisconsin what eight years of New Deal programs could not: it revitalized and rebuilt the state's economy. Milwaukee became known as "America's Toolbox." Shipbuilders in Manitowoc built dozens of submarines; Nash built engines for Jeeps; the army established the world's largest munitions factory near Baraboo; and Superior boomed by building merchant ships for the North Atlantic.

If the end of the war began an era of dizzying growth for Wisconsin's economy, it also led to political change. Wisconsinite Joseph McCarthy of Appleton became Republican senator in 1947 and initiated his infamous anti-communist crusade. Following McCarthy's death in May 1957, Democrat William Proxmire, originator of the Golden Fleece Award that revealed wasteful government spending, was elected senator and served for nearly 30 years. Democrat Gaylord Nelson, elected governor in 1958, went on to become Wisconsin's junior senator and is best known as the founder of Earth Day.

If the radical sparks in Wisconsin's fire had sputtered underground since the days of abolitionists and socialists, they flamed hot in the 1960s and 1970s, when the Civil Rights Movement and the Vietnam War sparked huge protests. Housing discrimination against African Americans outside Milwaukee's central city spawned the Fair Housing marches of the 1960s. Picketing by the Congress of Racial Equality began in 1963 and boycotts were initiated. Finally, in 1967 confrontations between blacks and a largely white police force erupted into eight days of riots, ending with four deaths and 1,500 arrests. A month later, Roman Catholic priest Father James E. Groppi led a few hundred protesters into Milwaukee's South Side, protesting the failure of the city council to approve open-housing laws. They were met by several thousand whites who pelted them with bottles, bricks, and stones. The marches continued for several months, and Groppi even took control of the State Capitol during one protest in Madison. Adoption of a tough open-housing ordinance in 1968 ended the protests and opened the door to direct political participation for African Americans. While problems related to long-term poverty remain, community, city, and state leaders have achieved marked success in righting past injustices.

Madison saw an extended period of protest over U.S. involvement in the war in Vietnam. Protests that grew from campus demonstrations became full-fledged riots in 1967, gaining national attention and requiring the presence of the National Guard. The anti-war movement was set back profoundly when a university building was blown up by extremists in 1970. Though the protests died off with the end of the war, a solid contingent of the counter-culture remains to this day. Many environmental and administrative law reforms date from this era, in part because so many protesters graduated from the university and immediately went to work to transform "the system." Today, Madison is in many respects a very conventional community that coexists easily with enclaves of people enjoying various "alternative" lifestyles.

Wisconsin's economy remained robust until the oil shocks of the 1975 oil embargo delivered a coup de grace to its aging industrial base. The recession of the late 1970s forced a restructuring of the economy, and Wisconsin has effectively returned as the economic star of the snowbelt, with low capital-gains taxes, superb public services, a strongly motivated and well-educated workforce, and an environment that has rebounded from the ravages of rapacious industrial growth. Politically, the state remains split between Republicans and Democrats with Milwaukee, Madison, Green Bay, the southeast cities, and the northwest leaning toward the Democrats, and the Republicans enjoying support in the suburbs, the Fox Valley, and the southwest.

*Governor Tommy Thompson (standing) with assistant Robert Trunzo in the State Capitol in Madison.*

# SEASONS OF THE STATE

## ■ WINTER

IT MAY SNOW IN OCTOBER. November can be cold, snow-blown, and windy. But winter never really arrives until the end of the first full week of December. After that, bone-numbing wind chills begin their dive to well below zero. Foreheads ache with cold, ears tingle, eyes tear—as much because of the wind as for the realization that no relief is in sight for four months. The night sky is India-ink blue, and ice forms clear and thick on the lakes, an inch a night. The lake waters flip over, a natural form of circulation in which the chilled top layer of water sinks to the depths. Water vapor pours off the surface like fog as heat is driven from the water. At the end of that first week of winter, loud groans and grinding squeals rise from the lakes as the great tectonic ice plates expand, popping and booming as their faces meet and cannot mesh.

The cold breath of winter remains until March, bringing a variety of winter weather that ranges from Arctic wind chills of 50 and 60 degrees below zero, to warm, spring-like days in the January thaw.

Three types of storms decorate the winter landscape. The first type arrives with a low-pressure system from the southern Pacific, sucking moisture from the Gulf of Mexico, and bringing deep, wet snowfalls in the teeth of a relentless northeast wind. The second type of storm slides in from the Pacific Northwest, with lows that linger at Turtle Mountain, North Dakota, before lumbering into northern Wisconsin and piling the shores of Lake Superior with enormous drifts of lake-effect snow. (Lake-effect snow extends only a short distance inland from lake shores.) The third type of storm, and perhaps the most dangerous, is the Alberta Clipper, an offspring of the permanent Arctic low. Screaming down the plains east of the Rocky Mountains, its characteristic counter-clockwise spiral packs 60-mile-per-hour (96-kmh) winds and sub-zero temperatures. The advancing cold front of an Alberta Clipper can bring heavy, dry snows, shaking every bit of moisture from the atmosphere. In its wake, a deep-blue sky and sunshine belie the below-zero temperatures. Nostrils freeze with each painful intake of breath, and ice masks form on scarves protecting faces. The squeak of the snow tells how cold it is; the higher the pitch, the colder the air.

Winter brings ice fishing to Wisconsin's 15,000 lakes, as it has since Native Americans first started spearing fish that they attracted with wooden lures. Modern ice anglers now use a tip-up, which sends up a flag to signal when an unwary perch, muskie, walleye, crappie, or pan fish has gobbled up the cutworm or minnow. Spearing for sturgeon, ancient denizens of the glacial lake, is permitted on Lake Winnebago. Famed for their size and roe (yes, caviar), sturgeon grow old, long, and heavy. They are difficult to spear, and though hundreds of anglers set up shanties to harvest the sturgeon, few come home with more than hopes for better luck next season.

*Long, cold, and snowy winters are the most notorious feature of Wisconsin's climate.*

# ■ SPRING

March may enter mildly, but the series of state high school basketball and wrestling tournaments which follow seem to have the uncanny ability to attract snow-bearing storm systems. It can snow as late as April, and frost may sting until mid-May. Certain forces cannot be restrained: about six weeks after the Sun Prairie groundhog sees its shadow, St. Patrick's Day is celebrated in the hopes of seeing more green and less white.

There are two infallible signs of spring that precede the arrival of Wisconsin's state bird, the robin red-breast. Long before the robin has booked its reservations to Wisconsin, the killdeer makes its arrival in prairies, and along rail corridors and other flat, open spaces. The killdeer sings the song of spring—a knifing *peep-peep-peep* as it cuts aloft in the evening sky. With a subdued entrance, the bluebird keeps to the protection of the woods to herald spring and the final thaw. Russet breast, piercing black eyes, back and wings of royal blue, the bluebird arrives a week or so ahead of the last full moon of winter.

When winter's back is broken, a great variety of birds begin winging their way north to begin the annual migration. Canada geese, launched from their southern sanctuary by lofty, warm tropical air pushing north, trace the ascent of the spring sun in northern skies. These intrepid travelers fly by the stars as well as by the sun, trumpeting the arrival of spring.

In late March, flocks of sandhill cranes glide their outstretched bodies into Wisconsin's heavens. These wide-winged, long-legged birds return in greater numbers each year, a population grown from the edge of extinction a few decades past. Family groups of cranes will work the edge of the fields and marshes, picking up amphibian meals. If alarmed, cranes stand still; their necks straighten, beaks to the sky to mimic the vertical marsh grasses around them. Cranes mate for life and pairs return to the same marshes year after year. In Wisconsin, they prepare for summer with wing-shaking mating dances, courting in the flat marshlands. As the air warms and the dawn comes ever earlier, the cranes greet the morning with voices like the musical chortle of wood chimes. Early in the day, their seven-foot (2-m) wings spread wide as they climb into the sky riding warm air vectors, circling thousands of feet into the troposphere.

Soon, flocks of herons fly north, joining the snowy egrets in the marshland, estuaries, sloughs, and river bottoms. There, they fish and rear their young in great colonies built in dead trees above the marshes. The herons fly with their necks wound into S-curves, their huge wings carving through blustery winds.

Spring is not always born full-grown. The best springs take time to build. The most unsatisfactory springs arrive in a hot southern wind around mid-March, leaping into sultry summer weather that lingers until September. The best come with snow-filled clouds, cold fogs, and stiff northeast winds whose rain lashes the trees, and makes the plants and animals fight for every step past winter's icy bite. The cool spring lets the floral bounty of the woodlands and prairies arrive at a leisurely pace. Deliberate springs gradually paint the landscape with a new coat of freshness. Yellow weeping willows and red dogwoods become early heralds of seasonal change, followed by the glowing silver-greens of fresh shoots on the verge of explosion, the red, swollen buds of the maples charging their limbs with red and yellow pigments, the sap running between the warm days and chilly nights, secreting sweetness to all who tap the tree for maple sugar.

Delicate white snowbells give way to the greening of the woodland. Bloodroot and trillium send up their white petals like prayers atop green leaves that unfold from tight tubes. In the prairies, delicate orchids attract varieties of flies and wasps to pollinate them in rare and ancient ritual. The leaves on the gnarled, arthritic oak trees swell to the size of mouse ears, signaling that morels are ready for picking

*Spring has always meant hard work for farmers, such as this country gentleman in Deerfield in 1874. (State Historical Society of Wisconsin)*

in the secret spots on the woodland floor. One of the finest of dinner fungi, the morel fruits most abundantly while the sunny days of mid-spring warm the forest floor, before the leaves unfurl to cloak all beneath in thick shade.

On the farm, tobacco hotbeds are filled with seedlings, last year's alfalfa fields are plowed and disked for corn, and a vast armamentaria of machinery is readied so farmers can produce enormous crops of corn and soybeans. Farmers hope to plant as soon as the fields are dry and warm enough to encourage seed germination, but the weather rules agriculture—hail, floods, drought, snow, or high winds can all show up on a fine spring day in Wisconsin. Spring also heralds tornado season, March to September. If all goes well, the green blades of corn knife their way through the soil by early May. The orchards of Wisconsin are a riot of flowers, especially the cherry orchards of Door County and the apple orchard region around Gays Mills. The warm wind is heavy with fragrance from fresh flowers and freshly turned soil warming with the return of the sun. So too are the bluffs of the Mississippi, where linden trees intoxicate the locals with an astounding fragrance that also provokes bees to make the most delicious honey in creation. (The linden was known as the bee tree.) With bees, birds, critters, and fish in motion, and the scent and substance of spring at their most dynamic, the wheel turns toward summer.

*In May, spring is in full bloom as flowers blanket country meadows, and morel mushrooms (right) pop up on the forest floors.*

## ■ SUMMER

The flowering of the locust and the catalpa, with their snowy, fragrant mounds of pea flowers, signals summer's arrival. Ducklings swim across the surface of ponds, a hen turkey shepherds her clutch of chicks through prairie grass, the wobbly legs of the fawn strengthen to skip its spotted frame through the woods to get a sip of water at dusk. The height of the summer sun beckons growth in farm, field, and woodland. Trees leaf out with verdant urgency, the deep-green oaks stretching their limbs to absorb all solar radiation within their reach.

In the cool evenings of the North Woods, the loons call out to each other with a cry that seems to fill the world with its resonance. In the marshes and wetlands, the chorus of spring peepers has given way to the deep chuckle of toads and the rumbling anthems of bullfrogs and leopard frogs, snacking on mosquitoes between each song and verse. Painted and snapping turtles carefully pick their way across the highways in search of the perfect spot to lay their eggs.

Summer is, of course, vacation time, and the baseball diamonds and volleyball courts at taverns and school yards get their well-deserved workouts. The fishing season brings out a flotilla of craft on every reputed fishing hole. Trout fishers use

*Watermelons and summer have long been associated with one another—*
*as this old photo testifies. (Murphy Library, University Wisconsin-La Crosse)*

the summer as a chance to find solitude and solace on the thousands of miles of trout streams in the valleys of Wisconsin. Hundreds of charter boats leave the ports of Lakes Michigan and Superior in quest of trout and salmon. Wood smoke from the fish boils of Door County means that another migratory animal, the Illinois tourist, is plentiful and at its summer roosting grounds in this Cape Cod of the Great Lakes. While there may be a few more churches than bait shops, there is no disputing which is more popular on a summer weekend. Outdoor music festivals fill the bandshells, gazebos, and greens of small villages and cities to entertain the locals in the early evening air.

Wisconsin's parks, bike trails, and forests get a workout every summer, mostly by state residents who have been cooped up for six months. Prairie flowers put on a summer-long display to highlight the million shades of green along highways and back roads with subtle touches of white, yellow, blue, pink, and orange.

The high days of summer pass all too quickly, and before long it seems that the sun has set before the ball game is over, or the day's fish limit reached. The muggy days of July and August may seem to linger like time suspended, but heavy dews fall on the cooler nights. The Perseid meteor shower of mid-August is the sign that

*Country entertainment at the expense of two turkeys. (State Historical Society of Wisconsin)*

things are about to change and summer soon shall pass. The vacationers begin to return to the places they came from, the cabins are shut down and boarded up, and school children return to school a little older and with another summer under their belts.

## ■ FALL

The ducklings of early summer are molted and fitted with an adult set of feathers; the turkey chicks, now full-grown, strut and peck at the light-brown grass seedheads. Songbirds are plucking up every bug they find and gobbling the wild seed. Flocks are congregating once more, riding the columns of warm air that ascend to the stratosphere; great vees of geese are passing south with a trumpeting chorus on high. The marshes fill with waterfowl from Canada and the far north, resting on their flight to escape the coming winter. For every pair of sandhill cranes that settled in April, the marsh now has three or four cranes exchanging chortling calls as they hastily nibble frogs, minnows, and crayfish. The weakening sun no longer sustains the vibrant green chlorophyll in every plant, and its subtle exodus brings

*Fall colors grace Twin Lake near Bayfield in northern Wisconsin.*

out the carotene and anthocyan, making yellows and reds—a brilliant prelude to the glories of autumn. Sumac turns shades of red usually relegated to the lipstick counter. Maples take on the hues of apricots, cantaloupes, watermelons, red beets, fuchsia, crimson, and blood. Cinnamon ferns change from green to cinnamon brown; oaks turn scarlet, red, and then golden brown. The palette of the hardwoods is contrasted by the permanent variety of green conifers, the spruces and white pines, whose sharp spires enhance the fall colors. All too soon the rugged skeletons of deciduous limbs and trunks shed their leaves.

As the days get shorter, farms are bustling. The moment of truth has arrived. The knives inside the gargantuan heads of corn-pickers have been sharpened and these green or red behemoths are ready for their final assaults through the fields. If the summer is bountiful and the ears of corn are full, the hot dry days of August and early September will change their kernels from "in dough" to "in dent." Soybeans will begin to rattle in their husks. The wheat and oats are golden and upright, despite the ferocity of summer winds that threatened to flatten them. Potatoes and onions emerge from the sandy fields, and sod-cutters seed their acres for the season to come. The combines and haybines make their final turns around the corners of the fields and then return to their sheds for another year.

*An Amish farmer harvests oats in a scene repeated every fall across the state.*

With the cooler days come the bow-hunters—rattling antlers, stalking deer, hoping for a clean shot at a buck. Hunting means venison, chops and sausage, and a chance to shed the mantle of the business world and deodorant, and stink like a doe in rut for a few days. Bow-hunting is a solitary art, requiring tracking skill and stealth so the hunter can get as close as possible to his prey. The gun season in November is a different type of hunt, with beaters chasing the deer through the woods so their pals in tree stands and blinds can get a shot off as their prey rushes by, afraid and half-crazed by the scent of does in heat. The gun season is a chance to get away from the job and family and hole up in a cabin for a week with a few other guys who hopefully play sloppier poker with every can of beer. Perfect conditions include a light snowfall on opening weekend, so hunters can track their deer before they find them and, more importantly, after they shoot. The best-tasting deer are the yearlings that grow up near cornfields, but killing a ten-point buck is the hoped-for prize.

The most unusual kill was recorded in the 1980s when a hunter shot a 14-point "trophy" buck with the rack and skull of a 12-point buck locked in its horns. The enormous buck had literally locked horns with another huge buck, killing it in the process, before severing its head with sharp kicks from its cloven hooves. The massive buck roamed the woods until his last, carrying the decaying headdress of his rival staring him down with unblinking eyes. The wheel of life turns to death in the fall, with winter soon to purify the countryside and ready the land for another cycle.

# FOX VALLEY AND DOOR PENINSULA

ARGUABLY WISCONSIN'S MOST HISTORIC and heavily used river, the Fox was once a highway for the Native Americans who plied its waters in search of shelter, food, and refuge, as well as a gateway to western Wisconsin and the Mississippi Valley for the French voyageurs. Following statehood, the forests of the Fox Valley and its cousin, the Wolf, gave birth and vitality to Wisconsin's lumber boomtowns of Neenah, Menasha, Appleton, Oshkosh, and Fond du Lac, all located along the shores of Lake Winnebago, into which the Fox River flows. After the forests were clear-cut, these cities readily turned their energies from processing lumber to the production of industrial goods, bringing great wealth to Wisconsin, and forging the character of the modern Fox River Valley.

Today, when the whistle blows in the factory towns along Lake Winnebago and the lower Fox River, Wisconsinites head for the millions of acres of surrounding wildlife preserves and regional parkland that still flourish in this area. No Fox River community, regardless of how heavily industrialized, is more than 20 miles (32 km) from active farmland, or the river's wilder heritage. Threading together work life and weekend pleasures are the thousands of restaurants and taverns that attend to the good life along the river. Badgers know how to party!

Though a trickle compared to the Mississippi or even the Wisconsin rivers, the Fox is a waterway of great character and importance, changing dramatically at every stage of its journey, from the shallow backwater marshes near Portage in south-central Wisconsin to its mouth many miles north and east at Green Bay. This great flood punches far past Green Bay into Lake Michigan, creating danger-ous currents at the tip of the Door Peninsula, which the French once called the *Porte des Morts,* Death's Door.

A traveler might wish to choose among **three very different trips** through this area. One might be a meandering drive through the **rural upper Fox country towns,** beginning with Portage, north of Madison, and continuing to Green Lake, Berlin, and Shawano. A visit to the lower Fox where it enters Lake Winnebago, then emerges to flow toward Green Bay is to enter **the heart of historic and indus-trialized Wisconsin.** The towns of Oshkosh, Appleton, and Green Bay are filled with history and dominated by some of the great names of American industry.

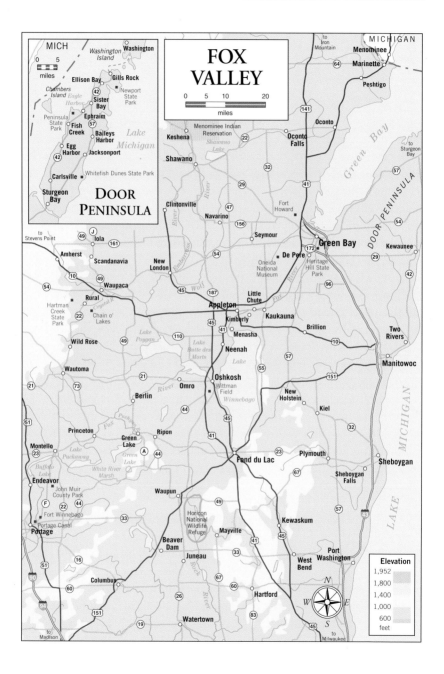

# FOX VALLEY

## DOOR PENINSULA

Beyond Green Bay lies the **Door Peninsula,** which juts like a thumb into Lake Michigan. This historic area is arguably the most beautiful in the state, with its cherry orchards, steep cliffs, lake views, and historic lighthouses.

## ■ UPPER FOX RIVER AND COUNTRY TOWNS

To follow this route is to drift through a landscape of open farmland alternating with woods and marshland, past charming small towns that enjoy a slow-paced way of life. This route turns north at the town of Berlin, crosses up toward the Wolf and Embarrass rivers, and over to the town of Shawano and Shawano Lake.

### ■ PORTAGE

In one sense the small town of Portage is the most important part of the Fox River Valley, for at this spot a narrow tract of land separates the placid Fox, with its connections to the Great Lakes, from the great Wisconsin River, with its connections to the upper Mississippi. Though the Winnebago and others knew about the portage, when French explorers Louis Jolliet and Father Jacques Marquette crossed it to follow the Wisconsin west to the Mississippi in 1673, the spot known as Portage arrived in the European consciousness. By the 1860s, steamboats were traveling back and forth between the two rivers through a channel built at this spot.

The mid-1800s brought even greater prominence to Portage, when the railroad stretched its elm timbers and iron rails across the marshlands to the sandy embankments between the Wisconsin and the Fox rivers. River clays were baked to brick, providing homes to the lumbermen, mill workers, and railroaders who hoped to prosper here at the edge of a great stand of pine. As the North Woods shrank back to the beat of a sharpened ax, a saw kerf at a time, the rivers brought pine into town and the railroad took finished lumber away to Chicago and Milwaukee.

Today, when most people travel by car and truck, they often roar up the freeway from Madison toward Portage on I-90/94, then turn northwest toward Eau Claire and St. Paul without ever visiting this historic town. Yet, those who head a few miles north on U.S. 51, then east on 33, will find themselves driving right into Portage. Downtown, the **Portage Canal** still joins the Fox and Wisconsin rivers, and it's worth getting out of the car and taking a look at the impressive quarried limestone slab walls of the canal. This is one of only two Wisconsin canals commissioned and completed before railroads made them obsolete.

Portage is a fine place to stop for a simple meal or to stretch after a long drive. Old stone and brick storefronts and a big Catholic church are visible along Main Street. Highway 33 East runs along the river where the canal joins the Fox. There are several parking areas here where you can get out to take a stroll along the riverbank of the Wisconsin River or launch a canoe and paddle up the Fox. Theoretically, it's possible to take a boat from here all the way to Lake Winnebago, north through the lake, and up through the old, hand-operated locks to the city of Green Bay at the mouth of Green Bay, an inlet of Lake Michigan.

Portage has been home to several interesting literary figures and intellectuals. **Historian Frederick Jackson Turner**, whose *The Frontier in American History* (1920) is one of the most widely read of American historical essays, was a native of Portage and winner of the Pulitzer prize in 1932. More famous in the literary world is **Zona Gale**, the Pulitzer-prize-winning author of *Miss Lulu Bett* (also 1920), a book (and later a play) about the relationships of a small-town gal. Gale's riverside home was at 506 West Edgewater Street. The best local literature was concocted by a Portage woman, **Margery Latimer**, and a poet, **Jean Toomer**, who together formed a small commune in nearby Briggsville that followed the teachings of the philosopher and mystic Gurdjieff. Together they shook the wrinkles out of this riverside town with Gurdjieffian conundrums.

Wisconsin artist **Georgia O'Keeffe**, who came to visit the commune from her hometown of Sun Prairie, was intrigued at first, but later grew critical of Toomer's group. As Toomer bled the local high-rollers of their cash to support his idyllic community, they became resentful of his control. What began as a social experiment to expand the consciousness of a small town ended with unfulfilled promises and broken dreams. Toomer, who later became the poetic "Prince of the Harlem Renaissance," took his young bride, Margery Latimer, and left Portage for California. Their story together ended sadly as rumors of Toomer's race (he was partly African American) made *Time* magazine, and Latimer died giving birth to Toomer's child. It was said that the house where she grew up was haunted for years by her ghost.

East of Portage on Highway 33 are the remains of an early American frontier fort and the home of an Indian agent. Indian Agency Road leads northeast of town to a rise above marshland and the frame house where Agent John Kinzie lived in 1832, as he began to arrange for treaties with the Winnebago that would

## JOHN MUIR'S WISCONSIN

*O*f all the great singers that sweeten Wisconsin, one of the best known and best loved is the brown thrush or thrasher, strong and able without being familiar, and easily seen and heard. Rosy-purple evenings after thunder-showers are the favorite songtimes, when the winds have died away and the steaming ground and the leaves and flowers fill the air with fragrance. Then the male makes haste to the topmost spray of an Oak tree and sings loud and clear with delightful enthusiasm until sun-down, mostly I suppose for his mate sitting on the precious eggs in a brush heap....

*America's great environmentalist, John Muir. (State Historical Society of Wisconsin)*

After the arrival of the thrushes came the bobolinks, gushing, gur-gling, inexhaustible fountains of song, pouring forth floods of sweet notes over the broad Fox River meadows in wonderful variety and volume, crowded and mixed beyond description, as they hovered on quivering wings above their hidden nests in the grass. It seemed marvelous to us that birds so moderate in size could hold so much of this wonderful song stuff. Each one of them poured forth music enough for a whole flock, singing as if its whole body, feathers and all, were made up of music, flowing glowing, bubbling melody interpenetrated here and there with small scintillating prickles and spicules....

One of the gayest of the singers is the red-wing blackbird. In the spring, when his scarlet epaulets shine brightest, and his little modest gray wife is sitting on the nest, built on rushes in a swamp, he sits on a near-by Oak and devotedly sings almost all day. His rich simple strain is *baumpalee, baumpalee,* or *bobalee* as inter-preted by some. In summer, after nesting cares are over, they assemble in flocks of hundreds and thousands to feast on Indian corn when it is in the milk. Scattering over a field, each selects an ear, strips the husk down far enough to lay bare an inch or two of the end of it, enjoys an exhilarating feast, and after all are full they rise simultaneously with a quick birr of wings like an old-fashioned church congrega-tion fluttering to their feet when the minister after giving out the hymn says, "Let the congregation arise and sing." Alighting on near-by trees, they sing with a hearty vengeance, bursting out without any puttering prelude in gloriously glad concert, hundreds or thousands of exulting voices with sweet gurgling *baumpalees* mingled with chippy vibrant and exploding globules of musical notes, making a most enthusiastic, indescribable joy-song, a combination unlike anything to be heard elsewhere in the bird kingdom; something like bagpipes, flutes, violins, pianos, and human-like voices all bursting and bubbling at once. Then suddenly some one of the joyful congregation shouts *Chirr! Chirr!* and all stop as if shot.

The sweet-voiced meadowlark, with its placid, simple song of *peery-eery-odical* was another favorite, and we soon learned to admire the Baltimore oriole and its wonderful hanging nests, and the scarlet tanager glowing like fire amid the green leaves. . . .

—John Muir, "A Paradise of Birds,"
from *The Story of My Boyhood and Youth,* 1913

transfer Indian lands to the United States. When the agent's wife, Juliette Magill Kinzie, arrived here on her wedding trip, she was the only white woman living in the territory. She recorded her experiences in a diary, published as *Wau-bun, Early Days in the Northwest.* Less than a mile farther is the site of **Fort Winnebago,** a frontier fort built about 1828, where Lt. Jefferson Davis served at the beginning of his career. All that remains are the surgeon's quarters—a log building on the banks of the Fox River. Inside are displays of native and frontier artifacts.

Turn north from Highway 33 onto Road F and follow the sign to **John Muir County Park.** Within its bounds is the farm where John Muir, America's preeminent environmentalist, spent his childhood. Muir was a determined, if sickly, son of a hard-working, mirthless Scottish father, whose farm was a ceaseless distraction from the natural abundance of plants, birds, and animals that filled the marshes and hills of this rolling region, and that absorbed the young Muir's attention in stolen moments between chores. Muir left the farm to attend the University of Wisconsin at Madison and gained early renown as a tinkerer and inventor of hand-carved wooden clocks and devices, one of which dropped books before students, then closed and refiled them at appointed intervals. It may have been a brief and transcendent encounter with a locust tree on the Madison campus that roused Muir to the wandering life of a botanist, but the sloughs, marshes, and hillsides of the Fox River's "university of the wilderness" taught him his first courses on the vitality and spirit of nature. It's interesting to note that many Wisconsinites became advocates of environmental preservation in the mid-nineteenth century as they watched lumbering and mining ravage a naturally beautiful landscape. Muir asked his brother to set aside a portion of their own farm as a natural area as early as 1865.

■ M O N T E L L O

County Road F continues almost due north to Montello from John Muir Park; the Fox itself curves east into the long narrow reservoir of **Buffalo Lake,** considered one of central Wisconsin's best fishing lakes. In its shallow water, northern pike, bass, and panfish meander under the weeds. Boat ramps for the lake are available in Montello and in the village of Endeavor.

After flowing through Buffalo Lake, the Fox River arrives at Montello, the granite heart of Wisconsin, famous for the elegant purplish-red stone that decorates Grant's Tomb in New York City, as well as the graves of millions of less-famous people across the country. The granite quarries have all shut down and are now silent granite monuments to dynamite, chisels, and plutonic intrusions. At the intersection of highways 22 and 23, in the heart of town, springs flowing over the stones of the old Montello Granite Quarry form a waterfall that feeds the growing Fox River. The river then slips past the backside of the brick and stone buildings on Main Street, built up on granite foundations. From the road, a restaurant and a tavern are visible across the river, giving the scene the ambiance of a European canal town.

West of Montello, on Highway 23 next to the county court house stands a remarkable **plum-colored mansion** that looks as if it had been built of stream-tumbled granite boulders. In fact, the home was built using fresh-cut granite from the quarry; masons chiseled the rounded appearance of the blocks once the stone had been mortared in place. In front of this house is **Wisconsin's largest tree,** a cottonwood, 24 feet (7 m) in circumference and 138 feet (42 m) tall, with its thirsty roots reaching through wet subsoil to the granite floor a few yards underground.

■ P R I N C E T O N

East of Montello, both Highway 23 and the Fox River reach toward Princeton. Wild rice marshes that have long since disappeared once grew along this route, feeding generations of native peoples. A bit north of here, Germania Marsh is still home to sandhill cranes, great blue herons, and bald eagles. The town of Princeton is a quiet, pleasant backwater that has recently become a center for antique shops and home to one of Wisconsin's largest outdoor antique flea markets, held every Saturday all summer long. The collection of older buildings along the town's main street, the former Tiger Brew brewery, the Stone House on Water Street, and the machine and farm implement buildings along the rail spur lend a nineteenth-century air to the scene.

## ■ GREEN LAKE

The road east of Princeton rides the top of hills, then drops down into Green Lake, set at the bottom of a bluff-lined valley. Green Lake was the site of a Winnebago village known as *Day-cho-lah,* or Green Waters. The French called it *Lac du Verde,* in keeping with the local tradition. Green Lake is one of Wisconsin's most famous resort lakes, a deep gash in the Wisconsin countryside carved down 237 feet (72 m) by glaciers. The Puchyan River flows from Green Lake into the Fox at the White River Marsh, north of Princeton, where more than 10,000 acres of marshy woodland shelter wildlife and game.

Around Green Lake there are several campgrounds and places to stay, the fanciest being the **Heidel House,** a modern hotel perched on a wooded hill overlooking the lake. Heidel House boasts one of Wisconsin's best restaurants, **The Grey Rock Mansion.** There are several golf courses in this area, including Tuscumbia Golf Course on Illinois Road, Wisconsin's oldest course. Highway A at Sunset Park cuts across the lake and from this route all of the lake is visible, including its marsh-lands and the maple-covered hills to the south. Biking is especially good in this southern area, and bike routes are marked on maps easily available in shops. Fishing is excellent everywhere, and as the lake is very deep, with abundant deep springs, many species of fish live here, including ciscoes, walleyes, panfish, large-mouth and smallmouth bass.

## ■ RIPON

The town of **Ripon,** located at the head of a valley and up on a ridge six miles (9.6 km) east of Green Lake, is significant in the political history of the United States. Once a stronghold of fervid anti-slavery sentiment, its citizens founded the Republican Party here in 1854, in a plain, white, clapboard building on the local college campus. Known as the **Little White Schoolhouse,** 303 Blackburn Street, it is clearly marked and worth a visit. At a time when southern Democrats favored slavery, the Republicans formed their party so that abolitionists, reformers,

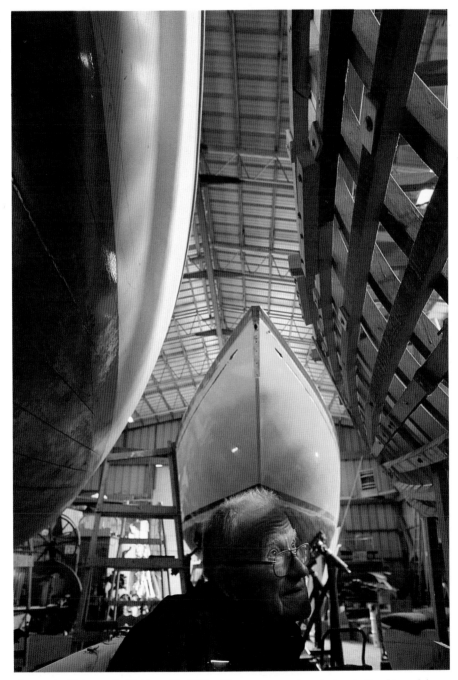

*Just north of Princeton in Neshkoro, "Red" Nimphius constructs and repairs boat hulls at his workshop.*

free-soilers, and Whigs could stand together against the extension of slavery into the expanding western frontier. Today, Ripon is a sort of a secular shrine for the Republican Party, a wailing wall for the party of Lincoln. To celebrate its claim as the Republican Party birthplace (an honor that other towns also actively claim, incidentally), the local party faithful regularly carry a scaled-down version of the Little White Schoolhouse of the Republican Party, like the Ark of the Covenant, at patriotic parades.

Along Ripon's Main Street is a collection of highly ornamented Cream City brick storefronts and warehouses that line the edge of the hill where Ripon College has held classes for nearly 150 years. The Congregational Church, atop a college knoll, is similarly ornamented and trimmed in deep French blue, accenting its Gothic lines and geometric brick design.

## ■ BERLIN

Few cities in Wisconsin have as lovely a collection of old homes as the Fox River city of **Berlin** (pronounced BUR-lin), founded in 1847. Located north of Green Lake on Highway 49 and perched atop the glacier-shaved stump of a prehistoric granite mountain, its site was first noted by the explorer Marquette. He stopped here in 1673 at a village of the Mascoutin Indians, who later fought the French for 100 years. The Mascoutin, like their Fox and Sauk allies, were displaced Michigan tribes fleeing the Iroquois and their fur-frenzy with the French. Today, Berlin is the leather and fur capital of Wisconsin, according to its self-promotion, and its refurbished and renovated downtown is filled with shops, restaurants, apartments, and taverns. Try the German restaurant, Café Schatzi, on West Huron.

A collection of luscious houses sit atop Berlin's granite knoll and around the town square. Homes on Park, North Huron, and North Adams avenues are textbook examples of Greek Revival, Italianate, Queen Anne, Second Empire, and other architectural styles. To find out more about them, pick up the guide to historic homes available along the town's main street.

# ■ WOLF RIVER VALLEY

Before the Fox River arrives at Lake Winnebago, it receives a massive infusion of fresh water from the highlands of northeast Wisconsin, thanks to the Wolf River. The pristine and hard-driven Wolf River leaves the North Woods behind at Shawano, joining the Little Wolf and Embarrass rivers to gently drain a basin formed by the western edge of the Green Bay glacier. The Wolf first fills Lake Poygan, then joins the Fox at Lake Butte des Morts and together they enter Lake Winnebago.

To travel into the western edge of the Wolf drainage, drive north of Berlin on Highway 49 past the marshland that helps to feed the Wolf. Here, the landscape is cut with streams and dotted with lakes that lie in a thin layer of glacial till only a few yards above the granite bedrock. The largest collection of lakes is called **Chain O' Lakes**, off Highway 22, a few miles west and southwest of Waupaca. Locally, this area is thought to rival the Lakes of Killarney in Ireland. Comparable or not, these wooded lakes are interconnected, so that travelers who seek to lose themselves in the woods have 22 bodies of water to explore and fish. Resorts, campgrounds, and boat-rental docks abound. **Hartman Creek State Park,** located at the western end of the chain, has hiking trails and a no-motor-boat rule, which makes swimming and canoeing especially nice. In winter, ice anglers cover the lakes, while snowmobiles and cross-country skiers rule the trails.

The **Crystal River,** a class three trout stream, flows out of Chain O' Lakes through the village of **Rural.** Most of the clocks here stopped about a hundred years ago. Yankees built this collection of homes starting in the 1860s, and now they are on the National Register of Historic Places.

The Crystal continues on to the city of **Waupaca,** located just north of U.S. 10, and named for elderly Potawatomi chief Sam Waupaca, who exhorted his tribesmen not to murder white settlers, and then fell dead trying to ride away after his speech. The settlers, grateful for his assistance, lived on to start one of the early potato-growing centers in the area's sandy glacial soils.

North of Waupaca, Highway 49 passes through two little Norwegian towns located on the Little Wolf River. They are **Scandinavia** and **Iola,** and both have great local cafes. **Iola Mills Museum of Pioneer History,** listed on the National Register of Historic Places, is located at 300 N. Main Street, and is devoted to Wisconsin's Norwegian heritage. Iola is also home to **Krause Publications,** the world's largest publisher of hobby magazines that focus on such subjects as coin collecting, antique autos, comic books, and baseball cards. Annually, on the weekend after the Fourth of July, the largest antique auto festival in the Midwest is held here, when over 100,000 people come to **Iola Old Car Show and Swap Meet.**

■ TIGERTON AND POSSE COMITATUS
The route from Iola to Tigerton along Highway J travels north past woods and fields dotted with what appear to be huge pink dinosaur eggs. Some of these rounded pink- and red-granite boulders have been set along the road by farmers trying to clear their fields. Once you arrive in Tigerton, take a look at their high school, arguably the prettiest Prairie-style high school in the state.

Tigerton signifies the beginning of the Wisconsin backwoods area. A few miles east of town are the Embarrass River watershed and the former **Tigerton Dells** resort (east of Tigerton and west of Shawano on Highway M). This region of woodland interspersed with potato cropland raised a particularly noisome new crop in the 1970s—a radical survivalist group known as the **Posse Comitatus,** started by a local potato farmer who got mad at the Department of Natural Resources (DNR) over a fine for unauthorized use of a stream to irrigate his farm. The Posse attracted attention with its characterization of the DNR as "Darn Near Russia," a popular anti-communist/populist position in a part of Wisconsin where U.S. Senator Joe McCarthy enjoyed solid voting support and long-lived mythic status years after his death. The Posse soon began to "discover" chilling connections between the DNR and other federal groups and policies that they claimed were not only communist-inspired, but thinly veiled conspiracies by non-whites to destroy or enslave White America. The white supremacy teachings spread among a faithful few from around the state, who gathered at the old Tigerton Dells resort.

Soon, the Rev. James Wickstrom of the Universal Life Church (which offered ordination through a classified ad post box) decided it was time for the Posse to take matters into its own hands. In defiance of local laws, they established an unofficial village, Tigerton Dells, as the capital of their fledgling empire. Posse members patrolled their compound armed with automatic weapons and handguns, and dressed in camouflage and surplus fatigues. Weapons and tactical training programs were conducted to prepare the growing number of Posse followers for the race war they believed to be imminent. Wickstrom became communications director and editor of the *Posse Noose Report,* their monthly newsletter, which chronicled the sell-out of America.

*Heritage Hill State Park near Green Bay preserves architecture from the not so distant past.*

The rise of the Posse coincided with the populist, anti-tax message of maverick Republican gubernatorial candidate Lee Sherman Dreyfus. Emboldened by Dreyfus's message of "let the people decide," the ragtag band of survivalists toted their guns in hip holsters when they visited local towns. The DNR wardens, county sheriff, and local authorities grew increasingly concerned with the collection of temporary buildings and bunkers growing up next to the old resort at Tigerton Dells. These stalwart survivalists failed to get zoning variances for the construction of their compound—a collection of old trailers, some barricades and trenches, and a few illegal latrines. Attempts to fine them for infractions only stiffened their resolve.

When Dreyfus declined to run for a second term and Democrats stumbled into the statehouse, a new effort was initiated to extricate the Posse. Rather than storm the compound and make martyrs out of the Posse, an alternate plan was laid. In Wisconsin, the establishment of any village must be approved by the state legislature—something the Posse had overlooked in building Tigerton Dells. This became the lever to dislodge the Posse from its compound and place its leaders in jail. Posse communications director, the Rev. James Wickstrom, was arrested, convicted, and jailed for establishing an illegal town and impersonating a public official (a serious offense). He served a few years in the state prison, then slipped away to anonymity once his prison term was over. The DNR and the local sheriff bulldozed the illegally constructed compound of house trailers and ramshackle buildings, returning the area to the deer and squirrels that initially held the property. Since then, Posse members have pretty much crept back into the woods and memories of Wisconsin's rural hollows.

## ■ SHAWANO

East of Tigerton off Highway 29 is Shawano (pronounced SHAW-no), settled in 1843 as the great lumber empires thinned the woods of the Fox River Valley and pushed settlers north. After Shawano's timber was cut, paper mills and a dairy industry took lumber's place in the economy. Today, it's a thriving recreational area, and the shores of nearby **Shawano Lake** are filled with vacation homes; neighboring villages sport the ubiquitous supper clubs and bait shops for the summer crowds. Since 1990, the lake has hosted the Zebco/U.S. Crappie Association tournament, meaning that devoted crappie fishermen come here from as far away as Oconee Lake in Georgia or Lake Eufala in Alabama. Devotees of other species angle for northern pike, largemouth bass, and walleyes.

The channel that connects Lake Shawano to the Wolf River recently regained its annual migration of sturgeon. These fish—some as big as five feet (1.5 m) long—come north to breed in the shallows of Shawano Lake between mid-April and early May, returning to Lakes Poygan, Butte de Morts, and Winnebago each fall. Water pollution has diminished the **annual sturgeon migration,** but anti-pollution laws (supported by the paper companies) are now getting good results. The annual spawning run can be seen at Shawano Dam on Richmond Street in town.

On Highway 29, northwest of Shawano along the Wolf River at the end of Franklin Street, the Shawano County Historical Society operates **Heritage Park.** Guided tours are offered of restored buildings, including a schoolhouse, a dairy building, and a log cabin. Nearby Sunset Island has picnic facilities, a fishing dock, and boat slips.

The Wolf River here has whitewater challenges for canoeists, kayakers, and rafters, and there are many local parks where you can put in your canoe or picnic. Several outfitters in the area offer raft trips on the Wolf River.

## ■ HISTORIC AND INDUSTRIAL CITIES

At the heart of the Fox Valley is **Lake Winnebago,** filled by the Fox and Wolf rivers to form a 215-square-mile bowl, 28 miles (45 km) long and 10 miles (16 km) wide, but only 20 feet (6 m) deep. This is the largest lake entirely within Wisconsin, and one of the state's most popular recreational locations.

*Kimberly-Clark Corporation began operations in October 1872 and went on to become one of America's largest multi-national corporations, producing a variety of paper products. The original Globe Paper Mill is pictured above.*

The cities around the lake—Oshkosh, Fond du Lac, Neenah, and Menasha—all enjoy lovely lakefront parks and marinas. These cities sprang to life to serve the timber industry. As ax and saw tore through the North Woods, millions of board feet of timber were floated each spring down the Wolf to the Fox, and into the mills at Oshkosh, Neenah, and Menasha, bringing great wealth to the fledging towns. They in turn shipped dimension lumber to the furniture, sash, and trim mills at Fond du Lac, Sheboygan, and Sheboygan Falls, and to the towns of Manitowoc and Sturgeon Bay for building the Great Lakes fishing and merchant fleets.

## ■ OSHKOSH

The city of Oshkosh was named for the Menominee chief Oshkosh, who had the misfortune to be the signer of the treaty that handed over the southeastern corner of Wisconsin to the U.S. government. Oshkosh was courted by Indian agents in the years preceding the treaty, after the territorial courts found him not guilty in the murder of another Indian. Oshkosh had fought on the side of the whites since his early years, but despite his loyalty the southern range of the Menominee was lost to an expanding nation. At the signing of the 1836 Treaty of the Cedars, Chief Oshkosh received a beaver and felt top hat with a red silk sash and feather. When he placed it on his head he was moved to say, "This is the way the white man's law fits the Indian. Don't I look awful?"

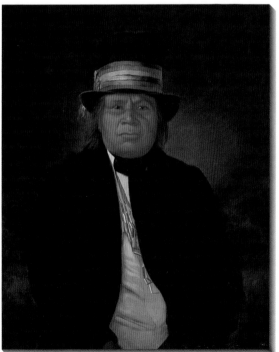

*Chief Oshkosh portrayed wearing his "awful" hat.*
*(State Historical Society of Wisconsin)*

Oshkosh was one of the first Wisconsin cities to experience the boom of the lumber business, and the downtown sprang up in a few years. It burned down in the 1870s, only to be rebuilt again. When the lumber floating down the Wolf River slowed to a trickle, lumberjacks disappeared from the streets of Oshkosh, and an industrial city emerged. Harsh lines were drawn between the working men and the factory bosses. Wood-working strikes were initiated during the 1890s, and by 1898 the strikes resembled riots in the bloody Third Ward of the city. Eventually, changes in manufacturing and increasing diversity of products served to diffuse the labor movement, while labor law improved the conditions of the working man.

**Paine Art Center and Arboretum**, at 1410 Algoma Boulevard, owes its existence to the labor strife that swirled through Oshkosh. Nathaniel Paine's sash and door plant, located on the Fox River down Algoma Boulevard, was the largest plant of its kind in the world. Paine was anti-union and resisted any union interference in his plant. Fond of grandeur and luxury, he began building a rambling Tudor Gothic mansion in the 1920s. Its construction was slow, due in part to his demand for rare materials, and in part to the craftsmen who shared sympathies with Samuel Gompers, who tried to organize a woodworkers union at Paine's sash and door plant.

When a 16-year-old boy was killed, famed attorney Clarence Darrow was brought in to defend the union leaders facing trumped-up charges for the death. In this highly charged atmosphere, years passed before the mansion could be completed, and rumors flew about how the ghost of the dead boy would harm Paine if he ever slept in the elegant home, or that Paine would die before the mansion was finished. Paine spent nearly a million dollars on the building, but never lived there, partly for fear of the rumors. Instead, he finally donated the building for use as a museum.

Industry still drives the city's economy. Oshkosh produces Oshkosh trucks—heavy-duty, four-wheel-drive vehicles preferred by the military and most common at airports for towing luggage carts and planes. If you are the parent of an infant or a toddler, the name Oshkosh is probably associated in your mind with "B'Gosh." The clothing manufacturer started by producing tough denim work coveralls, but the baby boomlet brought new opportunity to transform the tradesman's costume into baby pants with snap-in inseams. The pants became the hand-me-down of choice in families across America, and they are more popular in France than even Jerry Lewis. You'll find the **Oshkosh B'Gosh factory outlet** at the intersection of highways 44 and 41, in the huge **Manufacturers Marketplace**.

The town of Oshkosh is also enthusiastic about aviation. Every summer during the last week of July, Wittman Field in Oshkosh becomes one of the busiest airports in the world. Over the years the **Experimental Aircraft Association Fly-In** has been held at Oshkosh, where sport flyers, stunt pilots, and pilots of experimental craft join in this love-in for aviators. Vintage biplanes from the 1920s and 1930s mingle with aircraft used in World War II, and enormous jets. Tens of thousands of private pilots fly in and camp out with their aircraft for a few days. The EAA **Air Adventure Museum** is located next to the airport at 3000 Poberezny Road. Its exhibits show the history of aviation and include some full-sized planes.

## ■ APPLETON AND THE LOWER FOX

From Lake Winnebago, the Fox River turns 180 degrees north into a valley warped into the bedrock by the enormous weight of glaciers. Fortified by the 150-billion cubic feet of hydraulic power in Lake Winnebago, the Fox rushes down past Doty Island, between the dardanelles of Neenah and Menasha, dropping 15 feet (5 m) per mile over rapids at Appleton, Kimberly, Little Chute, and Kaukauna, and ripping through locks and dams to De Pere and Green Bay.

*Steve Wittman poses with his aircraft named Buster. A pioneer in aircraft design, Wittman embodies the spirit of the Experimental Aircraft Association, whose convention he helped bring to Oshkosh and which is now one of the leading such events in the world. (Oshkosh Public Museum)*

*Along College Avenue in Appelton during the 1880s ran the "Dinky," the nation's first commercially successful trolley. (Outagamie County Historical Society, Appleton)*

The power of the lower Fox was harnessed in the 1850s with a series of locks and dams, providing power for mills to saw up the plunder of the North Woods. When the pine woods began to falter after 40 years of intensive logging, the region was able to turn to paper manufacturing, thanks to an abundant supply of pulpwood and billions of gallons of water. In terms of *paper,* the industrial production of the region meets human needs from the cradle to the grave. Within a 15-mile (24-km) stretch of river, giants like Kimberly-Clark, Menasha Corporation, James River, Fox River, and Appleton Papers produce every conceivable paper and cardboard product. The sludge from their plants produced an overpowering stench that pervaded the valley until serious attempts were made to clean up the river. Although the DNR still recommends not eating the fish caught in these waters, great advances have been made.

Today, from De Pere Dam downstream to Green Bay, it's poignant to observe the eagerness of nature's creatures to return to their old haunts once man cleans up his act. Fishermen have been pulling in walleyes, smallmouths, white bass, catfish, crappies, and muskies; as a further sign of vitality, salmon and trout have begun to appear. A few northern pike come up the Fox, despite the degradation of the Green Bay shoreline where they spawn. Sediments in the river still carry heavy contaminants, so it's best to check locally about what fish are safe to eat. The local euphemism for the style of fishing encouraged here is "recreational fishing"; i.e., catch them, then put them back so you don't poison yourself.

**Appleton** is the flagship city of the Fox Valley, the central node of a paper-manufacturing empire that spreads out along the banks of the Fox. On its heights above the river, the handsome campus of **Lawrence University** stands amidst a vibrant and clean downtown area, which has grown out to meet the interstate. Appleton's wooded neighborhoods, and streets that trace Indian footpaths above the Fox, are among the most scenic residential areas in the valley, with architecture spanning the eras from Victorian to Bauhaus.

Nature lovers should follow College Avenue east to City A, and drive four miles (6.4 km) north to the **Gordon Bubolz Nature Preserve.** This white cedar swamp has fine trails, excellent for hikers and cross-country skiers.

To enjoy a brewery, turn east onto Olde Oneida Street to Between the Locks, a restored brewery, now a mall, which features a brewpub called **Appleton Brewing Company.**

Perhaps Appleton's most famous settlers were the Weiss and McCarthy families—better known throughout the country for spawning Harry Houdini and Joe McCarthy.

**Harry Houdini,** born Ehrich Weiss, was the son of a Jewish rabbi from Hungary who came over soon after Ehrich was born. Apocryphal stories abound: how Weiss learned to pick locks by raiding his mother's pie safe; how his father had killed a man in Europe and came to America a fugitive. Whatever the truth of these stories, Weiss was a genius with a third-grade education who designed some of the most sophisticated professional magic equipment ever invented. Using locks and handcuffs specially designed and made in his own laboratory, Houdini developed a hugely popular stage show. His opposable big toe allowed him access to a wide range of lock picks hidden in his shoes. Though Houdini left Appleton to join the circus, he is fondly remembered in his hometown. The **Houdini Historical Center at the Outagamie Museum,** 330 E. College Avenue, has an enormous collection of his posters and memorabilia, as well as an array of his trick cuffs and magical creations.

## HARRY HOUDINI

Harry Houdini, born Ehrich Weiss in Budapest, emigrated with his father, a rabbi, to Appleton at an early age. He became a circus trapeze performer at the age of eight and by the age of 26 had developed his reputation as the world's greatest escape artist. His uncanny ability to extricate himself from chains and locked boxes amazed the world and his performances often attracted thousands of spectators. In a typical act he would be handcuffed, bound in chains, placed in a locked box that was in turn roped and weighted before being submerged under water. A few minutes later he would rise unbound to the surface. Some claimed he had super-normal power—an assertion he strongly denied. In fact, Houdini campaigned against charlatans who claimed supernatural powers and wrote a book exposing their tricks titled *Miracle Mongers and Their Methods.* He died in 1926 from peritonitis as a result of a stomach injury he suffered when he was punched following a performance in Detroit.

*A 1911 poster promotes escape artist and magician Harry Houdini. (Collection of Dom DiMento, Oakland, CA)*

■ JOE MCCARTHY LAND

Memories of **Joe McCarthy** provoke mixed feelings in the Fox River Valley—most are negative, but he still has some solid supporters. Son of immigrant Irish farmers, the square-fisted Joe took to learning in his late teens, and graduated from four years of high school in one year. He went to Wisconsin's Roman Catholic bastion—Marquette University—to earn his law degree. But his fun-loving, pugilistic nature and understanding of the region's generally conservative working class and farm families, as well as business interests, directed him into politics. He enjoyed success in his race for district judge. During nominal military service during World War II, McCarthy played the publicity card astutely by posing for photographs as "Tailgunner Joe," even though his service to the nation consisted of practice bombing raids over coconut groves. With a war record in hand, McCarthy found immediate electoral success, using an early version of direct mail campaigning that went for the jugular against opponents. Wisconsin Progressives objected to McCarthy, but his career as an anti-communist sat well with the conservative Republican voters.

During his Senate career, McCarthy was an avid gambler and spent considerable money at the racetracks outside Washington, all too often burning up money sent

*"Tailgunner Joe" McCarthy used his brief military service as a publicity stunt to help his political career following World War II. (State Historical Society of Wisconsin)*

to fund his McCarthy Brigades. His charges denouncing State Department officials as communists hamstrung Presidents, destroyed careers, and left a permanent scar on U.S. foreign and domestic affairs. Until his army hearings outraged President Eisenhower and the Washington establishment, McCarthy was as unbeatable at home as his rhetoric was unchallenged nationally.

A few years after being chastised by the U.S. Senate, a disgraced McCarthy died of the effects of alcoholism. In Wisconsin, certain people still believe that he was right and it was only the drink that led him astray—the devil has his advocates. It is a permanent point of pride among the most conservative actors in Wisconsin's political scene that McCarthy invented anti-communism as a powerful political tool. In the 1980s, the John Birch Society moved its national headquarters to McCarthy's birthplace of Grand Chute, a short trip from his Appleton grave site, the object of veneration for annual pilgrimages by faithful devotees of "Tailgunner Joe" McCarthy.

## ■ GREEN BAY

Having hoped to discover the Northwest Passage to China, the French explorer Nicolet found Green Bay and the Fox River a great disappointment. Little did he realize that he was, in many ways, successful; he had stumbled upon a real northwest passage to the American interior.

The missionary and trading encampment founded after his arrival at La Baye Verte (the Green Bay) was the first permanent European establishment in Wisconsin, and it fulfilled its French colonial manifest as a headquarters-in-the-field for men in search of furs and souls.

Though much warmer than France's primary wilderness outpost in Montreal, La Baye Verte remained a backwater of the colonial empire. Local natives burned down the St. Xavier Mission above the De Pere rapids in 1687, but the French remained persistent colonists. By the late 1700s, families settled "ribbon" farms stretching back from the banks of the Fox. Green Bay was home to Charles de Langlade, part French and part Ottawa, whose military savvy and command of Indian forces deterred British expansion during the French and Indian War, and later, American efforts in the War of 1812. Charles de Langlade remained an important local figure in this trading outpost when the British melted back into Canada, and the fur trade continued for a few more years under John Jacob Astor.

Green Bay's position as trade center continued when the Yankees arrived. As the Fox Valley matured into an industrial basin, goods came down the Fox through

Green Bay's port to build the Western frontier. Land speculation in the 1830s platted the cities of Navarino and Fort Howard on opposite sides of the Fox River. Those farms, cabins, and a fort at the jaws of the Fox became Green Bay, whose 96,000 residents today make it Wisconsin's third-largest city.

The history of Green Bay is captured best at **Heritage Hill State Park** on the Fox River above the suburb of De Pere (Highway 57 at 2640 S. Webster Avenue). Heritage Hill has exhibits of a replica of a bark chapel used by Jesuits, log cabins that housed fur traders and frontier lawyers, military buildings from Fort Howard, and the Roi-Porlier-Tank Cottage, the oldest extant building in the city. The **Neville Public Museum** of Brown County, at 210 Museum Place, has several exhibits describing Wisconsin geology, glaciers, and natural history. You can still see Charles de Langlade's uniforms, journals, and other personal artifacts, as well as pictures, newspapers, pottery, weaponry, and other items that provide a thorough picture of early life in Wisconsin. In response to recent federal laws, the skeletal remains here belonging to native tribes will be returned for reburial; spiritual relics will also be returned.

The **Oneida National Museum**, at 886 Highway EE, tells the story of the Oneida nation of the Iroquois confederacy, which left New York state in the mid-1800s

*Octoberfest in full swing at the Riverside Ballroom in Green Bay.*

and purchased reservation land in Wisconsin. The Oneida have transformed some of their reservation land west of Green Bay into a profitable, popular **casino and bingo hall complex** located at Irene Moore Activity Center, Highway 172 across from Austin Straubel Airport.

Green Bay is also "Titletown U.S.A.," the home of the **Green Bay Packers,** and the smallest U.S. city with a National Football League (NFL) franchise. The club was started in 1919 over a couple of beers in a tavern by Curly Lambeau, a triple-threat back from Green Bay High who played a year for Knute Rockne at Notre Dame. Lambeau talked the Indian Packing Company into sponsoring the club in 1919, and it bought a franchise in Jim Thorpe's American Professional Football Association (APFA). The APFA became the NFL after George Halas brought a team to Chicago and named it the Bears, igniting a rivalry with the Packers that stands to this day. The Packers joined the NFL in 1921. (Soon afterwards league president "Papa Bear" Halas pardoned the Acme Packing Company's club for illegally fielding college players.)

The Packers won league championships in 1929, 1930, and 1931, but financial problems forced the team to dissolve briefly in the 1930s. The team was saved in 1935 by the people and businesses of Green Bay, who bought shares of stock

*Fish boils—a specialty of Green Bay and the Door Peninsula—consist of whitefish, potatoes, carrots, onions, and cabbage boiled over an open fire.*

## COACHING THE GREEN BAY PACKERS

*W*hen I served as backfield coach at West Point under Earl Blaik, I learned more from him than I have ever learned from any other man. One of the things that Blaik used to say was: "To beat the Navy, you have to hate the Navy."

What kind of game is this, then, that requires the constant conjuring up of animosity? Each year, and probably more than once a year, I tell our team that, during the football season, there are only three things in which each man should be interested: 1) his family; 2) his religion; 3) the Green Bay Packers. I coach this game, however, at no small cost to my family. I am a religious man whose religion, as all true religions, is based on love of fellowman, and yet each week, as I talk about our opponents, I almost always snarl against them . . . .

"The day of a game," my wife Marie has said, "Vince hates everybody connected with that other team, but after the game—win, lose or draw—it's over."

I don't think that's true, I *know* it's true . . . .

That's our game, though, this game for madmen. It arouses such violent emotions, and those emotions feed latent prejudice. In our NFL championship game, when our daughter Susan heard the epithet "Wop!" screamed down at me, she cried . . . .

The better and more successful we are, of course, the worse this becomes. That is the irony associated with success in this business. It doesn't make your life any easier. Everybody in the league is shooting at you, on the field and off, which is expected, but there is also an unexpected alteration in attitude on your own team . . . .

In coaching you speak in clichés, but I mean every one of them. There is only one yardstick in our business and that is winning. Second place is meaningless. You can't always be first, but you have to believe that you should have been—that you are never beaten, time just runs out on you. When any one of my ballplayers is tired of winning, or tired of paying the price winning demands, he will have a one-way ticket on a plane from Green Bay, no matter who he is.

If I am going to instill in my team this ravenous appetite for success and then maintain it against the constant threat of self-complacency, it must be deeply ingrained in me.

—Vince Lombardi and W. C. Heinz,
"A Game for Madmen," *LOOK,* September 5, 1967

through the American Legion to make the team a municipal asset—tax-exempt and non-profit—owned by the city of Green Bay.

The modern years of Packer Glory began when a New York Giants offensive coach, Vincent T. Lombardi, was hired in 1958 to rejuvenate the cellar-dwelling Packers. He raised them up in two seasons to win the NFL championship in 1961; in 1967 and 1968 they won the first two Super Bowls. During these glory years, Wisconsin priests shortened Sunday sermons so the faithful could get home in time for the games. Lombardi became the model corporate motivator, whose motto (winning isn't everything, it's the only thing) was im-

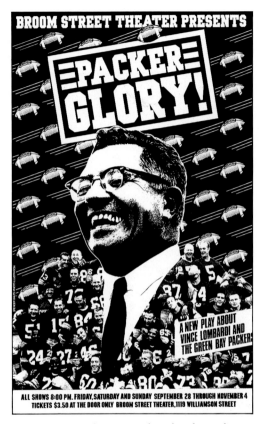

**BROOM STREET THEATER PRESENTS**

**=PACKER= GLORY!**

A NEW PLAY ABOUT VINCE LOMBARDI AND THE GREEN BAY PACKERS

ALL SHOWS 8:00 PM. FRIDAY, SATURDAY AND SUNDAY SEPTEMBER 28 THROUGH NOVEMBER 4 TICKETS $3.50 AT THE DOOR ONLY BROOM STREET THEATER, 1119 WILLIAMSON STREET

*The Green Bay Packers were in their glory during the late 1960s when the football team won the first two official Super Bowls in 1967 and 1968.*

printed on Americans like a psychological tattoo. In the NFL, Lombardi is a mythic figure; in Wisconsin he is patron saint, whose chapel is the **Packer Hall of Fame** next to Lambeau Field at 855 Lombardi Avenue. Tours of the stadium are available in the summer.

# ■ DOOR PENINSULA

Walling in the *bay* of Green Bay on the east, a sharp slab of limestone juts into Lake Michigan like the thumb of a mitten. Seventy miles (112 km) long, and 13 miles (21 km) wide, the peninsula has a maritime heritage of fishing and boat-building that invites comparison to Cape Cod, which it exceeds in attributes such as developmental restraint, picturesque cliffs, sandy beaches, dunes, numerous parks, Victorian charm, and abundant orchards. Farther north than Minnesota's Twin Cities, its position between Green Bay and Lake Michigan blesses the peninsula with late falls, early springs, and a climate perfect for growing fruit.

The apple and cherry orchards of Door County and Kewaunee County (to the south) once earned them the reputation as the California of the north, blessed with fertile soil, a gentle climate, and lots of kids willing to live in camps and pick cherries and apples until schools reopened in fall. Some migrant camps were chaperoned to prevent young women from sneaking out at night to consort with men they met in the orchards—fitting concerns, as most of the orchards were family-run.

*Cherry orchards crisscross the Door Peninsula, and their blossoming every June is a major tourist attraction. (Photo by Jerry Stebbins)*

*Freddie Kodanko of Bailey's Harbor displays his drumming talent as well as his perfect Door County potatoes.*

Washington Island at the tip of Door County was once home to the Potawatomi, who moved into the area after most of the Winnebago there died from contact with the French and their diseases. The Potawatomi farmed land near the ancient effigy mounds built by earlier Indian tribes. The treacherous currents between the tip of the peninsula and Washington Island were described by the French as *Porte des Morts,* Death's Door, where many ships have sunk trying to cross the straits, and from which Door County got its name.

The entire peninsula is alive with tourists for most of the summer, and inn-hopping, eating, and shopping vacations have replaced the fishing and camping of generations past. The shops are filled to overflowing, many featuring the work of local painters and artisans. Restaurants cater to visitors and cuisine might best be described as "hearty." So many places offer the Door Peninsula's specialty, fish boils, that it's impossible to escape the smell of burning firewood and stewing fish when the sun starts to sink into Green Bay. A "boil" is made by filling a large pot with white fish, potatoes, carrots, onions, and sometimes cabbage, and cooking it all over a fire. After the stew is made, it's served up with bread and butter. The fish boil is reputed to be an old Scandinavian custom handed down from the original immigrants on the peninsula, who settled to fish the surrounding waters in the late 1800s. Their descendants invented an alcoholic brew called Cherry Bounce, that, according to one Wisconsinite, involves the following: At the height of the cherry harvest in July, get two big fistfuls of ripe cherries and put them in a large bottle. Pour in a fifth of vodka and a half cup sugar. Drink at Christmas.

Hardy, outdoor types enjoy the parks on the peninsula, which still provide summer camping and winter cross-country skiing. (The moist lake air provides ample snow and a second tourist season during the winter.) Reservations for lodging are recommended for weekend trips, whatever the season, for despite the inevitable tourist kitsch, the charm of Door County's small towns endures.

A tour of Door is to follow one of the most scenic drives in the U.S.: high lime-stone bluffs with views of offshore islands and fishing boats, historic lighthouses, fields of wildflowers, and stone fences. From the city of Green Bay, follow Highway 57 north to Sturgeon Bay. On this side of the peninsula the weather is apt to be warm and sunny, the water fairly calm, and the landscape well settled.

**Sturgeon Bay,** located halfway up the peninsula, is a shipbuilding center where you can see ships, yachts, and boats being constructed. Drop by the Information Center or the Door County Chamber of Commerce office for a free self-guided tour of the downtown and the residential historic districts. Cherryland Brewery, located in an old railroad station at 341 N. Third Avenue, has a microbrewery. Door County Maritime Museum, at the foot of Florida Street next to Sunset Park, is located adjacent to a shipyard, and documents the region's maritime heritage.

Highway 42 meanders up the Green Bay side of the peninsula past lots of Victorian houses that now are used as bed and breakfasts or boutiques. Towns along the way include **Egg Harbor** and **Fish Creek**. Just north of Egg Harbor, at the site of an old dairy farm, is the **Birch Creek Music Center,** where well-known artists come in the summertime to teach young musicians, and evening concerts are performed for the public.

To experience a traditional peninsula fish boil try **The White Gull Inn** at 4225 Main Street in Fish Creek. North of Fish Creek at **Peninsula State Park,** there's a magnificent view from Eagle Bluff, and in summer you can visit the park's nineteenth-century Eagle Bluff Lighthouse, still in use. The only state-owned golf course in the area is here, the 18-hole Peninsula Park Golf Course.

As you drive along, you'll see many signs for fishing tours and charters. In the town of **Ephraim** you might wish to try Eagle Harbor Charters; for a sailing cruise, Bella Sailing Cruises. When you drive into this town, founded in 1853, you'll see why it's also known as "White Village." White wooden houses and churches rise in tiers on the hills above Ephraim's bay.

As the road continues northeast, it passes cherry orchards and some abandoned farmland. In spring and summer, unplowed fields fill up with Queen Anne's Lace, Indian paintbrush, mustard, knapweed, chicory, and daisies. **Ellison Bay,** a little town founded in 1870 and located near the tip of the peninsula, is a lovely spot to go biking and hiking, as the backroads are quiet and picturesque. **The Clearing,** just off Highway 42 in Ellison Bay, is devoted to the study of Danish folk tradition. Located on a lovely bluff-top site, its residential school is open in the summertime. Camping is available nearby at **Newport State Park.**

A little further north at **Gills Rock,** a passenger ferry crosses to Washington Island (a car ferry leaves from Northport) through *Porte des Morts.* In rough weather, this can be an exciting trip.

Approaching **Washington Island** you'll see steep bluffs rising gradually toward the center of the island. At its edges the island is thickly wooded; inland is farmland tilled by a population of mostly Scandinavian descent. From Washington Island another ferry leads to the high rocky promontory known as **Rock Island.**

A heavily wooded little mountain with a lighthouse at its tip, Rock Island is home to a lovely, "unimproved" state park excellent for backpacking and cycling, and for generally getting away from it all.

Travelers returning south down the peninsula along the Lake Michigan shoreline will find it foggier and stormier, its water rougher, and landscape more rugged than the Green Bay shoreline. Highway 57 branches southeast past **Cana Island Lighthouse,** built in 1870. Located about a quarter mile offshore, it is reached via a stone causeway when the water is low. Just beyond is the **Ridges Sanctuary,** where rare plant communities—including all 23 orchid species native to the state —thrive in the ridges and swales along the shoreline. Nearby woods are a mix of conifers and hardwood, and vivid with color in autumn. On sunny days Lake Michigan is as blue as the sky. Stormy days are green, gray, and growling, the lake water tossed with froth and white caps. Beaches along the shore are sand and rock—white-fawn sand and gray-black stone mixed with some red and pink.

The village of **Bailey's Harbor,** founded by a sea captain who sheltered here in 1840 during a fierce storm, is set inside a wooded arm of land curving into the lake. It has a few restaurants and two boat docks. If fishing in Lake Michigan interests you, try Bailey's Harbor Charter Fishing Association.

**Bjorklunden Chapel** on Chapel Lane, a replica of an ancient Norwegian *stavkirke* (wooden church), is worth a visit. Call ahead to (414) 839-2216, if you'd like a tour.

Just past Bailey's Harbor in Jacksonport you'll cross the 45th parallel and be exactly halfway between the equator and the North Pole. A few miles farther south is **Whitefish Dunes State Park,** a perfect place to loll on a wide sand beach or take a hike along lakeside trails or remains of ancient Indian cultures.

*Pilot Island Lighthouse rests on a lonely rock in the Porte des Morts passage, across which the Washington Island ferry traverses. (Photo by Jerry Stebbins)*

*Villa Gottfried, built by brewing tycoon, Wilhelm Gottfried in Elkhart Lake, is typical of the country mansions built in southeastern Wisconsin by Milwaukee and Chicago captains of industry. (Sheboygan County Historical Research Center)*

# SOUTHEAST WISCONSIN

WHEN SETTLERS FIRST ARRIVED in southeastern Wisconsin, they found a sandy, rock-strewn shoreline along Lake Michigan, rising to a plateau above the lake. Natural harbors lay at the mouths of rivers flowing from a mysterious interior, which, they soon discovered, was an inviting oak savanna and grassland rolling up to tree-covered hills, later known as the kettle moraine.

The kettle moraine, which forms the backbone of southeast Wisconsin, is a gently curving, 100-mile (161-km) line of hollows and hills created when two competing glacial lobes from Lake Michigan and Green Bay rubbed up against one another, mounding up the ground and debris along their common edge. Stippled with "kettles," glacier-carved hollows in the hills, the moraine holds hundreds of lakes, bogs, and marshes, a mix of aquatic habitat and hardwood forest that is a haven for wildlife.

To the west, beyond the kettle moraine, meandering rivers—the Yahara, Rock, Bark, Crawfish, and others—drain a vast area of glacial debris. The rivers rise in marshes amid drumlins and eskers—hills and narrow ridges of sand, gravel, and boulders deposited by streams flowing beneath the glaciers.

In 1971 the Ice Age National Scientific Reserve was created, preserving the distinctive glacial landscape of Wisconsin and providing recreational enjoyment. The reserve consists of nine separate units spread over the state, as well as the Ice Age National Scenic Trail.

## ■ SETTLING THE SOUTHEAST

In the early years of the Wisconsin territory, a handful of surveyors dreamed of bustling cities and prosperous villages as they platted the wilderness westward from Lake Michigan. Once the Winnebago signed treaties with the U.S. government, these lands opened for settlement, and beginning in the 1840s, large numbers of Irish, Cornish, Swiss, and German immigrants began arriving in Wisconsin. The emigration of Scandinavians from 1860 to 1880, and the arrival of Italians and Eastern Europeans by the turn of the century, made Wisconsin the most ethnically diverse state in the union. With these settlers came a great variety of religions. The

English and Yankees were mostly Episcopalian; Germans and Scandinavians primarily Lutheran. The Irish, Italians, Poles, and many Germans remained loyal Roman Catholics. As they outgrew the early log and frame churches, they replaced them with hundreds of Gothic and Romanesque stone and brick churches, whose steeples still rise above the hearts of small villages.

Milwaukee and other southeast settlements became golden cities made of Cream City brick, first fired in 1836 from deposits of lacustrine clay along Lake Michigan. Glacial deposits of clay allowed dozens of brick factories to flourish in the river towns of the southeast. Masons from Europe and the East Coast cut the multi-colored field stones of granite, basalt, and rhyolite into foundations for homes and barns. Limestone, sandstone, and dolomite outcroppings were transformed into homes, churches, commercial buildings, wells, and cisterns. To this day, the cities and villages of the southeast have fine churches, homes, and main street buildings of brick and stone in designs spanning Federal, Gothic, Victorian, and European, as elegant and solid today as when they were first built.

Along with railroads, steam-powered engines transformed the industrial base of Wisconsin. As water-powered mills adopted steam, cities like Milwaukee, Racine, Kenosha, and Janesville became industrial centers, making industrial pumps, tractors, cars, machine tools, rail cars and locomotives, and food products. Foundries sprang up to smelt the ore from the northern part of the state, supplying finished iron for the factories. The most heavily developed part of Wisconsin is the corridor of cities along Lake Michigan's shores, from Sheboygan in the north to the Illinois state line in the south. The densest industrial core extends from Milwaukee south to the Lake Michigan port cities of Racine to Kenosha. Smaller cities and villages sprang up on the river banks and also developed industries—at first, saw and grain mills, and brick and wagon factories; and later, breweries, cheese factories, foundries, and tanneries. This industrial heritage made Wisconsin one of the top manufacturing states in the Union.

## ■ MANITOWOC

Set on Lake Michigan below the Door Peninsula and at the mouth of the Manitowoc River, this city was known for its shipyards and in the nineteenth century for its schooners. Later, submarines and landing craft were built here. A visit to the

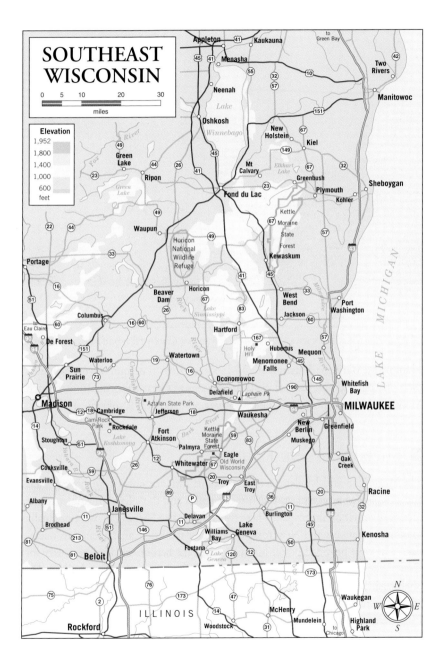

*A bird's-eye view of Sheboygan Falls in 1880. (Sheboygan County Historical Research Center)*

**Manitowoc Maritime Museum** at 75 Maritime Drive, is definitely worthwhile, as their photographs and displays explain 100 years of Great Lakes maritime history. Moored beside the museum is the USS *Cobia*, a World War II submarine.

## ■ SHEBOYGAN AND KOHLER

The Sheboygan and Mullet rivers join a short distance outside Sheboygan Falls and tumble down together through rocky rapids and the village of Kohler to the industrial center of Sheboygan. These two villages, like Sheboygan, were originally founded by Yankees and New Yorkers soon after the Erie Canal opened its operation. The river provided power for mills, while the harbor provided sanctuary for Great Lakes merchant vessels. Charles Cole built an inn and other buildings at Sheboygan Falls, preserved today by the Sheboygan County Historical Society across the river from the old knitting mills (Water Street and County Highway PP). German immigrants formed the dominant culture as the Yankees followed the new railroads out of town.

## ■ KOHLER INDUSTRIAL EMPIRE

The Kohler family of Sheboygan built an empire from cast iron and porcelain. Starting out with a foundry producing farm implements, they later switched to enameled plates and cups. When inside plumbing became the rule after outhouses fell from fashion, Kohler's factory grew big producing toilets, tubs, sinks, and bath fixtures. Their products are said to be flushed with pride. Another branch of the Kohler family owns Vollrath Corporation, which makes stainless steel cookware and industrial products. Together the two companies are among the largest employers in Sheboygan County. Being wealthy didn't hurt them in politics, either, as two members of the Kohler clan served terms as governors of Wisconsin (Walter Kohler, Senior and Junior).

Unfortunately, what was good for the Kohler family business was not always enjoyed by the workers. Labor strife infected its workshops from the 1930s to the 1960s. National Guard troops fought with strikers in 1934 to protect the village of Kohler from an angry mob of workers. Two protesters were killed in that strike, trying to organize the Kohler workers. Labor unrest divided the community for over 30 years, setting brothers, fathers, and other family members at odds with

*Walter J. Kohler (in straw hat) crosses a picket line at his plant on July 16, 1934. Labor strife was endemic until the 1960s. Kohler enjoys a reputation of producing quality porcelain and steel products. (Sheboygan County Historical Research Center)*

*Sheboygan's three "Cs": chairs, cheese, and children. (Sheboygan County Historical Research Center)*

one another. Labor peace returned in the 1960s, and Kohler remains one of Wisconsin's premier privately held companies, with a reputation for craftsmanship and design excellence.

The **Kohler plant** in Kohler on Highland Drive is a masterpiece of art deco industrial design, and it's possible to tour it weekdays by calling (414) 457-4441. From the pleasing proportions of the smokestacks, evenly arrayed above a massive factory, to the elegant brick residential complex that once housed European porcelain workers employed by the company (now the five-diamond American Club Resort), the Kohlers emphasized fine design in every product they made. Each year Kohler invites artists from all over the country to explore their artistic inspiration using porcelain and cast iron. The artists display their finished work at the **Kohler Design Center**, 101 Upper Road adjacent to the factory in Kohler, and at Sheboygan's **John Michael Kohler Arts Center** at 608 New York Avenue. The latter's interest in art extends throughout Wisconsin and beyond: they have purchased and preserved works of art where they stand, such as the farmyard sculptures at Hollandale, southwest of Madison, and the Wegner Grotto north of Sparta, Wisconsin.

## ■ ROAD AMERICA AND BRATWURST

Tucked in the northern kettle moraine west of Sheboygan is **Elkhart Lake,** and several miles south of town on Highway 67, Wisconsin's premier auto-racing track, **Road America.** The lake became a resort area in the late 1800s and still offers visitors lodging in elegant Victorian hotels and mansions.

Road America was born of a wider vision by a German immigrant who made it big in America—Chicago brewer Wilhelm Gottfried. German plays were performed in his own theater, while elk and deer wandered freely on his 400-acre estate. One of Gottfried's favorite diversions was car racing. He brought the first hopped-up cars to race on his estate, but soon drivers were racing on the winding streets of the town of Elkhart Lake. In the mid-1950s, in response to state laws forbidding racing on state roads, a special track was built outside of town, and called Road America. The track is best known for its European-style Grand Prix race cars, but a full slate of motorcycles, Indy cars, and other fuel-breathing machines test their wheels on the twisting, picturesque track set in the hilly moraine south of the lake.

*Road America races in progress during the summer of 1967. (Sheboygan County Historical Research Center)*

While the Yankees may have controlled the early politics of the towns and villages of Wisconsin, it was the beer and food of German immigrants that created the cultural ambiance of the state. In this region of Wisconsin, one of the most lasting German legacies is the **bratwurst**, a mildly spiced smoked pork or veal sausage. Perhaps the finest place to sample this culinary phenomenon is in the tiny village of **Mt. Calvary,** west of Elkhart Lake and nestled in the shadow of a hilltop Roman Catholic seminary dominating the surrounding landscape. The butcher store in Mt. Calvary occasionally holds a brat fry (as do hundreds of other towns and neighborhoods in this part of Wisconsin) to benefit Little League teams, 4-H clubs, snowmobile clubs, or some other cause. It's better by far to fall prey to the lure of mustard, onions, and fresh bratwurst than the gut-numbing mediocrity of fast-food fare somewhere down the road.

The small village of **Greenbush,** at the northern end of the Kettle Moraine State Forest, was founded by Yankees in the 1850s when the town was the main overland stop between Fond du Lac and Sheboygan. Their inn—the **Old Wade House**—a blacksmith shop, and the **Wesley W. Jung Carriage Museum** capture the essentials of life in the mid-1800s. When the railroad bypassed Greenbush, the plank-road traffic ebbed, and the village faded into the landscape until it was renovated by the Kohler Company and presented as a historic site to the State Historical Society. It is one of the few places in Wisconsin where you can still travel by horse-drawn carriage.

## ■ NORTHERN KETTLE MORAINE

The kettle moraine forms an arcing backbone that runs from north to south, separating Lake Michigan from Lake Winnebago, the Horicon Marsh, and the well-watered valley of the Rock River. Driving through the kettle moraine can be an almost hypnotic experience, as drumlins slip behind eskers, tamarack trees sweep past kettle bogs. The landscape is pocketed with marshes and lakes and stippled with rolling hills. The oaks that once ruled the lonely hills now are thick with invading buckthorn, box elder, honeysuckle, red cedar, and sumac. Two of the finest sectors of the moraine are preserved in the Kettle Moraine State Forest: the northern sector to the west of Sheboygan, and the other to the southeast of Milwaukee. (See "Southern Kettle Moraine" later in this chapter.) A fine driving trip through this area would begin west of Sheboygan on Highway 23 where it intersects with 67. Turning south, the road travels through the Kettle Moraine State Forest—which is popular for cross-country skiing and snowmobiling in winter and for hiking, camping, and fishing in summer.

## ■ HORICON MARSH

From the northern kettle moraine it is a short trip west along Highway 49 to Horicon Marsh, an extinct glacial lake that is now the largest freshwater cattail marsh in the United States.

Every spring and fall, millions of waterfowl—ducks, swans, cranes, herons, and over 200,000 Canada geese—fly over the expansive Horicon Marsh, once lush with wild rice in its wetlands. The marsh is part of the Horicon National Wildlife Refuge and is a haven for the bird-watchers and hunters who flock to the flyway each spring and fall for the breathtaking sight of thousands of birds beating their wings against the sky. Honks, whistles, chortles, and quacks fill the air from the sun's first glimmer until its evening fall to the west. The **Wild Goose Trail** tracks along this flyway and is a stunning place to witness the avian congregations on their seasonal migration.

On the banks of the Rock River and the highlands surrounding the marsh, prehistoric Mound Builders were active about 1,200 years ago, and dozens of their effigy mounds line the low ridges.

Today the city of Horicon sits on the hills above the Rock River, and its many parks afford pleasant views of the wild wetlands of Horicon Marsh.

## ■ PORT WASHINGTON TO HARTFORD

Port Washington, located midway between Sheboygan and Milwaukee, is one of several fishing ports on Lake Michigan. The city climbs the rising limestone bluff above the lake, providing beautiful views. A large park stretches north from the marina, with fine views of the lake and St. Mary's Church, perched on a high ridge overlooking the harbor. The main street is well maintained, although the view to the south includes a huge electric power plant. The Ozaukee County courthouse

*(following pages) Dairy cows and Wisconsin have been synonymous for almost a century. The counties of southeast Wisconsin are some of the finest dairy country in the world.*

and the old county buildings, just off the main drag, are handsome Victorian buildings and only a short walk from the lake.

The fishing industry is probably Port Washington's most popular diversion, thanks to the introduction of coho salmon, a tasty, large fish. It's a good fighter; so if you're game, prepare for a battle, strap yourself into your chair, and have the burly, cigarette-smoking boat captain wrap his arms around you to help haul in the fish. A great number of charter boats are available, and the city has hundreds of moorings for all forms of lake-craft. Port Washington also boasts the world's largest fish fry, sponsored by the Veterans of Foreign Wars. It's held in a band shell next to the harbor in July. Call (414) 284-0900 for information.

The city's no pushover for heavy industry, either, even though its greatest claim to manufacturing fame is the long-gone Kewpie Doll. Sold in dimestores and awarded as prizes at county fair arcades, literally millions of Kewpie Dolls found their way from Port Washington to mantles, nightstands, and doll collections across America. Port Washington is also the home of the Simplicity lawn tractor (hated adversary of the suburban dandelion) and the Allen-Edmonds shoe company, purveyors of elegant footwear.

### ■ WEST BEND

West of Port Washington and south of the Kettle Moraine State Forest's northern sector, the Milwaukee River flows through the hills of West Bend. Built of Cream City brick in the 1880s, the Victorian house of correction and the Romanesque, turreted courthouse still crown this hilltop town magnificently. Both buildings are restored and open to the public. The jail now serves as the Washington County Historical Society.

The downtown area along Main Street, called **Old Settler's Triangle,** has been extensively renovated. Graced with elegant brick buildings, it houses a great variety of shops, restaurants, and other businesses. The Milwaukee River flows a block east of the main street behind the Treveriani Hotel and Saloon, the Schagel Bakery, and Eagle Brewery—built in 1856 (and merged with the West Bend Brewery, which closed in 1972). West Bend is home to West Bend Appliances, long the prize of choice on game shows like "The Price is Right." To tour a local cheese factory, visit **Bieri's Cheese Factory** at 3271 City P in nearby Jackson.

# CHEESE

Cheese-making: One of those creative break-throughs most of us can imagine evolving on the edge of a hillside where a dawn-of-time Heidi and her beloved grandfather sit staring at a wooden bowl full of souring goat milk, sorry to see good food go to waste. They know that soon the souring milk will curdle, forming acid curds and watery whey. If only the residue were edible!

Suddenly, on the edge of that fateful hillside, Heidi comes up with an idea as to how to achieve this end, and after a lot of enthusiastic yodeling, others hear the news, and cheese-making is born. Thousands of years pass. Fabulous regional cheeses developed all over Europe. People express passionate feelings about them. Then they emigrate to America, begin to farm its valleys, raise cows, and remember how cheese was made in their particular Old Country.

*News Item, Nov. 14, 1935: "President Gets Giant Cheese As Gift. Said to be the largest piece of cheese ever seen in Washington, D.C., a huge 1,250 pound lump of the creamy substance, today was presented to The President by Wisconsin cheese producers." (Underwood Photo Archives)*

Cheese-making was first brought to Wisconsin by Yankee settlers in the 1830s, who made it from milk cooked in kettles over the kitchen fire. By the 1870s, cheese manufacturing was booming in Wisconsin; Sheboygan County alone boasted 20 factories. Today, there are over 200 cheese factories in the state, making 100 kinds of cheese.

Among the classic Wisconsin cheeses are **Wisconsin Swiss**, introduced by Swiss settlers in the New Glaris-Monroe area, and both sharp and mild English **cheddars**. A French company has introduced **Brie** in Belmont; **Colby**—described by some as a cross between crumbly cheddar and firmer muenster—was invented in Wisconsin at the Colby Cheese Factory. **Limburger**, an aromatic, semi-soft cheese, is still made at Monroe, the last factory of its kind in the state.

All over Wisconsin you'll see signs inviting you to tour cheese factories. A short list of these appears under the heading "Cheese Factories" in the "PRACTICAL INFORMATION" chapter.

## ■ CEDAR CREEK SETTLEMENT

Between West Bend and Hartford is a historic farmstead—Cedar Creek Settlement —with stone barns and German half-timber houses that were built in the 1840s and 1850s. Of interest are the Cedarburg gristmill, one of the finest mills in the Midwest, and the Cedarburg Woolen Mill, built during the Civil War. For information, call the Cedarburg Chamber of Commerce at (414) 377-5856.

## ■ HARTFORD

Westward across the kettle moraine from West Bend is the manufacturing town of Hartford. The Kissel Car Factory, one of the many automobile manufacturers that once operated in Wisconsin, is memorialized with an elegant and rare antique automobile collection at the **Hartford Heritage Auto Museum.** If you're a deerskin clothing afficionado, take your preserved deerskins to the **W. B. Place Company,** and they'll make you the jacket of your dreams. The enormous wooden tanning tuns outside the front door are artifacts of Wisconsin's tanning industry, a once significant part of the state's economy.

For a scenic, hilly, curving drive south of Hartford, travel Hogsback Road, four miles (6 km) west of Hubertus, just off Hubertus Road and roughly two miles

(3 km) from Holy Hill. It traverses a magnificent narrow ridge of sand and gravel formed under glacial ice and known as an esker.

### ■ HOLY HILL

When surveyor Increase Lapham first looked over this area from a high point south of town, he reported finding three Indian mounds on top of the hill. A few years later, a large, wooden cross was erected here. Soon afterward, a monk from Quebec, praying beneath the cross, experienced a miraculous cure of his paralysis. The top of this hill, one of the highest points of southern Wisconsin at 289 feet (88 m), rises above the hills and swales of the surrounding countryside. A log church was begun on the hilltop in 1863, and 20 years later, a Gothic brick church was built to house a growing congregation and shelter the original wooden cross. The Discalced Carmelite fathers later took control of the site and founded a monastery, now visited by thousands of pilgrims each year. **Holy Hill National Shrine of Mary**, at 1525 Carmel Road in Hubertus, is open all year round.

Old Monastery Inn Cafeteria is open daily from June to October, and is a fine place for a bowl of soup and a light meal before tackling the stations of the cross

*South of Hartford, on one of the highest hills in southern Wisconsin, rests the Holy Hill National Shrine of Mary. The church's spires rise 192 feet above its foundations.*

and exploring the beautiful grounds. The Romanesque, redbrick church has twin spires that stand 192 feet (59 m) above the top of the hill. Inside, a special chapel is decorated with crutches and canes, leg braces and wheelchairs from the faithful whose prayers for healing were answered. The hill itself and surrounding grounds are gorgeous in all seasons, and magnificent in spring.

## ■ WAUKESHA COUNTY AND LAKES

Heading south from Hartford along the arc of the kettle moraine, drivers follow Highway 83. Nearby, the Oconomowoc and Bark rivers thread their way through two separate strings of resort lakes in Waukesha County, comprising a total of 17 lakes. The Bark connects La' e Nagawicka with Upper and Lower Nemahbin lakes, while the Oconomowoc joins North Lake, Okauchee, Oconomowoc, and Lac La Belle. Both rivers join the Rock River at separate points. Formed by giant ice blocks left by the glacier, the lakes are now surrounded by vacation homes and residences. **Oconomowoc** is a resort city, with boating and fishing among its main attractions. Lakes Oconomowoc and Okauchee are best known for the mansions built by the Milwaukee beer barons on their own private beaches, far away from the industrial grit of Milwaukee.

Nearby are the old villages of Nashotah and Delafield, that grew up around a stage stop along the Watertown Plank Road and later a rail stop on the Milwaukee & Mississippi. **Nashotah** is home to an 1842 Episcopalian mission to the Indians which later became a seminary for Episcopal clergy.

**Delafield's Greek Revival Hawk's Inn,** built in 1847, is one of the oldest stage-coach stops in Wisconsin. It was moved and renovated in 1960 and still functions as an inn. The Hawk's Inn Dance hall was built in 1850. Later, soberly faced with stone, it served as a shoe factory, then a post office, and finally the Delafield town hall. The **Red Circle Inn** is the oldest stagecoach inn in Wisconsin and is still serving food to travelers. South of Delafield is Lapham Peak, one of Increase Lapham's highest vantage points for surveying the kettle moraine region. Now a park, it is used for cross-country skiing in winter and hiking in summer.

The village of **Eagle,** south of Delafield on 67, is a suitable base of operations for a foray into the kettle moraine, whatever the season. The **Kettle Moraine Nature Center,** west of Eagle, helps visitors identify and understand the area's wildlife. For a glimpse into the life of pioneer Europeans who came to Wisconsin, visit **Old World Wisconsin,** a seasonal, outdoor exhibit just south of Eagle. The 600-acre site includes about 50 houses, barns, and other buildings built between 1830 and 1880 by German, Norwegian, Irish, and English settlers. Costumed guides re-create village life on the frontier and explain their "daily" activities on the farm using pioneer techniques, and the crafts and trades of early Wisconsin. Highlights include the Scandinavian Midsummer Festival at the summer solstice; steam-threshing of grain during the wheat harvest; and a Civil War encampment.

**Palmyra** lies six miles (10 km) west across the moraine and was once a mecca for health-conscious visitors seeking the curative power of its hot springs. Several large hotels were built to accommodate the crowds but the tourist trade ended at the turn of the century, and the hotels fell into disrepair and were torn down by the 1950s.

West of Palmyra lies a large, flat, lacustrine basin left by the glacial meltwater—prime muck-farming land where onions, carrots, and other garden staples are grown by the ton. The **lakes of Palmyra,** whose dammed-up springs once attracted the masses, lie on the western edge of the southern unit of the kettle moraine, where trails and campgrounds offer hikers a view of Wisconsin's most lovely hill-country. The hills and hollows are lush with conifer and hardwood, teeming with songbirds, raptors, and deer.

*The Bidwell house in Palmyra, built in 1878, was one of several resorts in the area which featured "health-giving" springs and luxurious accommodations. (Fort Atkinson Historical Society)*

## ■ SOUTHERN KETTLE MORAINE

The southern kettle moraine stretches southwest to the Whitewater Recreation Area, a pair of lakes split by a large moraine hill southeast of Whitewater on County Highway P, off of Highway 12. From there the trails form part of the **Ice Age Trail** —which stretches across Wisconsin's glacial landscape, following the length of the moraines that mark the furthest advance of the last glacier in the state. (The Ice Age Trail is part of the Ice Age National Scientific Reserve.) The quiet country highways and backroads here are fine places to cycle in summer and cross-country ski in winter.

## ■ WATERTOWN AND ROCK RIVER DRAINAGE

The Rock River rises from the highlands south of Lake Winnebago and gently drains the great basin of Horicon Marsh, flowing south past Horicon to feed Lake Sinnissippi. The Rock dodges drumlins and cuts through Watertown, Jefferson, and Fort Atkinson, to enter Lake Koshkonong, where it swells, rushing past Janesville and Beloit to Illinois and the Mississippi.

*The importance of German culture in southeastern Wisconsin can be experienced every year at Octoberfest celebrations.*

Watertown was primarily settled by Germans. Until World War I dampened America's enthusiasm for German culture, this city was a place where many conducted business in German, and where the language was spoken in homes and taught in schools. English was a second and infrequently used language.

A leading figure in the German-American community, **Carl Schurz** (1829–1906), arrived in Watertown in 1855 after engaging in revolutionary activities in Germany. Germany's loss was America's gain. Schurz later moved to Milwaukee, where he soon passed the bar. He volunteered in the Civil War, and rose in the ranks to major general in 1863. After the war, Schurz was elected U.S. Senator from Missouri, and later became U.S. Secretary of the Interior and editor for the *New York Evening Post,* where he campaigned vigorously for honesty and high ethical standards in government. A noted writer, Schurz was the toast of Watertown.

Outside of Watertown, however, the legacy of the woman who married Carl Schurz is much more widely known than her husband's. In 1856, Margarethe Meyer Schurz began a unique school for the youngest of children. She called her experiment a "children's garden"—using the German word, *kindergarten.* The

*Summer afternoon on a Wisconsin farm.*

*The Octagon House in Watertown looks much the same today as it did when this photo was taken in the late nineteenth century. (The Watertown Historical Museum)*

experiment was more successful than she could have dreamed. Today, kindergarten is considered an essential first year of school for children in the United States.

The building that housed the **first kindergarten** is on the grounds at the **Watertown Octagon House,** built by John Richards in 1854. Three stories tall, with a 440-foot-high (134-m) spiral staircase, indoor plumbing, a wood-burning furnace that provided central heating, and a ventilation system that cooled the house in summer, the Octagon House was a marvel of its time. It commands a wonderful view of the Rock River from the top of the highest hill in Watertown.

On the banks of the Rock River is the public park, **Tivoli,** a riverside resort area that was popular among the German citizens of Watertown. They believed that Sunday afternoons were best spent sitting in a park with friends and listening to bands, drinking beer, holding shooting contests, singing, and playing games with children. Tivoli Park retains a sense of the pleasures of that era.

## ■ AZTALAN

South of Watertown and three miles (5 km) east of Lake Mills on County Highway B lies the mysterious remains of an ancient Indian village. A series of round burial mounds overlook what was once a 15-foot (3-m) mud-brick stockade. Two pyramids that appear to have been astral and solar calendars rise at opposite ends of the compound. The largest pyramid is 13 paces square at the top level, 26 paces square at the second level, and 52 paces square at the base—a tally that possibly corresponds to the number of moons, fortnights, and weeks in a year. The creation of the settlement is believed to have occurred shortly after a supernova in the Crab Nebula constellation lit up the nighttime sky for several weeks in A.D. 1054, and it's possible that such an event might have inspired a small group of Cahokia mound-builders in Illinois to move here and build the northernmost platform pyramid mounds in North America.

The body of a hunchbacked woman was unearthed from an elaborate Aztalan grave by archaeologists from the Milwaukee Public Museum between 1920 and 1932. The preparations for her afterlife were unlike any other found in Wisconsin. Adorned with three bundles of clam-shell beads, beaded clothing, and beaded

*Aztalan Indian village contains the northernmost platform mounds found in North America. Constructed by emigrants from the Illinois area in the eleventh century, it flourished for 200 years before being burned and deserted.*

boots, she may have been the shaman who led the Cahokia colonists out of Illinois and up the Rock River.

Aztalan remained occupied for about 200 years, but suddenly the stockade was burned and all residents departed. Excavation of the Aztalan mounds turned up the charred remains of human bones, along with those of deer, fish, and raccoon. Whether the human bones indicate cannibalism or expedient sanitation isn't known, but the end of Aztalan was swift and deliberate.

## ■ JEFFERSON

The Crawfish joins the Rock River at Jefferson, settled in 1836 by two men from Milwaukee. Soon a dam was built and a mill erected, and the process of building a city began. Jefferson grew into a manufacturing center that produced furniture, woolens, boots, shoes, bricks, farm implements, wagons, cheese, beer, and sausage. Today the town is typical of a river-front city in the late 1800s, with brick warehouses lining the riverfront. Local brick was used for the gristmill, the Neuer Brewery at the corner of Racine and Main, the storefronts, the courthouse, the jail, the schools, two towering churches (Lutheran and Roman Catholic), the Jefferson Liberal Institute, and dozens of homes and stores.

Jefferson was home to **Adam Grimm, a pioneering beekeeper** who introduced the gentle Italian honeybee to America. He popularized beekeeping in America, helping to sweeten the hard life on the prairie. His beehive-shaped grave marker is in the local graveyard, a sort of unofficial shrine for honey-lovers.

Below Jefferson, the Rock River is lined by river-front taverns and boat landings that support bass addicts and other anglers.

## ■ FORT ATKINSON

The town of **Fort Atkinson** was founded in 1832 as a stockade by Gen. Henry Atkinson, who was in Wisconsin pursuing Chief Black Hawk. During a later cholera epidemic, the stricken army stockade "surrendered" to the local Winnebago when the soldiers became too sick to carry their arms. The Winnebago helped nurse them back to health and then surrendered the fort once more to the army. (This was the tribe who later obligingly moved north to Wisconsin Dells.) In the 1830s, several Yankee and New York families moved to the area and put up their cabins and a tavern near the Rock River and the old fort.

Milo Jones, one resident, set up a brick factory in 1847 on property that now houses the **Hoard Dairyman Farm.** One of his sons began the Jones Farm meat-packing plant, which still produces their famous Jones breakfast sausage. You can buy the sausages at the Jones Dairy Farm and take a tour of the packing plant.

Jones's original brickyard on Merchant was eventually sold to W. D. Hoard, who later became governor of Wisconsin. Hoard achieved fame as a promoter of dairy farming through his newspaper, still issued as *Hoard's Dairymen.* He also introduced the French version of the silo to the United States as a means to provide feed to cattle year-round. Hoard's efforts went a long way toward transforming Wisconsin into "America's Dairyland," and the top producer of all milk products in the United States. The Hoard Dairyman Farm offers tours.

*The Friedrich Schumacher cabin of Fort Atkinson in the 1870s, wearing its implements inside out. (The Watertown Historical Museum)*

## ANTIQUITIES OF WISCONSIN

*Increase Lapham, an early surveyor, wrote extensively about the ancient villages and Indian mounds of Wisconsin in 1852. Lapham was the first president of the Wisconsin Historical Society and father of the Weather Service.*

The Rock River country is favorably know as among the most fertile and beautiful in the broad West . . . A few miles above Fulton, the [Rock] river expands into a broad and shallow lake, known by its Indian name of Koshkonong, said to mean "the lake we live on." . . . At the time of our visit (July 1850), wild rice (*ziziana aquatica*, Linn.) was growing abundantly over almost its whole surface, giving it more the appearance of a meadow than a lake. Fish and mollusks also abound in its waters, finding plenty of food in the warm mud beneath, and among the roots and stems of grass and rushes (*scirpus lacustris*).

*Increase Lapham, early surveyor of Wisconsin and father of the Weather Service. (State Historical Society of Wisconsin)*

The locality being thus abundantly supplied with the means of subsistence relied upon in a great degree by the American Indian— rice and fish—we were not surprised to find numerous traces of Indians on the banks of the lake, which were known to have been occupied until a very recent period. There are two prominent spots projecting into the water from the south shore, which were favorite spots with the natives . . . .

On Thebean Point are traces of mounds; and a little further up the lake commences a series of works extending about two miles along the high lands which border upon that portion of it . . . As happens in many other cases, these mounds are placed on high and commanding situations; evincing a taste for beauty of scenery, or a watchfulness, perhaps, rendered necessary by the proximity of enemies . . . .

❖  ❖  ❖

The American race is now, and probably always has been divided into numerous distinct tribes or nations, occupying different portions of the country and each having to some extent its own peculiar habits, customs, religion, and even language. Many of the tribes were of a roving disposition, with no fixed place of abode; while others were more permanent, only leaving their villages for the purpose of war or the chase. Since these nations have been known to us, and their history recorded, we are cognizant of numerous and important changes in the location of different tribes and even nations. We know of tribes that have become extinct, and of others that have gradually united with their neighbors, adopting their habits, religion, and language.

We may, therefore, without assuming any far-fetched theories, suppose that a nation or tribe of red men formerly occupied the country now known as Wisconsin, whose superstitions, ceremonies, and beliefs, required the erection of mounds of earth of the various forms represented on the plates accompanying this work; and that these tribes may have emigrated, or been driven off by others having no veneration for their ancient monuments. These subsequent tribes may or may not be the same that until very recently occupied that country. They extended their cultivation over the mounds with as little feeling of respect as is manifested by men of the race who are now fast destroying them. It is quite certain that these later tribes continued the practice of mound-building so far as to erect a circular or conical tumulus over their dead. This practice appears to be a remnant of ancient customs that connects the mound-builders with the present tribes.

The extent of the ancient works in the West indicates a condition of society somewhat different from the purely savage or hunter state: for to accomplish the labor required for the completion of such large structures, it would be necessary to accumulate the means of subsistence; and this could be done only by an agricultural people, or at least agriculture must have been among the pursuits of a people capable of constructing those works . . . .

The animal-shaped mounds appear to be peculiar to Wisconsin; for a few obscure instances noticed in Ohio by Messrs. Squire and Davis, can hardly be deemed an exception to this remark. They indicate a difference in the character of the people occupying these regions, but not greater than often exists between the neighboring tribes or nations.

—Increase Lapham, *Antiquities of Wisconsin,* 1852

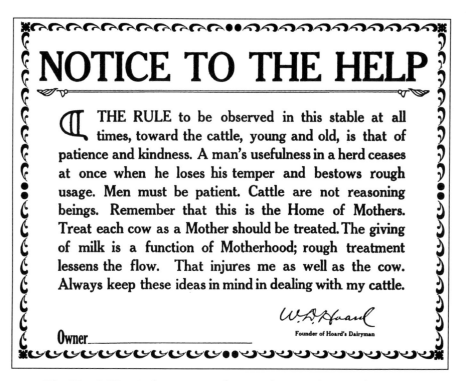

# NOTICE TO THE HELP

⊄ THE RULE to be observed in this stable at all times, toward the cattle, young and old, is that of patience and kindness. A man's usefulness in a herd ceases at once when he loses his temper and bestows rough usage. Men must be patient. Cattle are not reasoning beings. Remember that this is the Home of Mothers. Treat each cow as a Mother should be treated. The giving of milk is a function of Motherhood; rough treatment lessens the flow. That injures me as well as the cow. Always keep these ideas in mind in dealing with my cattle.

*W. D. Hoard*

Founder of Hoard's Dairyman

Owner_____

**The Hoard Historical Museum and Dairy Shrine** at 407 Merchants Avenue presents the history of dairying in Wisconsin, an extensive collection of native artifacts, and the history of the Black Hawk War.

### ■ CAMBRIDGE AND ROCKDALE

The villages of Cambridge and Rockdale, northwest of Lake Koshkonong, provide another time capsule of mid-nineteenth-century architecture in their main streets and residential neighborhoods. **Cambridge** always has been at the crossroads of well-traveled routes. Highway 12, which cuts through diagonally from the northwest to the southwest, passed first as an Indian trail, then a military road, then a stage road to Madison from Chicago. Highway 18, which cuts through from the east to the west, began as a trail from Milwaukee to Jefferson and Madison. The heights around Lake Ripley and along Koshkonong Creek have many effigy mounds, the work of a native population a thousand years ago. Cambridge is best known for salt-glazed earthenware. The Rowe pottery outlet still manufactures salt-glazed crocks with cobalt-blue designs, fine for pickles and sauerkraut. Pottery shops, craft stores, and restaurants fill the stone and brick storefronts along the main street.

The Koshkonong flows south to **Rockdale**, a tiny village built above a dam on the creek. The town once had dreams of attaining the grand prize of the 1848 state legislature in Belmont—becoming Wisconsin's state capital. But Rockdale earned a life sentence of remaining picturesque.

■ LAKE KOSHKONONG

Bolstered by the marriage of the Crawfish and Bark rivers, the Rock flows down to **Lake Koshkonong.** Broad-bladed spear points of nomadic hunters, exquisitely worked from flint and stone, provide evidence that native populations moved through this area for over 10,000 years. Over 40 groups of effigy and burial mounds surround Lake Koshkonong, and nearly 500 of 1,500 known mounds in Jefferson County overlook the lake. One rare effigy, the **Panther Intaglio Mound** (Route 106 at the western edge of Fort Atkinson), was scooped out of the ground rather than built above it. Extensive garden plots of the Woodland and Oneota people have been found on the east and west shores of the lake. The Winnebago had two large, permanent villages in the area—Burnt River about two miles (3 km) east of Fort Atkinson, and White Crow on the north side of Lake Koshkonong. White Crow had as many as 2,800 Winnebago before the arrival of the European settlers. When the land treaty was signed after the Black Hawk War, Chief White Crow, known as Kay-ray-kaw-saw-kaw, moved the tribe from Lake Koshkonong to the north side of the Wisconsin River between Portage and Sauk City.

# ■ YAHARA RIVER VALLEY

From Lake Koshkonong, the Rock sends its flood south toward Janesville, taking in the water of the Yahara River. Once known as the Catfish, the Yahara drains the wetlands north of Madison to feed the four lakes of the capital city before heading south through Lake Kegonsa to join the Rock River, south of Stoughton.

■ STOUGHTON

South of Madison and east of I-90 off U.S. 51 is the unofficial Norwegian capital of Wisconsin, where Norwegian Independence Day and Christmas are celebrated with true Norwegian abandon. Stoughton was born with Yankee roots in 1847, when Luke Stoughton of Vermont traveled up the Rock River from Janesville to settle a piece of property he had purchased from Daniel Webster. The wagon manufacturing businesses and tobacco warehouses that developed along the banks of the Rock River south of Lake Kegonsa prospered with the arrival of Norwegian immigrants. As the Yankees moved west, the Norwegians who settled their vacated lands used their extraordinary carpentry skills to build a beautiful collection of ornate Queen Anne homes, appointed with stained glass, turrets, and wedding cake trim. At Christmas time, the townspeople still dress up in Victorian garb and stroll the streets while carolling. Syttende Mai (17 May), Norwegian Independence Day, is Stoughton's grandest holiday. The King of Norway has even shown up to cheer on his long-lost countrymen. A marathon footrace starts at Madison's Capitol Square and winds 17 miles (27 km) south through country lanes to Stoughton where the celebration overtakes the town for the entire weekend. On the main street, a stop in the local cafe will introduce you to Norway, American style. Norwegian rosemaling, the traditional decorative painting of flowers and other designs on trunks, plates, spoons, houses, and other surfaces, is readily available down the street. Lutefisk (preserved codfish), rice puddings, and lefse (fried potato bread)—hallmarks of the "white" cuisine of Norway—can be enjoyed at local Lutheran church dinners.

South of Stoughton, Badfish Creek runs down the western edge of the prairie to join the Yahara. On its banks lies **Cooksville**, an unspoiled Yankee village filled with Greek and Gothic revival buildings set amidst an oak copse on the prairie. The vermillion brick buildings of the town, built by the self-taught Yankee craftsmen, were laid with locally fired brick. Like much of Wisconsin in the 1840s, the land was subject to speculation. Its most famous absentee landholder was Daniel Webster, who sold it to Dr. John Porter, who settled there along with other

# TOBACCO TRIANGLE

As dairy farming developed in Wisconsin, dairymen began to depend on corn, silage, and hay to feed their herds. This "dairyman's trinity" of crops handily supplied feed and bedding for the cattle, and were far more forgiving in Wisconsin's predictably unpredictable weather than wheat or other grains. Hay and silage crops could be cut on the first day following a storm, and the crop could be dried and baled before the next storm system arrived. Corn could dry on the stalk and be picked at any time. In the region around Stoughton, Edgerton, and Evansville tobacco developed into the dairy farmer's perfect cash crop, because it sandwiched so nicely with corn, silage, and hay. At one point in the late nineteenth century, Wisconsin became America's leading producer of tobacco, after the soil of Virginia and North Carolina became depleted and cultivation of the crop moved westward.

Today's tobacco harvest still follows the old routine. After the stalks are chopped, five or six are pierced and skewered with a strip of wood lathing. The tobacco-laden lathing strips are then suspended on tamarack poles arranged on three levels of a long, narrow tobacco shed. These long, red sheds have adjustable side panels, so air can pass through the barn and dry the tobacco leaves. In January, when the thaw replaces the arctic cold for a few days and fogs etch the landscape in hoarfrost, the tobacco shed is a buzz of activity. This is casing weather, when the leaves are stripped from the stem, smoothed out, and carefully stacked and bundled for sale at the tobacco warehouses in Stoughton and Edgerton. Most of the crop is destined to become chewing tobacco in the mouths of baseball players; some is used to wrap cigars puffed in the mouths of bankers.

*Wisconsin tobacco is used primarily for cigar wrappers.*

Yankees, Pennsylvanians, and immigrants from Ireland, Scotland, and England. By 1850, Cooksville's population crested 150, as nearby tall-grass prairie was converted to wheat land. The prairie soils didn't support wheat for long, and by the 1880s the farmland supported dairy cows, corn, and tobacco.

The buildings that make up the core of Cooksville have been cited either by the National or the State Register of Historic Places. These include a general store, a mill, and more than 20 vermillion-brick and frame houses built before 1850. Cooksville remains small and untouched by development. Since the 1940s, the people of Cooksville have renovated their homes as part of an informal restoration project. The wagon road, with its windbreak of oak and maple trees, extends east across marshes and prairie from Cooksville to Janesville.

## ■ LOWER ROCK RIVER VALLEY

More than 160 different manufacturers once built cars in Wisconsin: Chrysler, Hudson, Excalibur, Nash, Rambler, American Motors (AMC), and lesser-known companies like Kissel. They faded one by one; and today Wisconsin's only automotive production line, a Chevrolet plant, is in **Janesville** (pop. 53,000). The presence of General Motors in Janesville means related work for local manufacturers that supply materials. Free tours of the plant at 1000 Industrial Avenue can be arranged. Call (608) 756-7681 for more information.

Janesville also is home to Parker Pen, the manufacturer of the pens that U.S. Presidents use to signs bills into law and finalize treaties with nations around the world.

Janesville was founded in 1836 by Henry Janes, a Virginian with the itchiest pair of pioneer feet in the Wisconsin territory. He first built a cabin in Racine county in 1835, but seeing smoke from another pioneer cabin he packed up his family and headed west. Settling on the Rock River at the edge of a large prairie, Janes set to work becoming a one-man town. He petitioned the state legislature in Belmont to let him set up the post office and mail route, and start a ferry service across the Rock River. The city fathers of Janesville eventually recognized the value of Janes's parcel and bought him out. When the sun finally set on Janes, he continued west to California to escape civilization.

Downtown Janesville has been restored, and many older buildings are interspersed among the modern storefronts that line the north bank of the Rock River.

Mansions adorn the heights overlooking the Rock River, which flows through the center of the city. On the west side of the river are the Tallman Restorations, home to William Tallman and Mabel Walker Tallman of Racine. Built in 1854, the buff brick home is an ornate, antebellum, Italianate structure. Tallman was an ardent supporter of the abolitionist movement, and the house was a stop on the Underground Railway, providing shelter for run-away slaves. Abraham Lincoln was a guest there during his 1859 presidential campaign when he debated Stephen Douglas. The buildings on the site have been returned to their mid-nineteenth-century splendor and now house the **Rock County Historical Society.** The extensive Victorian housing stock downtown is quiet testimony to the prosperity of earlier days. True to this city's industrial heritage, Janesville continues to attract factories and businesses.

The Rock River separates Wisconsin from Illinois at the industrial town of **Beloit.** At that point, the river is a broad, flowing stream, with parks along its banks that make the thought of a picnic ever so inviting. The **Bartlett Museum** has an extraordinary collection of Native American artifacts, collected across the Americas. The town suffered from the industrial decline that hit the Midwest in the 1970s and 1980s, but is recovering thanks to food-processing companies like Frito-Lay, which makes Cheetos, Doritos, and Ruffles; and Hormel, which makes Spam.

## ■ SOUTHEAST LAKE DISTRICT

East of Beloit, the inland sectors of Kenosha and Racine counties, as well as Walworth County, back up to the kettle moraine. The land is sprinkled with lakes, and has become a prime vacation spot for the citizens of the southern Lake Michigan shore.

The town of **Delavan** is situated between two lakes, and from 1847 to 1894, twenty-six circuses wintered here. The first was the Olympia Circus, whose owners, Ed and Jeremiah Mabie, stopped in the area to hunt prairie chickens and ended up buying 400 acres. The idea for the Ringling Brothers and Barnum & Bailey Circus was developed here in 1879, as was the idea to tour the circus around the country by railroad rather than by wagon. This innovation helped make Ringling Brothers the largest circus in the country. (For more about Ringling Brothers see "Baraboo" in the "SOUTHWEST WISCONSIN" chapter.)

The main downtown area of Delavan is vibrant with brick streets and Victorian-era storefronts overlooking the lake. The cemetery at the west edge of town is a study in granite and limestone teeth popping from green, landscaped gums with a hardwood canopy shielding the thousands of gravestones. The circus laid many of its performers to final rest at this graveyard. The circus campground covered several acres in a valley west of the city, on the grounds of what is now the Wisconsin School for the Deaf. The **Clown Hall of Fame**, at 212 E. Walworth, takes itself seriously memorializing such comics as Red Skelton and Emmet Kelly, Sr.

**Lake Geneva** was known as "*Kishwauketo*" by the Potawatomi Indians who settled in this region long before the lake became a resort and retreat for well-to-do Chicagoans in the mid-1850s. Kishwauketo means Big Foot Lake in Potawatomi, and it was carved by glaciers, which also deposited the Elkhorn moraine that blocks the southwest end of the lake. Lake Geneva is 172 feet (52 m) deep and surrounded by hills that rise more than 200 feet (61m) above its surface. The north shore is dotted with exquisite mansions and horse breeding farms, set in woods and meadows along Snake Road.

*Detail of the Tallman House in Janesville. During the Civil War it was used as a stop on the Underground Railway.*

Lake Geneva's popularity was assured when the Wrigley family (of chewing gum fame) built a summer home, Green Gables, on the lake's north shore. The roads in this area are private and closed to the public; thus the mansions that line them remain out of sight. Dedicated gawkers can get a glimpse of these grand houses—fancifully named Deadwood, Wychwood, Villa Hortensia, Wadsworth Hall, Flowerside Farm, the House in the Woods, the Narrows, and Bonnie Brae)—from the public lake path, or by taking a tour with Gage Marine Boat Tours and viewing them from the water.

The city of **Williams Bay** is located at the north shore of Lake Geneva, and commands a choice view of the rising and setting sun on the lake waters. Restaurants, boats launches, and accommodations are close at hand, and a small city park hugs the waterfront. The **Yerkes Observatory** on Geneva Street, built for the University of Chicago Department of Astronomy in 1897, offers free tours on Sundays.

## ■ KINGDOM OF VOREE

Northeast of Lake Geneva, and west of the town of Burlington, once lay the Kingdom of Voree, a Mormon colony from the 1840s. When the Mormons were driven out of Illinois after their founder, Joseph Smith, was murdered, most followed Brigham Young to Utah. Unfortunately for Mormon unity, Smith had died before appointing a successor who could lead the Mormons and resolve the rift over polygamy. A second leader, James Jesse Strang (1813–1845), claimed to be the real prophet, and led a party of Mormons north to Voree, Wisconsin. On Mormon Road in 1845, near the top of a hill outside of Burlington, Strang unearthed a small, wooden box that contained three copper plates. The plates proved that he was the true successor to Mormon founder Joseph Smith. Strang convinced his sect of Mormons that the Lost Tribes of Israel had left the copper plates on that very spot, and he and his followers founded the Kingdom of Voree—the "garden of peace"—and built a small stone church overlooking the White River. The rift between Mormon sects became so volatile, however, that Strang soon took his community to Beaver Island, Michigan (near Mackinac Island), possibly to limit contact with other Mormons in the Walworth County area. Though he originally denounced polygamy, Strang became attracted to young Elvira Field, who he disguised as a boy so he could take her on his travels without his wife knowing of his extracurricular appetite. After his wife left him, Strang changed his mind about polygamy and married several more women at the same time. Strang was twice elected to Michigan's State Legislature with the captive Beaver Island vote, but was eventually shot and mortally wounded by two disgruntled former colonists. The injured Strang return to Voree, where he died and was buried in 1856. You can see the grave in a small cemetery on Mormon Road.

## RASCAL

*Sterling North's classic of juvenile literature,* Rascal, *stars a pet raccoon . It is set in and around his boyhood home of Edgerton near the shores of Lake Koshkonong during World War I.*

*T*here were no superhighways in those days to streak impersonally toward some distant goal, scoring the countryside with ribbons of unfeeling concrete. In fact there was scant paving of any kind, only friendly little roads that wandered everywhere, muddy in wet weather, dusty in dry, but clinging to ancient game and Indian trails, skirting orchards where one might reach out to pluck an early apple, winding through the valleys of streams and rivers, coming close to flower gardens and patures of clover that one could smell all the good country smells, from new-mown hay to ripening corn.

We started early next morning, my father, Rascal, and I in our usual places on the front seat. Turning northward toward Fort Atkinson, we passed our old farm and the Kumlien place as we ascended the Rock River valley. Finding sources of streams was a passion with me. I had followed Saunder's Creek all the way to its first spring nearly ten miles north of Brailsford Junction, and I had always wanted to follow the Rock River to its source. So we went by way of the Horicon marshes, as romantic to me as Sidney Lanier's Marshes of Glynn.

At some point in this neighborhood we crossed the divide between waters pouring down the Rock River to the Mississippi and waters pouring into Lake Winnebago and the Fox River to Lake Michigan, and thus down the Lakes to the St. Lawrence and the Atlantic. When we saw the first creek running northeastward I felt like the early French explorers of this region.

—Sterling North, *Rascal,* 1963

# ■ EAST TROY

Northwest of Burlington on Highway 120 is the small community of East Troy, once the end of the line for the East Troy Railroad & Trolley Line. In the summertime the trolley is still in operation. Catch it in town at the **East Troy Trolley Museum** (County Road ES) and ride it to the Elegant Farmer, a combination pick-your-own-vegetable garden and farmers' market.

East Troy's Cobblestone Inn on the square is a fine example of elegant 1840s architecture. Built of hand-selected lake stones and limestone and granite quoins, it was the inspired design of Milwaukee architect and builder Samuel Bradley (who, being in debt, disappeared soon after the building was finished).

North of East Troy is the Beulah Lake resort area, and campgrounds surrounding seven nearby lakes.

# ■ RACINE AND KENOSHA

**Racine,** a major Lake Michigan port south of Milwaukee, has a large Danish population. Its most famous contribution to Wisconsin cuisine is kringle, a Danish pastry made of feather-light, buttery piecrust shaped like an "O," filled with fruit, and iced to perfection. Kringle makes all other breakfast pastry taste like sawdust. Sure, bakeries call them Danish pastries, but one bite of kringle will prove that you have been swindled at the breakfast counter for years.

The Italian community in Racine celebrates the world's largest boccie tournament in August: the **Roma Lodge Boccie Fest.** Like something out of Italy, with the older gentlemen barking out, "botch him outta there, knock him out," to the bowlers trying to place their balls on the green, this annual scene is not to be missed.

To the south of Racine stands one of **Frank Lloyd Wright's** most famous corporate projects, the **Johnson Wax Company** building. The company, which began as a wood-finishing products manufacturer and eventually became one of the world's largest home-product giants, seemed the perfect venue for Wright's distinctive American style. His innovative architecture incorporates glass and graceful columns that suspend the ceiling high above the office floor. The work spaces themselves are artfully modern, modular units that lend an open uniformity to the workplace.

The Johnson Wax Company building was constructed just before Wright drew his plans for the Guggenheim Museum in New York City, and his bold use of concrete here may have inspired Wright to conceive of the elastic flow that typifies the Guggenheim design. Free tours of the Johnson Wax headquarters, at 1525 How Street, are offered Tuesday through Friday, and on summer weekends.

Wright also designed a magnificent 14,000-square-foot home, **Wingspread,** for Johnson Wax magnate Herbert Johnson, in 1937. The beautiful brick house, with cantilevered roof line, brick columns, and sprawling living quarters, hugs the top of the bluff overlooking Lake Michigan. The fours wings of the house meet like the spokes of a wheel at a central hearth—a Wright trademark. The home is located north of Racine (33 East Four Mile Road) and is now a conference facility that can be toured when not in use.

A few miles down the coast from Racine is **Kenosha,** a city that has lately become a suburb of Chicago. Kenosha has been settled since the earliest days of the Wisconsin territory, and was once the home of Olympia Brown, a notable orator whose lifelong efforts to gain women the vote began when she arrived as a Universalist Church minister here in 1880. Her political work culminated with the Nineteenth Amendment to the Constitution.

Kenosha blossomed early, thanks to a deep port at Pike Creek and the advance of industry. Although the city has suffered with the closing of automotive production lines, it's still the destination of Wisconsin's cranberry crop, processed here by the Ocean Spray Company. And Kenosha is the home of Jockey International, a business whose undergarments help America and the world keep their privates private.

*Milwaukee skyline.*

# M I L W A U K E E

IT MAY HAVE BEEN BEER that made Milwaukee famous, but it was manufacturing that made it rich. Bucyrus Erie power shovels dug the Panama Canal. Pumps and valves from the E. P. Allis Company sucked groundwater from the iron mines up north. Briggs and Stratton trimmed America's lawns. Milwaukee breweries made beer, while coopers built millions of barrels to ship that beer around the country. Harley-Davidson put a power motor between the legs of men.

Factories in place, hard-working people from all over Europe came to labor in them. More ethnic patchwork than melting pot, it was a city in which each immigrant group settled in its own neighborhood. Irish and Yankees remained among the primary entrepreneurs and industrialists. Germans, the largest community, contributed hard work and an extraordinary sense of civic responsibility. Added to these were the Poles, Serbs, Croats, Hungarians, and Czechs, each attending

*Harley-Davidson's big break came when it won contracts to supply police departments across the United States with motorcycles. (Underwood Photo Archives)*

their separate churches and celebrating their separate festivals. The old Jewish neighborhood, where Israel's prime minister Golda Meir grew up, is now part of the city's expanding African American core. Recently, Asians and Hispanics have moved into the old Polish south side. Milwaukee is a vibrant, diverse, exciting city, with fine parks, an Olympic-quality ice rink, interesting neighborhoods, and a deep and refined cultural mix.

## ■ EARLY HISTORY

Before Europeans arrived, the Menominee tribe, and later the Potawatomi, Fox, and Sauk visited this area to hunt, fish, and harvest wild rice. Their landscape was defined by three rivers, the Kinnickinnic, Milwaukee, and Menomonee, which ran together in a great marshland marked by high bluffs and a swamp that fronted Lake Michigan. Together these formed an enormous habitat for birds, and the fish in the rivers and estuaries were bountiful. All about these bodies of water, in a land of great natural beauty, lived deer, bear, muskrat, mink, beaver, and raccoon.

By the end of the French and Indian War in 1760, other tribes had settled in the area, as much to avoid the conflicts raging farther up the Great Lakes as they were drawn by abundant wildlife and stretches of wild rice. The name "Milwaukee" is thought to mean "good land" or "rich land" in Menominee or Potawatomi.

During the eighteenth century, Milwaukee was visited regularly by French fur traders, but they didn't settle permanently, preferring to operate out of Green Bay. It was not until the 1820s that two such fur traders, Solomon Juneau and Jacques Vieau, made a permanent settlement in the Milwaukee region.

## ■ ENTER THE UNITED STATES

In 1831, Indian tribes ceded the southeastern part of Wisconsin to the United States, and the newly opened land brought settlers and speculators. In the 1830s, an enterprising attorney, Morgan Martin, came upon the cabin that had belonged to the French fur trapper Juneau and thought the area surrounding it would make a perfect site for a city. Set on a spit of land on the east bank of the south-flowing Milwaukee River, with Lake Michigan at its back, the settlement became known as

Juneautown. Meanwhile, Byron Kilbourn arrived, surveyor's sextant in hand, intent on plotting the development of the west bank of the Milwaukee, and a settlement called Kilbourntown. When Virginian George Walker, with his surveyor's sextant, lent his name to Walker's Point on the south side (where the Menomonee River joins the Milwaukee and flows to the lake) the groundwork was laid for the city.

The summer of 1836 saw a furious scramble, as settlers tried to establish claims on property before the federal land sales could take place. Cabins went up within weeks and more than a thousand people staked claims over a two-month period. A few individuals, acting as lenders to the scrambling squatters and speculators —Byron Kilbourn, Ephilet and William Cramer, Martin O. Walker, and George Smith—ended up with the highlands behind Milwaukee. The city established in 1846 was more a confederacy of three competing villages separated by water, than a unified municipality, and the old divisions of the city can be seen today, in bridges that cross the rivers at odd angles because the three towns couldn't agree on how to align the streets.

## ■ IMMIGRANT ERA

Samuel Freeman's *The Emigrant's Handbook,* published in 1851, provided vital information about Milwaukee for prospective residents. There were six hotels, a fire department, six newspapers (two published in German), a list of churches, and brief descriptions of the various cities and regions of the state. Freeman warned travelers to avoid "friendly strangers" along the way, particularly at gaming houses in New York.

Between 1840 and 1880, Milwaukee's population grew by 70 to 80 percent every 10 years. Its first immigrants were British, Irish, Norwegians, and Germans who arrived between 1840 and 1850. A free black community was established in the mid-1840s and 1850s. German '48ers arrived in this era—displaced revolutionaries whose unsuccessful revolt against the German monarchy forced them to flee. By 1880, the city had become one of the most popular destinations for Polish Roman Catholics and Jews, Bohemians, Ukrainians, Russians, Armenians, Serbs, Croats, Italians, Bavarians, Swedes, Norwegians, Danes, Dutch, and Romanians. Until 1910, at least one-third of the population was foreign-born.

# ■ POLITICS AND PARKS

Politically, Milwaukee became civic minded and progressive in spirit, a legacy of idealistic Germans who'd fought monarchies at home. At the beginning of the twentieth century, Milwaukee socialists stood for reform. Labor's support was rewarded by projects dedicated to employing people and beautifying the city. Lake and riverfront were preserved for public use and magnificently landscaped. Public transportation helped the work force get to their jobs, and Milwaukee's trolley system was beyond compare. Milwaukee gained, and has kept, a reputation as a clean and tightly run city.

Perhaps the finest example of enlightened city planning is Milwaukee's park system. The popularity of the German recipe for *Gemüthlichkeit*—beer, sausage, and fresh air—gave rise to beer gardens sponsored by breweries. As Milwaukee grew, city leaders had the foresight to develop some of these areas into parkland before they were eaten by development. In the 1880s, the Milwaukee Parks Commission began to create and establish parks that would serve as the "lungs of the city," and they employed some of the great landscape architects of the age, including Frederick Law Olmstead and Horace Cleveland. This approach eventually led to continued annexation of lands beyond the city to serve as parkland, and to cooperation and imagination in planning mass transit, sewerage, and other city services.

# ■ LAY OF THE LAND

Milwaukee is located on the shores of Lake Michigan in southeastern Wisconsin. It lies directly north of Chicago on I-94 and east of Madison, also on I-94. Milwaukee was first settled at the shoreline, now the downtown, where many important buildings and museums are located. North of downtown, along the lake, are fine neighborhoods and stately old mansions built by Milwaukee's industrial barons. To the west of downtown are suburbs, stadiums, a famed ice rink, and the zoo. At the south end of the city is the old industrial center and ethnic neighborhoods. In wintertime, Milwaukee battens down; in the summer its citizens enjoy festivals, parks, and museums. The sites of the city described below flow from the central city northward, then westward, and finally, to the south. Central Milwaukee has many one-way streets, so drivers may find routes more circuitous than will pedestrians.

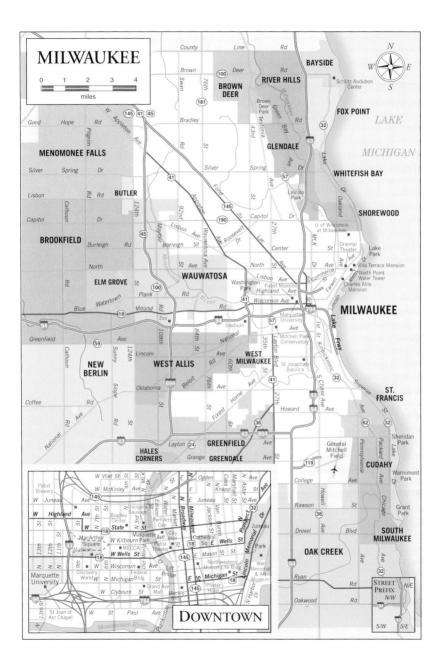

# ■ EAST SIDE

To explore Milwaukee, it's best to begin where settlement began. At the heart of the east side lies what was once "Juneautown," the village established between the Milwaukee River and the bluffs above Lake Michigan. The gateway to this area is the **Wisconsin Avenue Lift Bridge,** whose hydraulic system of pulleys and weights rises with the water of the Milwaukee River.

Milwaukee's renovated theater district is in this area, its finest light being the **Pabst Theater** at 144 East Wells at Water Street. Known for its fine acoustics, it is architecturally interesting—a Victorian Baroque delicacy with orange terra-cotta, ornamental sheet metal, and wrought iron. One block west at 200 East Wells is **City Hall,** home to all Milwaukee's German-inspired civic mindedness and a collection of Socialist mayors. Its 393-foot- (119-m) tall bell tower holds the third largest bell in the world: impressive but useless. It can't be rung because its vibrations are such that they weaken the building structure.

The **Performing Arts Center** near the Milwaukee River at 929 North Water Street is a modern rectilinear marble and steel building whose impressive halls host local performers and guest artists from around the world. The center is surrounded by sculpture and a chestnut grove where, in summertime, performances are held outdoors.

As it heads south, Water Street crosses Wisconsin Avenue and enters the old Third Ward neighborhood, set on the spit of land that slopes from the Milwaukee River down to Lake Michgan and the Summerfest grounds. Today the area is dominated by older 8- to 10-story buildings interspersed with skyscrapers.

From Water Street take a left on East Michigan Street. Along it lie some of Milwaukee's grandest buildings. The **Mitchell Building** at 207 East Michigan is a stunning example of Second Empire architecture, trimmed with rich ornamentation for its owner Alexander Mitchell, the banking, rail, and insurance magnate who became one of Milwaukee's earliest and most influential power-brokers. The building's stone-carvers graced it with lion-headed keystones and winged horses, and its entrance is tended by a pair of sheet-metal griffins. It was built in 1876 by Edward Townsend Mix, Milwaukee's busiest architect.

Nearby, at 225 East Michigan, is the **Mackie Building,** and on the second floor the opulent **Grain Exchange Room,** the first "trading pit" in the country. Wheat traders took themselves seriously! The carved likeness of Mercury, messenger to the gods and also the Roman god of trade and commerce, stands wedged between the granite pillars flanking the entrance to this 10,000-square-foot room. Three-story-high columns reach toward painted ceiling panels featuring Wisconsin wildflowers. Models for the classical figures representing Trade, Industry, and Agriculture in a lush mural were the city's society ladies.

Despite its utilitarian air of Victorian perfunctitude, there is an elegance to the exterior of the building, achieved in the design by Edward Mix. Outside, the pillar-framed entrance supports a frieze of carvings with locomotives, boats, and various Wisconsin motifs.

North of the Mackie Building, at 517 East Wisconsin, is the **Federal Building,** a gray, granite Richardsonian Romanesque building designed by that style's strongest architectural proponent, Henry Robson Richardson of Boston, whose somber gray arches, gables, and turrets are rife with an eccentric collection of carved stone gargoyles, faces, and leaves.

At the east end of Wisconsin Avenue at the lakefront, the controversial Di Suvero sculpture in O'Donnell Park is set in a spot with a prime view of Lake Michigan. Nearly everyone in Milwaukee has an opinion about this enormous orange-painted sunburst built of construction materials—and opinions vary considerably.

Along the lakefront above Lincoln Park is the War Memorial Complex, at 750 North Lincoln Memorial Drive, and within it the **Milwaukee Art Museum**— Eero Saarinen's 1957-modern rectangular structure that captures the Lake Michigan view and provides a gleaming receptacle for a choice art collection. The museum has a great collection of German Expressionist pieces, modern masters, seventeenth- and eighteenth-century American decorative arts, and paintings from that visionary American movement—the American Ash Can School.

The hill to the west of the museum is **Yankee Hill,** long ago covered with Indian mounds and later with the homes of Milwaukee's industrial barons. Wisconsin Avenue forms the southern border of Yankee Hill, and at 720 East Wisconsin Avenue is the massive, monumental **Northwestern Mutual Life Insurance Company** building. Out front is one of the biggest and finest fountains in a city famous for its fountains. What you see, if you stand before it, is 42,000 gallons of water cascading a distance of 25 feet (8 m) to a reflecting pool.

**The Wisconsin Gas Company building,** at 626 East Wisconsin Avenue, was one of the city's first skyscrapers. The three-color flame on the top of the building tells you what the weather will be. Red means warm; gold means cold; blue means no change; and a flickering flame, snow or rain.

**Pfister Hotel**, at 424 East Wisconsin Avenue, is a Victorian-era gem. A fine collection of nineteenth-century paintings graces its lobby, and pure Victoriana bedecks each floor. The hotel's English Room is a posh spot for an evening meal.

From the Pfister Hotel turn north on Jefferson two blocks to **Cathedral Square,** a quiet park across the street from **St. John's Cathedral.** The first Roman Catholic cathedral in Wisconsin, it was dedicated in 1853.

**Old St. Mary's Church,** two blocks west at North Broadway and Kilbourn at the western edge of Yankee Hill, was built in 1846. The first German Catholic church in Milwaukee, it served as a school and centerpiece of the German community until a finer and larger church was built 40 years later. Its altar displays a painting of the Annunciation, a gift from King Ludwig I of Bavaria.

Well-to-do Yankees prayed and thanked God for their blessings at the Gothic revival **All Saints Episcopal Cathedral** at East Juneau and North Cass (a few blocks north and west of St. John's Cathedral). It was designed in 1862 for Congregationalists who were forced by hard times to sell it to the better-heeled Episcopal congregation. This Cream City brick structure has decorative brick molding rising to a sheet metal cornice topped by a fish-scale slate roof.

Nearby, at 1060 East Juneau Street, is the **home of George P. Miller.** An amalgam of troglodyte whimsy—squat turrets, carved stone, copper ornamentation,

*The renowned Milwaukee Symphony performs at the Pabst Theatre in Milwaukee.*

*The Wisconsin Gas Company building features a three-color flame on its roof that tells the weather forecast—the blue in this case indicating no change in the weather.*

stained glass, brick, brass, and wrought iron—it was built in 1885 by department store magnate T. A. Chapman for his daughter when she became Mrs. George Miller and joined the beer-making clan.

## ■ PROSPECT AVENUE GOLD COAST

In the Prospect Avenue area, just north of downtown, are some of the finest mansions and choicest museums in Milwaukee. The **Charles Allis mansion** (1801 North Prospect Avenue at Royal Place) houses the extensive art library and the fabulous art collection of Charles Allis, the first president of the Allis-Chalmers Company. It's nice to think people actually lived here once and looked up at the three-tiered stained-glass window by Louis Tiffany when they came in from walking the dog. Their money came from farm implements.

At North Avenue and North Farwell, the **Oriental Theater** stands proudly as the last of Milwaukee's movie palaces, built in 1927 during the golden age of film. Tile, wrought iron, Oriental carpets, silver-sheathed elephant heads, golden Buddhas, minaret towers, and terra-cotta trim were combined to create this near-mythic temple to the not-so-silent screen. Attached to the theater is the **Oriental Drugstore** with its wonderful diner counter—*the* place to eat a cheap lunch in art deco surroundings.

To the east on 2220 North Terrace is the Mediterranean-style **Villa Terrace mansion.** Set on bluffs overlooking the lake, it is now a decorative arts museum with a delicate wrought-iron doorway and terra-cotta roofed courtyard. Its 1,000-foot- (305-m) deep garden drops down to the lake, its choice plantings, waterfall, and a stone staircase framed by well-trimmed, stately hedges.

North of Prospect Avenue, Prospect Hill and North Point hug the bluff above the shore of Lake Michigan. The **Frederick Bogk residence** on 2420 Terrace Avenue in North Point is a private home visible from the street, designed by Frank Lloyd Wright in 1916. It has Wright's characteristic wide roof overhang and a green tile roof. Its leaded glass windows are deeply recessed into the buff-colored brick and cast concrete lintels, an excellent example of Wright's Prairie-style design.

**North Point Water Tower** on North Avenue at the top of the bluff above Lake Michigan was built in 1873, and is a twin to one in Chicago. It's a favorite landmark, set in Water Tower Park, near a neighborhood of old-time lavish mansions—a good place to stroll around and imagine life in a more genteel era. Across from the water tower is **St. Mary's Hospital** with its lovely fountain. St. Mary's was Milwaukee's first hospital, established in 1848 by the Sisters of Mercy of St. Joseph. Later it became the first public hospital in Wisconsin.

North of St. Mary's on the shore of the lake is **Lake Park**, once a resort and beer garden, known as Lueddemann's by the Lake. Two artful cast-iron bridges guarded by life-size stone lions, cross parallel ravines. The beacon from **North Point Lighthouse**, which stands guard on the bluff, can be seen for 25 miles (40 km). Along the path to the north you can see boccie ball being played, and farther on, an old Indian burial mound.

The mansions continue up the lakeshore for the next several miles until North Lake Drive hits Brown Deer Road. There one can visit the **Schlitz Audubon Center**, 185 acres of unspoiled woodland that includes beach, meadows, and ponds. Donated by the Schlitz Foundation as an educational nature center, it is located at 1111 East Brown Deer Road; (414) 352-2880.

*The Schlitz Palm Garden in better years, when patrons could visit the brewery and sip beer among palms as it snowed outside. (State Historical Society of Wisconsin)*

# ■ KILBOURNTOWN AND WESTERN MILWAUKEE

Kilbourntown, just west of the Milwaukee River and north of the Menomonee River, was once a wild rice swamp. Commerce Street was the Rock River Canal, providing water power to flour mills. The typewriter was invented on State Street, and the *Milwaukee Journal and Sentinel* is published at the Journal Company Building at 333 West State Street, just a few doors down the street. For a tour call (414) 224-2120.

Just west of the Wisconsin River on West State and Old World Third Street, you will see **Pere Marquette Park,** a fine place to relax mid-town. Both sides of the river in this old section are busy in summer, especially at noon, when downtown workers lunch in nearby parks and public areas. There are many places to eat in this area. At 1030 North Old World Third Street is **Usinger's Sausage Factory,** a link to Milwaukee's German heritage. A turn-of-the-century German store, it sells more than 60 kinds of sausage.

Old World Third Street leads south to **Grand Avenue Mall,** which in turn joins the historic Plankinton Arcade in an urban shopping mall three blocks long. West and north is the **Mecca** (Milwaukee Exposition and Convention Center and Arena), and the **Bradley Center,** home of the Milwaukee Bucks. The Bucks won

*Usinger's Sausage Factory still supplies America with some of its best German sausage. (Courtesy of Usinger's, Milwaukee)*

the 1970–1971 NBA championship with the help of the unstoppable skyhook of Lew Alcindor, later known as Kareem Abdul-Jabbar.

Collections and exhibits at the **Milwaukee Public Museum** (800 West Wells at North Seventh) present the modern face of Wisconsin's Native American tribes; the natural history of Wisconsin from the age of dinosaurs to the modern era; and studies in the environment, particularly the tropical rain forest.

**Discovery World,** a block south at 818 West Wisconsin, presents the world of modern technology in a hands-on way so that no visitor can fail to grasp the significance of technological innovation.

The area just to the north was once a major beer-brewing area. The Schlitz Brewery was located on West Galena until, in the 1970s, Schlitz changed its recipe. No one liked the new taste and within three years Schlitz had closed down. The oldest brewery building still remaining in Milwaukee, the **Gipfel Brewery,** was built in 1843, and is on 423 West Juneau. **Pabst Brewery** still brews beer at 915 West Juneau and tours of its facilities are available.

Just west of I-43 is **Marquette University,** an urban campus founded in 1864. One of the most important Catholic universities in the United States, it has an enrollment of 11,600 students. Marquette's **Saint Joan of Arc Chapel** was reconstructed from a Rhone Valley chapel built in the fifteenth century. **Patrick and**

*Grand Avenue Mall, a downtown shopping mall three blocks long, is entirely enclosed, protecting its visitors from the elements.*

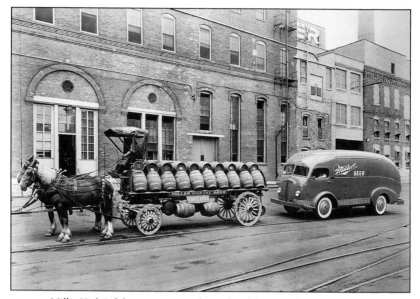

*Miller High Life beer wagon poses along side a delivery truck of 1939. (State Historical Society of Wisconsin)*

**Beatrice Haggerty Museum of Art,** located on the east mall of the campus, has an extensive collection of Asian, tribal, and decorative arts, as well as a fine collection of Renaissance, Baroque, and modern painting and sculpture.

The 37-room **Pabst Mansion** was built in 1892 at the west end of Wisconsin Avenue in the days when the street was lined with magnificent elm trees. It was built by German-born Frederick Pabst, a steamship captain on the Great Lakes. At the age of 24 he came to Milwaukee and married Maria Best, daughter of the owner of Best's Empire Brewery. The mansion is located at 2000 West Wisconsin Avenue, and it is open limited hours to the public.

West and north of Marquette, at 4251 West State Street, is the **Miller Brewery,** founded here in 1886. Not only is the Miller Brewery an important part of the economy, it has always been a great contributor to the arts in Milwaukee, particularly in its sponsorship of the **Miller Jazz Oasis** during Summerfest.

South of the Miller brewing complex lies **Pigsville,** a moniker applied to a Menomonee Valley farm. It became home to Croats, Serbs, Czechs, Poles, and Russians, who worked as laborers and tradesmen in this area.

**Milwaukee County Stadium,** located just west of Highway 41 and south of I-94 (at 201 South 46th Street) is home to baseball's Milwaukee Brewers. If the team is out of town, take this opportunity to visit the stadium. Make reservations in advance by calling (414) 933-4114, and you can sit in the dugout, and learn how technicians control more than 30,000 lights on the scoreboard. The Green Bay Packers favor County Stadium.

In the northwest corner of the cross formed by I-94 and Highway 45 is the **Milwaukee County Zoo.** One of the finest zoos in the world, it houses about 4,000 animals and birds. Within the zoo is a Children's Zoo, where kids can pet and feed baby and farm animals. A narrated tour of the grounds is offered by the Zoomobile, and there's a miniature train ride, and pony, camel, and elephant rides.

## ■ SOUTH SIDE

Due south of downtown is Walker's Point and the South Side, gateways to Milwaukee's industrial heritage and ethnic neighborhoods. The construction of **St. Josaphat's Basilica** at West Lincoln Avenue at South Sixth Street, with the

*The 1903 factory of the Harley-Davidson Company where the first three of its world-renowned motorcycles were constructed. (Courtesy of the Harley-Davidson Company)*

world's sixth-largest dome, was perhaps the greatest recycling effort of all time. Lavish in style, it was built by thrifty Polish parishioners from a demolished Chicago post office. Father Wilhelm Grutzka purchased its limestone blocks, marble, granite columns, and woodwork for $20,000 and had them shipped north in 500 train-car loads. The post office was reconstituted into the shape of the cross, under a gilt dome, to serve the Polish Catholic neighborhood in 1900. Inside are relics and portraits of Polish saints and leaders, stained glass, and fine wood carvings.

A few blocks away twin towers rise above **St. Stanislaus,** the third Polish parish in the United States when it was built in 1873. Its gold-leafed aluminum domes shine brighter than the original copper dome, thanks to a 1962 remodeling. The neighborhood also has a statue and park (located at West Lincoln near South Ninth Street) honoring Gen. Tadeusz Kosciuszko, the Polish hero of the American Revolutionary War. The Polish neighborhoods are now home to an expanding Hispanic population, which has added Latin rhythm and Mexican food.

Neighborhood companies like the Allen-Bradley Corporation sprang from humble roots to become Milwaukee's largest employers. **Allen-Bradley's famous clock,** at 1201 South Second, towers 300 feet (91 m) above the street and is a Milwaukee landmark. Supposedly, Allen-Bradley's is the largest four-faced clock in the world, and not surprisingly, ships use it as a navigational reference point.

*The clock tower of the Allen-Bradley Corporation rises 300 feet above the street and features the largest four-faced clock in the world.*

Other great companies in this area are, or have been: The Bay View Rolling Mills, E. P. Allis Company (later Allis-Chalmers), and Pawling & Harnischfeger. The West Milwaukee Carshops, west of the 35th Street viaduct, forged the steel that went into the manufacture of more than 666 locomotives, 151 passenger cars, and over 65,000 freight cars for the Milwaukee Railroad. On the margins of the Menomonee Valley, long narrow loft buildings provided space for Milwaukee's garment and textile industries, producing finished goods like gloves, wallets, coats, and leather goods. Other industries, like International Harvester, gave America's farmers some of their finest tractors, and Red Star yeast leavened America bread. These industries moved to the suburbs after World War II, leaving a trail of empty industrial space in Milwaukee's iron and brick core.

One of high points of the South Side industrial area is **Mitchell Park Conservatory** just off Highway 57, graced with a huge, English-style greenhouse that now has three, seven-story-tall geodesic domes that house a beautiful collection of tropical, desert, and flowering plants. The triad of geodesic domes is an excellent place to hide from the icy blast of winter on one of those January Sundays when the world looks especially bleak. There's even a tropical aviary and birds flying overhead, singing and chatting with one another while it snows outside.

**Serb Memorial Hall** at 5105 West Oklahoma is the center of a closely knit community, and offers bowling and Friday fish fries. Inside the hall are held huge, wonderful, Serbian weddings, great luncheons to honor visiting politicians and local heroes, and copious amounts of delicious food. This is one of the great ethnic treasures in Milwaukee and should not be overlooked.

Soccer players and soccer fans take their game seriously in this part of town and one of the best attended is that between the Serbs and Croats.

## ■ FESTIVALS AND PARADES

Festival season begins in Milwaukee to the sound of accordions and polka music that drives the two-step until dawn. In late June Milwaukee celebrates Summerfest, which combines all kinds of music, ethnic food, and Milwaukee beer. The Great Circus Parade, when Ringling Bros. and Barnum & Bailey take their animals and clowns out to show the city, is held in mid-July, followed by the French celebration of Bastille Day with great food and hot jazz. Festa Italiana takes place the next week, followed by Germanfest a week later.

The Kho-thi dance troupe explores the African American heritage of rhythm and movement, recreating traditional dances during African World Festival in late July. While the Wisconsin State Fair celebrates Wisconsin Agriculture in early August, the Irish ready the children of Eire for North America's largest Irish Fest, ceoli dances, and superb Irish music. In August, Fiesta Mexicana brings out the Mexican community, delicious Mexican food, norteño and mariachi music, and traditional dances. In September the Indian Summer Festival is brought to life with the beat of the drum, and Milwaukee's large population of Menominee, Potawatomi, Winnebago, Chippewa, and Oneida put on leather, ribbons, and feathers and dance on the Summerfest grounds. For more information see "Festivals and Events" in "PRACTICAL INFORMATION" or call (414) 799-1177.

*The Great Circus Parade of Milwaukee takes place every July and is one of America's best attended parade events.*

*The Mitchell Park Conservatory has three giant geodesic domes that house a tropical aviary as well as desert and flowering plants.*

# BEER

Historically, Wisconsin has been the beer capital of the United States, and no city took its leadership role more seriously than the city of Milwaukee. When fire burned down Chicago in 1871 and its water supply was knocked out, Milwaukee's Schlitz brewery donated hundreds of barrels of beer to help the locals slake their thirst. The fortunes of Milwaukee's beer barons rose in the nineteenth century, only to plummet when Prohibition was enacted in 1919. When fervor for temperance flagged, Americans couldn't wait to guzzle again, and Milwaukee was up to the task of helping them do it. During World War II, the army served the drinking man Miller. In the 1950s, nation-wide television advertising promoted the beers brewed by Pabst, Schlitz, and Miller, making them economic giants and eroding loyalty to local breweries. Bigger was better when it came to beer.

Enter the 1970s, and the new American fascination with "cuisine." If wine became de rigueur at dinner, more informal, but somehow high-class occasions

*Brewery workers pose for a company portrait at Mitchell's Brewery in La Crosse, circa 1880. (State Historical Society of Wisconsin)*

*Students in Madison demonstrate in favor of Prohibition in the 1920s, a scene quite out of character for this city and likely never to be seen again. (Underwood Photo Archives)*

seemed to call for imported beer—real beer, made in accordance with German purity laws, with only hops, barley malt, yeast, and water, and devoid of the extracts and additives used by the big breweries. Once the taste for imports caught on, it was only a few years before micro-breweries began producing a fresher, and at times superior beer. If the goliaths of the beer industry continued to produce millions of barrels a year (much to the delight of undemanding palates across the country), the small breweries have found a niche providing a number of German-style lagers including weiss (a wheat beer), black Bavarian, dopplebocks and fest beers, such as an Octoberfest or Marzen, as well as Pilsners.

You can find these isles of brewing sophistication in many places in Wisconsin. In Middleton (near Madison) at **Capital Brewery,** 7734 Terrace Avenue just off Highway 12. In Milwaukee, two fine micro-breweries produce some beautiful beers and ales: **Sprecher Brewing Company** at 730 W. Oregon Street, just south of the Menomonee River; and **Lakefront Brewery** at 818A East Chambers Street, just west of the Milwaukee River on the near North Side.

A new brewery was opened on Highway 69 in New Glarus in 1993, the **New Glarus Brewing Company,** run by Dan Carey, a brew master who developed the Kessler Beers in Helena, Montana.

*continues*

The **Huber Brewery,** on the edge of the Driftless area in Monroe, recently signed an agreement to brew Chicago's favorite German-style lager, Berghoff, for the Berghoff Restaurant. Huber once brewed a similar lager, Augsburger, when the brewery was owned by a former Pabst executive who sold the label to Strohs. Huber has more than made up for the loss with the Berghoff arrangement and its stable of several Wisconsin labels, its flagships Huber and Huber Bock, and other regional labels such as Rhinelander, Hi Brau, Braumeister, and Walters' that would have been forgotten if the Huber had not preserved them in barrel and bottle. The Huber bock beers have an old-time taste, somewhat hoppy and malty, and are among the lowest-priced beers of this kind available.

**Point,** an independent brewery in the Central Sands community of Stevens Point, has a loyal following across Wisconsin. Point is famous in the industry for selling 60 percent of its beer within a 50-mile (80 km) radius of the brewery.

In Chippewa Falls, between the Upper Coulee Country and the North Woods, **Leinenkugel's** enjoys similar standing and reputation. The brewery was purchased by Miller Brewing, which allows Leinenkugel's to continue its traditional labels. The marketing and distribution folks at Miller have added punch to Leinie's muscle and market penetration in Wisconsin. Like Point, Leinie's brews seasonal beers, such as bock, along with their lagers, and both

*continues*

produce some "bigger," maltier products that pack a slightly stronger punch. It is not uncommon to find bars and restaurants in Chicago offering these labels for consumption; no small accomplishment considering the tight hold the big breweries have on this enormous market. They may not like the Packers in Chicago, but they sure like Wisconsin beer.

## BREWPUBS

The development of brewpubs is a logical step in melding restaurants with on-site brewing of beer. In Door County, the **Cherryland Brewing Company** brews its own at 341 N. Third Avenue in Sturgeon Bay. In Milwaukee, the **Water Street Brewery** and its restaurant is located at 1101 North Water Street. The **Appleton Brewing Company** is at 1004 South Olde Oneida, in Appleton. **Brewmaster's Pub** is found in Kenosha at 4017 80th Street. In Chilton, **Rowland's Calumet Brewery and Brewpub** is located at 25 North Madison Street. These operations are part of a national trend toward handmade beers; some made with grains and some with elixirs and syrups; all are big and flavorful.

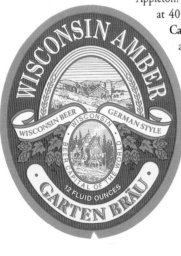

*Madison was built upon an isthmus between two lakes. Here on Lake Mendota, a small steamboat takes on passengers at a floating dock, ca. 1900. (State Historical Society of Wisconsin)*

# M A D I S O N

THE FOUR LAKES REGION, as Madison and its environs are known, sits in a naturally glorious setting, where once the Winnebago (and the mound-building people before them) fished, hunted, and camped. Wisconsin's capital city stands astride an isthmus between two lovely glacial lakes, and a fifteen-minute drive from downtown finds farmland and wildlife close at hand. Few spots in the city are more than a mile from one of its nearly 200 parks, and the city holds three lakes within its boundaries.

The citizenry of Madison borrowed Algonquian names for their lakes. Lake Mendota, the largest and deepest, fed by the Yahara (Catfish) River, marks the northern edge of Madison. Lake Monona, second in size, borders on the south side of the isthmus. Lake Wingra, the smallest, is spring-fed and surrounded by the University Arboretum. These three lakes flow into a fourth, Lake Waubesa (outside the city limits), before emptying into Lake Kegonsa, the Rock River, and eventually the Mississippi.

If Madison is a gem finely set in southern Wisconsin, it is known as much for its shopping, music clubs, bars, and restaurants as for its natural beauty. With the state capital and one of the world's great universities at its heart, its citizens tend to be well educated and tolerant. Its landlords, restaurants, and retail shops cater not only to a permanent regional population of a quarter-million, but also to a transient population of legislators and over 40,000 university students.

State government and the University of Wisconsin, the largest employers in the region, drive the local economy, followed by credit unions and insurance companies. Before state government and the university grew so big, Oscar Mayer (you remember the Wienermobile, don't you?) was the largest employer in Dane County. Madison has been corporate headquarters for the company since 1955. Cows and pigs from surrounding farms still find their way into the heart of the abattoir, coming out smoked, ground or chopped, spiced, and neatly packaged for shipment throughout the United States.

# ■ RADICAL BRAND

Madison's well-known reputation throughout the rest of Wisconsin for being liberal, even radical, was forged in the late 1960s and early 1970s, when the university campus was known for its anti-war student protests, and its population of Marxists. Four events marked the heyday and passing of the anti-war protests—the Dow Chemical Demonstration, the Mifflin Street Block Party, the takeover of the State Capitol, and the Sterling Hall bombing.

The demonstrations against the Vietnam War polarized the campus and community in 1967. Madison police were called to a campus building (ironically the Commerce building) to remove students protesting the presence of recruiters from the Dow Chemical Corporation, which manufactured napalm. Police used nightsticks and fists to forcibly remove the students. A crowd grew and a riot ensued. The National Guard was called in to calm the campus, while days of rioting flared up and down State Street and in some downtown student neighborhoods.

*Police grapple with demonstrators during the campus protests against Dow Chemical Company in 1967. (State Historical Society of Wisconsin,* Daily Cardinal *photo)*

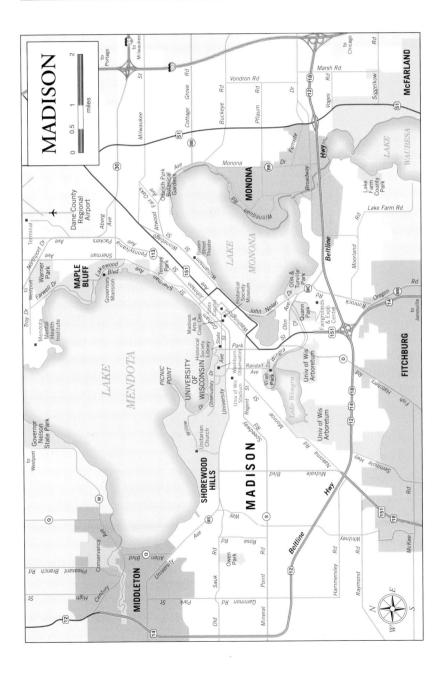

The following spring, police attempts to close down an illegal May Day "block party" on Mifflin Street sparked another confrontation. A young man from Chicago, Paul Soglin, who had been active in that neighborhood, was roughed up by police and arrested during the altercation that followed. Soglin used his popularity to become the student alderman from the downtown wards, a fly in the ointment for the conservative mayor.

Later that year, another demonstration united the campus community in an all-out, shut-the-place-down riot that began with the takeover of the state capitol by a Milwaukee Roman Catholic priest, James Groppi. His march for fair housing standards for African Americans in Milwaukee combined the civil rights crusade with the youthful explosiveness of the anti-war movement, the likes of which have not been seen since. These events gave Madison a reputation across Wisconsin of being a dangerous place where radicals lurked.

The anti-war demonstrations and riots continued in earnest over the next few years. The town was in tatters, and its reputation became that of a haven for radicals. Plywood replaced windows broken on State Street. A supermarket, Kroger's, was burned down by arsonists. The irregular skirmishes ebbed and flowed, and protests were as much an adventure in hormone fulfillment as they were serious political dialogue. The invasion of Cambodia and the Kent State killings (in which four student protesters were killed in Ohio by anxious National Guard troops), however, convinced a few students that the "non-violent" approach was not succeeding.

A single final event clinched and defiled Madison's radical reputation in one fell swoop. In 1970, two brothers and two accomplices decided that violence was needed to stop the University Army Math Research Center from helping the military calculate bomb trajectories. The center was located in the physics building, Sterling Hall. Under cover of darkness, they drove into an underground garage beneath Sterling Hall in a van filled with fuel-oil-soaked nitrate fertilizer. Identifying themselves as the New Year's Gang, they telephoned the laboratories and campus police to warn of the impending explosion. The blast that disemboweled Sterling Hall shattered glass in buildings for blocks around, rocked Madison and the campus, and could be heard 15 miles (24 km) away. The bomb also killed Robert Fassnacht, a young husband, father, and graduate student in physics, who worked late into the night on a physics research project. Karl Armstrong, the eldest of the two Armstrong brothers, was the first member of the gang apprehended. His prison term was the longest and harshest of the four. Dwight Armstrong and

David Fine were also caught, but the fourth accomplice, a member of the University of Wisconsin crew team named Leo Burt, was never found.

Following the bombing, the Army Math Research Center continued its work in new facilities. Plummeting public approval for the local anti-war movement destroyed the coalition that organized teach-ins and non-violent protests against the war. Rather than energizing the local anti-war movement, the bombing shocked the public and served to breed distrust among the protest-group members.

Ironically, three years after the bombing, the alderman from the student ward, Paul Soglin, was elected mayor of Madison. The man whose political ambition, once aimed at galvanizing the student community, now reigns in his fifth term as mayor of one of the most popular small cities in the United States.

# ■ STATE CAPITOL

In 1846, James Doty convinced his fellow legislators at their lonely Belmont outpost to move the state capital from Belmont to Madison. The beauty of the natural setting was as crucial to earning their votes as the promise of profits from land speculation. Doty held significant interest in his landholdings on the isthmus, and his dispersal of choice lots to undecided legislators, as well as to other congressmen, governors, and judges, helped him realize his plans for Madison. In a few months' time, the town consisted of a log cabin serving as tavern and lodging for the workmen hired to transform the wooded isthmus into a city.

The legislators claimed the highest hill on the isthmus for the site of the new capitol building, which rose in 1852, using local sandstone and a frame dome covered with tin. In 1857, a replacement was built and served the state until 1904, when a gas lamp in a cloak room touched off a ceiling fire, and the entire building soon was engulfed in flame. As it was February, no water could be pumped from fire hydrants around Capitol Square. To replace the building, ground was broken in 1907 for construction of a neoclassical design by George Post. The splendid marble and granite capitol, built around a steel frame, was completed in 1917.

The exterior of the capitol is flanked with enormous granite and marble columns, while the dome's interior is decorated with a painting, *The Resources of Wisconsin*, and four remarkable mosaics representing *Legislature, Government, Justice,* and *Liberty.* Four gilt badgers peer out from above the supreme court, assembly, and senate chambers. The exterior pediments of each of the four wings, supported by enormous granite columns, are decorated with classical, bas relief sculpture. Recent interior and exterior renovations have painstakingly modernized and preserved the decor of the original building with marble from 60 countries. An observation deck is open spring, summer, and fall, providing gorgeous views of the city, lakes, and surrounding countryside.

Wisconsinites can watch their tax dollars at work by visiting the state assembly and senate during public debates. The verbal free-for-all can be remarkably entertaining. In the state assembly, look for the replica of **Old Abe,** a bald eagle captured by a young Chippewa in the wilds north of the Flambeau River in 1861, and one of Wisconsin's most beloved Civil War heroes. Old Abe became the mascot of the Eagle Regiment, later to become the Marine Corps' Screamin' Eagles of the 101st Airborne Division. Old Abe was trained to perch on a standard carried around by the soldiers during parade review, and off he went with the troops to fight the Rebels of the Confederacy. In 39 battles, Old Abe would take to the skies, crying fiercely as he circled the battlefield. The greater the din of battle, the louder Old Abe would scream, bringing joy to the Wisconsin Eighth Infantry and woe to the rebels. He survived the Civil War and returned to Wisconsin, where he

*"Old Abe," a bald eagle that became the mascot of the Civil War Eagle Regiment later to become the Marine Corps' Screaming Eagles 101st Airborne Division. (Chippewa Valley Museum, Eau Claire)*

*The State Capitol of Wisconsin was built as a smaller scale replica of the nation's Capitol in Washington. The dome's interior is decorated with a painting,* The Resources of Wisconsin.

lived out his days dining on fresh meat in the basement of the capitol in Madison. Old Abe died in 1881, and was stuffed and mounted above the assembly chambers, until the building burned in 1904.

A **farmers' market** is held on the capitol's sidewalks every Saturday morning from April to November, providing seasonal fruit and vegetables, steaming coffee, pastry, plants, and treats from a variety of carts and stands set up by local farmers, growers, and cooks.

## ■ STATE STREET

State Street, which runs between the capitol and the university, is the commercial heart of the downtown. Amid the bars and restaurants you can also find Madison's cultural heart—the **Madison Art Center and Civic Center,** which provides an artistic vision safe enough to soothe the savage taxpayer, who funds its activities. The shops along State Street help to give Madison its special character—hip and trendier than the standard mall fare.

The **Wisconsin State Historical Society** is at home at both ends of State Street. Its **museum** at the corner of State Street and the Capitol Square, has an extraordinary permanent display of Native American artifacts, and ever-changing exhibits of interesting things historic from the Badger State. One of its most curious possessions is a clock hand-built by John Muir, the famed naturalist and founder of the Sierra Club, when he was a student at the university; the clock is designed to regulate study by dropping a succession of books on a student's desk at prescribed intervals. (An inveterate inventor, Muir once built a clock that tipped him out of bed in the morning, and another that would light his schoolroom stove.) The **State Historical Society Library and Archives,** at the campus end of State Street, contains one of the largest genealogical collections in the United States, of interest to those seeking to find their immigrant roots. The archives contain a treasure trove of materials, from personal papers, to photographic and film collections, newspaper collections, maps, periodicals, and public records.

## ■ UNIVERSITY CAMPUS AREA

The University of Wisconsin is considered one of the finest universities in the United States, and with more than 44,000 students, it has an enormous impact on

*Between May and October a farmers' market is held every weekend on the sidewalks surrounding the State Capitol Building.*

EXTRA
LARGE
ET RE
PPER
25
5-$100

a city of just under 200,000 people. If the tenor of campus life has changed since the radical '70s—perhaps less exciting and more congenial—so has the status of the football team. In the '70s the Badgers groveled at the bottom of the Big Ten, and students couldn't have cared less. In 1993, Wisconsin's football team won the Rose Bowl, and the campus resounded in celebration.

From the foot of State Street and three miles (5 km) west, a walk or a drive around campus is a prerequisite for understanding Madison. Not only are its grounds the setting for a vibrant student life, they also contain fragments from all stages of Madison's history, from the early Mound Builders to the Civil War, past Vietnam, and into the Space Age.

Built on the southern shore of Lake Mendota, the campus covers about six square miles of beautiful shoreline in a park-like setting that everyone can enjoy. The southern lakeshore of Mendota, preserved in as pristine a condition as could be expected in these modern times, abounds with waterfowl in season. In spring, the campus is alive with flowering trees and shrubs. Gardens are packed with flowering bulbs, annuals, and perennials, calculated to stay in bloom until the frost of

*The class of 1876 poses in front of Bascom Hill. (State Historical Society of Wisconsin)*

autumn. It is a horticultural display befitting an agricultural land-grant university that commands the highest amount of federal research funding of all public universities in the United States.

The university's oldest buildings stand on **Bascom Hill,** the heart of the upper campus, with splendid views over Lake Mendota. **Bascom Hall,** flanked by North and South halls, was built in 1857, and now houses administrative offices. **North Hall,** the oldest building on campus, dates from 1851 and used to be a dormitory. John Muir lived here when he was a student at the university in the 1860s. A locust tree near the dorm nourished his lifelong love of plants, while forays into the libraries of his professors taught him of botany, Emerson, and the humanities. Muir left Madison to study medicine at Michigan, but a final trip on the Wisconsin River sent him off instead to the "university of the wilderness."

On Observatory Hill stands **Washburn Observatory** and the sandstone home of the Observatory Director, which now houses the **La Follette Institute,** a progressive think-tank. An adjacent glacial hill is decorated with several effigy mounds and an enormous glacial erratic called **Chamberlain Rock**—a huge chip off some granite crag, taken as a souvenir by the ice lobes that marched down across the state.

The **Elvehjem Museum,** on University Avenue just east of Park Street, has a fine collection of Asian, ancient Greek, and Etruscan art complemented by contemporary and visiting collections. To learn about the glaciers that shaped Wisconsin, and their fossil records, visit the **Geology Museum,** located in Weeks Hall at the corner of Charter and West Dayton. It houses an excellent collection of semi-precious stones and crystals, and some fine dinosaur and prehistoric mammal skeletons, including a great mammoth unearthed at Boaz, Wisconsin. Every campus tour should include a visit to the **Memorial Union.** With its sweeping terrace affording Madison's finest lake-level view of Mendota, studded with sailboats and ducks, it is best enjoyed on a bright summer day with a cold local beer on tap. (Guest passes are available.)

For more vigorously attained views over Lake Mendota, walk, bike, skate, or jog from the campus down the lakeshore path to **Eagle Heights and Picnic Point,** a lovely peninsula reaching into the lake. In its pre-glacial period, Picnic Point was a mighty rock promontory looming 400 feet (122 m) over the primeval Yahara Valley, now flooded with the lake. In winter, hardy ice-fishers angle for panfish, perch, muskies, and walleye in University Bay and across the lake. (Preserve the magic—keep a few fish to eat and let the rest return.)

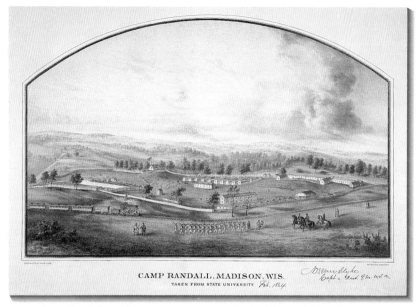

CAMP RANDALL, MADISON, WIS.
TAKEN FROM STATE UNIVERSITY *Feb. 1864*

*Camp Randall served as an internment camp for Confederate soldiers when this lithograph was drawn in 1864. (State Historical Society of Wisconsin)*

The Civil War brought thousands of conscripts and soldiers to Madison to follow their bald eagle mascot, Old Abe, against the Confederate army. **Camp Randall** was established to quarter the 70,000 Wisconsin recruits, who camped and marched in close-order drill on what is now the football field. Soldiers cut every tree in the dense oak and hickory woods for firewood, clearing the crown of University Heights and the area around Vilas Park and Monroe Street. Nearly two out of every three Wisconsin men joined the Union cause and fought in campaigns at Bull Run, Gettysburg, and down the Mississippi, where they participated in the capture of Memphis, Little Rock, Mobile, and Vicksburg. The Memorial Arch, 36 feet (11 m) high, has stood here in their honor since 1912.

Later in the Civil War, Camp Randall became a prisoner-of-war camp for unfortunate Southerners who were caught and brought north by Union troops to shiver in the sub-zero winters. Their prison cages remain on display, along with several Civil War-era cannon at Camp Randall Park.

Camp Randall today encompasses the University of Wisconsin Stadium, home to the Wisconsin Badgers football team, Rose Bowl Champions of 1993, who scrimmage on the field where the recruits once marched. Nearby stands the Field House, home of the basketball Badgers.

## ■ MADISON'S WEST SIDE

One of the finest neighborhoods in the city, **University Heights** was the first residential subdivision to be built outside the central part of the city, in the 1890s. This is Madison's fanciest enclave of late-Victorian and Prairie-style homes. Perched atop the hill is the Gilmore House by Frank Lloyd Wright. On Summit Avenue are two homes designed by Wright's mentor, Louis B. Sullivan, whose most enterprising Madison design is the Sigma Chi fraternity house at Prospect and Van Hise streets.

From the University of Wisconsin Stadium at Camp Randall, Monroe Street heads out southwest through a pleasant commercial strip of shops and restaurants, past Edgewood College. At Knickerbocker Street, turn south to find the shores of

*A University Heights house designed by Louis B. Sullivan, who is credited as being Frank Lloyd Wright's architectural mentor.*

Lake Wingra and the **University Arboretum**, which preserves Wisconsin's prairie and woodland landscape as it is believed to have been. A springtime walk here is a calming respite from the swirl of life outside. Points of interest in the arboretum include the McKay Center, which describes the rare plant species collected over the past 50 years; Curtis Prairie, a dry prairie restored with existing plant species used by native herbalists; Green Prairie, a beautiful, wet meadowland chock-a-block with prairie orchids; and Gallistal Woods, where native effigy mounds near spring-fed beds of watercress signify the spiritual value of the springs to the Woodland peoples. To see the arboretum from the lake, rent canoes or wind-surfing equipment from the City of Madison Parks Department at Knickerbocker Park, at the end of Knickerbocker Street, off Monroe Street.

Miles of excellent and well-planted walking trails branch from the arboretum around the lake, with connections to the **Madison Zoo**. The adjacent lagoons and beach of **Vilas Park** are excellent in all seasons, especially in winter for skating; this was the training ground for Wisconsin's Olympic Gold Medalist speed skaters, Eric and Beth Heiden.

Heading west on Regent Street from Camp Randall, you arrive at one of the state's most beautiful graveyards, **Forest Hill Cemetery**. It's most worthwhile to see the final resting place of prominent Madisonians and American veterans in a beautiful setting of oak, maple, hickory, and flowering shrubs.

At the end of Speedway is Mineral Point Road, which once connected the state capital with the prosperous lead-mining region of the southwest. **Mineral Point** is most notable for the University Industrial Park at the former Charmany Experimental Farms, and the home base of Credit Unions International—a complex of modernistic buildings that may be one of the most influential financial centers in the world, charting the control of trillions of dollars in assets for hard-working credit-union members everywhere. Farther out on Mineral Point is Madison's version of Edge City—**West Towne Mall**—and its commercial progeny that have sprung up over the past 30 years on this former farmland and glacial out-wash. The strip continues to push new development at the edge of Madison on annexed portions of the town of Middleton, where modern hotels, banks, and residential neighborhoods invade a panoramic oak-prairie savanna. Suffice it to say that the Madison area is growing, both in abducted territories at its margins, and by sparking development in the neighboring villages. Because of its educational system, retail base, and tolerant, well-educated population, and opportunities for white-collar employment, this is one of the most popular areas to live in Wisconsin.

## ■ MADISON'S EAST SIDE

**The Isthmus,** comprised mainly of filled-in marshland between Lakes Mendota and Monona, is an active social and residential area for renters, students, and urban professionals. The shore of Madison's **Lake Monona** is almost entirely devoted to public park, swimming, fishing, and boating, not to mention the popular winter-time variants of ice-fishing, skating, and (snow permitting) cross-country skiing. Public parks stretch along Lake Monona from Turville Point and Olin Park to Law Park and B. B. Clarke Beach, past the old Third Ridge neighborhood, and then across the Yahara to Yahara Park, the effigy mounds, and Olbrich Park.

The cultural organs of Madison's near east side are hipper, a bit more brash, and more adventurous than the more moderate and broader offerings at the Civic Center on State Street, or on campus. To enjoy this part of town, walk past *The Isthmus Weekly's* offices at the southeast corner of Capitol Square. This irreverent tabloid pales in comparison to the dozens of left-wing and underground papers that once appeared on the campus, but in these staid times it provides a welcome alternative to the daily papers.

A block away, wander into the **Argus Bar** at East Main and Hamilton, a tavern with a beautiful tin ceiling, which housed the first newspaper in Madison. The next stop, two blocks south, is the **Fess Hotel,** which once afforded a man and his horse a week's lodging for six dollars. Now a restaurant, and refurbished inside, the Fess interior is trimmed nicely in wood, glass, and brass. Its brick and ivy terrace, cloistered away from the din of the city, is a summertime must.

Across the street is a complex of state office buildings, the site of the original log cabin built in Madison by Eben and Rosaline Peck, who moved into the isthmus from Blue Mounds to operate a hotel for the workers who would clear the woods and build the new capital city. The Pecks' cabin was Madison's first frontier hotel. Nearby this historic ground, the legacy of Wisconsin's Progressive tradition continues at the offices of *The Progressive* magazine, published at 300 West Main Street, in the shadow of the capitol. *The Progressive,* founded by Wisconsin's Populist majordomo, Fightin' Bob La Follette, still is a stalwart proponent of iconoclasm in all things. Head south to the **Cardinal Bar** at 400 Wilson, an older, tile-floored work-ingman's bar, retrofitted in the disco-'70s, and now a harbor from the workaday world. By night it becomes a downtown dance magnet for single youth and the aging hip-oisie.

Walk east past the old Fauerbach Brewery building to 900 Williamson Street, under the Pharo Grocery sign (from the 1920s) and peek into the old Wieden-bock Grocery. Here, **Survival Graphics**, an artists' collective, cuts through life's material dross to refract society in photos, prints, sculpture, crayons, and paint. They offer instruction and a gallery; openings are good fun.

Histrionics abound at 1119 Williamson, where **Broom Street Theater** has taunted and tantalized Madison with 20 years of original theater under the command of Joel Gersmann. Gersmann has penned more than 90 plays, crafted from his voracious reading of everything under the sun—ancient, modern, and in-between. The kinetic, actor-oriented theater, with the cheapest ticket prices in the United States, framed the New Testament as a Western (*The Jesus Gang*), the nuclear holocaust as a review (*Bombs Away Enola Gay*), and explored Wisconsin's favorite sons—Houdini (in *The Jew from Appleton*), Vince Lombardi (in *Packer Glory*), and Joe McCarthy (in *Joe: A Life, or Angel on the Edge*).

*Halloween on State Street is one of the most popular events for students and locals alike.*

*The Unitarian Meeting House in Shorewood Hills (top) is considered one of Frank Lloyd Wright's most beautiful buildings. Windsurfing on Lake Mendota is one of the many pleasures of life in Wisconsin's capital city. (bottom)*

There are several bars along the Williamson/Winnebago/Atwood stretch; each caters to a different stripe of east-side humanity, so take your pick. If it's music you want, try the **Crystal Corners Bar** at Williamson and Baldwin, or the **Harmony Bar** at Atwood. A more formal venue is the purple-roofed **Barrymore Theater,** a branch of the Civic Center and the local neighborhood association.

## ■ AROUND LAKE MENDOTA

There are many other excursions throughout the city and in the surrounding areas. One of the best is around Lake Mendota, the largest of Madison's lakes. This trip consists of a counter-clockwise journey from Tenney Park (a great place to skate in winter) to Lake Monona. You can bike or drive around Lake Mendota by heading northeast through the community of Maple Bluff.

**Maple Bluff** was a favorite campground for the Winnebago, and even though government policy had forced them out of Wisconsin in the 1800s, they kept returning to this campsite of their ancestors. The stands of maples that give this village its name were protected from the prairie fires the Winnebago set to keep the prairie productive. Of the expensive and large homes now found there, the Governor's Mansion gracing the shoreline on Cambridge Drive is worth note. Fightin' Bob La Follette's Italianate redbrick Victorian farmhouse, overlooking the Maple Bluff Country Club, was built in 1876 by Norwegian fire insurance magnate Halle Steensland.

The ride around Lake Mendota takes you past the former State Hospital for the Insane (now the Mendota Mental Health Institute), built in 1858 from pale local brick. Mendota State Hospital is set amid oaks and effigy mounds on Mendota's northern shore. It was made famous in *Wisconsin Death Trip,* a compilation of local photos, news clippings, and entries from the asylum's logbook.

The road continues through the town of Westport, past the condo-maniacal incursion at the mouth of the Yahara and the **Cherokee Marsh,** where herons, cranes, hawks, and kingfishers share the lake with a population of ducks, geese, coots, and the occasional loon. Head west on County Trunk Road M to **Governor Nelson State Park,** where more mounds are found on the lake bluffs, protected in parkland named for former Wisconsin governor and U.S. Senator Gaylord Nelson, who founded Earth Day. Watch the traffic on County M as you round

Middleton and head back into Madison on Allen Boulevard, past Marshall Park, and onto University Avenue.

Take a left on Capital Avenue and coast downhill to Lake Mendota Drive for a lakeside jaunt on the final leg of the Mendota loop through **Shorewood Hills,** which, like Maple Bluff, is an island of large homes on wooded lots away from the din of the surrounding city.

Frank Lloyd Wright's elegant use of stone and glass is beautifully expressed in his most spectacular Madison design—the **Unitarian Meeting House,** on University Bay Drive in Shorewood Hills. Wright's father was a Unitarian minister who helped to found the Madison Society of Unitarians in 1879. This close association with the Unitarians produced one of Wright's most beautiful buildings, its rising copper roof shooting up to heaven, a sweeping stained glass window—like the prow of a crystal ship splitting stone-walled seas—splintering morning light above the rostrum and diffusing it into the congregation meeting room. To save construction costs, the members of the society volunteered their time and labor to stack rock near Prairie du Sac, and hauled over 1,000 tons of limestone 30 miles (48 km) to the Shorewood Hills location.

Lake Mendota Drive connects with the University Campus and its Eagle Heights housing complex, and gently brings you to Picnic Point and back to the west campus lowlands of the University of Wisconsin.

*(following pages) An overview of downtown Madison illustrates the fact that the city rests on a narrow isthmus only a mile wide between Lake Monona to the south (right) and Lake Mendota to the north (left). The building in the foreground is Bascom Hall, in the heart of the university campus.*

# SOUTHWEST WISCONSIN

ICE AGE GLACIERS CARVED out the boundaries of what is known as the Driftless area of southwestern Wisconsin two million years ago, but while the cold white sheets swept as far south as the Ohio River and Kansas, this sedimentary highland stood tall above the lobes of ice. Having avoided this glacial leveling, the Driftless area has more of an irregular, even rugged, character than the rest of Wisconsin. Wisconsin's Driftless area covers about 8,000 square miles of rolling countryside, where undulating roads and tidy farms (and the occasional slice of hillbilly heaven) are tucked into tight valleys, or crown the rocky ridges and plateaus. The valleys and glens of these higher lands are striped with rivers and creeks, though lakes (which in most of Wisconsin were gouged by glaciers) are rare. The Wisconsin River links a handful of riverside cities and villages as it flows through the Driftless area, from a few miles below Wisconsin Dells (see "CENTRAL SANDS" chapter) to Prairie du Chien on the Mississippi. The blend of farms, woods, and wildlife melds with the ever-changing sandbar complexion of the river. From Richland Center north to Westby on U.S. 14, and from Ontario down the Kickapoo River,

*A family hams it up for the photographer in the small southwestern town of Christiana-Pleasant Springs in 1875. (State Historical Society of Wisconsin)*

and in the highlands above the coulee valleys, clean, fresh, farmland is planted with silage, hay, and corn for dairy cattle. After milking in the morning, the cows wind their way down to twisting, wooded stream valleys to snack on grass and spend the day before returning uphill for the evening milking. The pace of farm life, with its rhythms and schedules, is "Driftless area standard time."

The Driftless area embraces many distinct regions and terrains: the river valley of the lower Wisconsin River; the Wisconsin's largest tributary, the Kickapoo; the lead-mining plateau of the southwest highlands; the magnificent Mississippi Valley; and the broad valleys of Upper Coulee Country (see "UPPER COULEE COUNTRY").

## ■ BARABOO

The glaciers that scoured most of Wisconsin were blocked by the Baraboo Range, a low series of quartzite hills that still blocks the path of the Wisconsin River, forcing it to make a 40-mile (64-km) hook around the range to the east. Rising above the river, the Baraboo Range and the eastern highlands of Sauk County are packed with hidden glens and heights.

When an ice block dammed the Wisconsin River during the glacial age, the river jumped its bed. The rush of grit-filled ice-melt unleashed from a glacial lake atop the Central Sands cut through the range. When the ice melted and the Wisconsin River took its present course, the 400-foot (122-m) gash through the range remained. Filled with water, it became **Devil's Lake.**

One of Wisconsin's largest state parks, the varied terrain at **Devil's Lake State Park** is a mecca for rock climbers, hikers, campers, and cross-country skiers. The most scenic approach to this area from Madison is to take Highway 113 northwest from Lake Mendota and cross the Wisconsin River on the free ferry at the town of Merrimac.

Devil's Lake is surrounded by oak and hickory woods that blaze with color in autumn, a torch-lit maple canopy of Promethean intensity. On three sides of the lake, sheer rugged bluffs rise 500 feet (152 m) above clear water. As no gasoline motors are allowed, it's a fine place to canoe, row, or sail, or if you're up to it, enjoy peace and quiet.

The park is part of the Ice Age National Scientific Reserve, nine separate areas spread in an arc from Lake Michigan to the St. Croix River that together tell the story of how glaciers shaped Wisconsin's topography.

East of Devil's Lake State Park are two hidden clefts in the Baraboo Range—**Parfrey's Glen** and **Durwood's Glen.** These quiet ravines, shaded by hardwood canopies and overgrown with moss and ferns, allow the hiker to travel millions of years with each ascending step. The steep cliff walls exhibit layers of sediment, fossil deposits, and different size stones—conglomerate stone—layers all laid down randomly in ancient, shallow seas. A millennia of erosion cut through this sediment.

The Sauk County seat of **Baraboo** is nestled into the Baraboo Range. The town's most famous native sons are the brothers Ringling—better known as the Ringling Brothers, whose circus wintered in Baraboo during the late-nineteenth and early twentieth century. The Ringling brothers—Arthur, the juggler, and four others—combined their father's skill in harness-making with their own imagintion to develop a circus featuring riding acts, juggling, and snake charming. By 1907 the Ringlings had merged with the Barnum & Bailey Circus and soon they were the biggest circus in America, not to mention the Greatest Show on Earth. Traveling between towns by railway, the circus staged a parade from the depot to their tenting grounds, drumming up excitement and business.

Ringling Brothers circus wagons are still loaded onto trains that snake their way across the Wisconsin countryside to Madison, and then east to Milwaukee, where

*The Circus Museum Band of the Ringling Brothers puts on an impromptu performance before taking their Greatest Show on Earth on a road trip.*

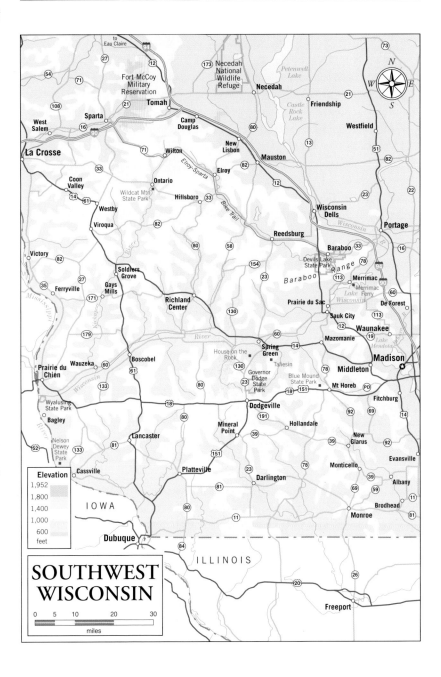

SOUTHWEST
WISCONSIN

they perform the **Great Circus Parade** in July. The sight of beautiful wagons hitched up to teams of horses, and filled with lions, tigers, hippos, and apes, and topped with brass bands, is nothing less than magnificent.

The **Circus World Museum** at 426 Water Street in Baraboo, maintains an exquisite collection of circus wagons and memorabilia.

For the non-zoo view of animal life, visit the **International Crane Foundation** at E11376 Shady Lane Road in Baraboo. The foundation is devoted to rearing, and returning to the wild, cranes from all over the world. (Also see "CENTRAL SANDS" chapter for more on the foundation and on environmentalist Aldo Leopold.)

Just north of Baraboo, along Man Mound Road, stands a rare and unique figure, the **Man Mound Effigy.** At 150 feet (46 m) long, it is the largest human effigy in North America, comparable to the grand figures on the Peruvian plain of Nazca that served ceremonial and astronomical ends. If the Man Mound could stand on its feet, it would rise fifteen stories tall. Its significance long forgotten, it remains a quiet and extraordinary link to the mind of the Woodland people that made it more than a thousand years ago.

Seven miles (11 km) west of Baraboo at **North Freedom,** the **Mid-Continent Railway** is the perfect antidote for train buffs in need of a real steam locomotive fix. Several working steam locomotives pull passenger cars along the Baraboo River Valley lines each summer, and some even pull duty on the winter snow trail. The scenery is lovely and the trains are a must for families with young children. Adults will marvel at the engineering craft that went into the grand old machines that spanned the continent. The train leaves from the Mid-Continent Railway Museum on Walnut Street; (608) 522-4261.

**Reedsburg** is a pleasant town on Highway 33, with an older downtown area. The **Norman Rockwell Museum** there (at 227 Park Street) has hundreds of pieces of his artwork, which is great for Rockwell aficionados in the Midwest—though Rockwell's Stockbridge, Massachusetts, studio still has the better collection of the artist's original works.

# ■ LOWER WISCONSIN RIVER

After its detour around the Baraboo Range, the Wisconsin River flows into Lake Wisconsin, a reservoir dammed two miles (3.2 km) above Prairie du Sac. The shore of the lake is dotted with summer cottages and boat launches, catering to the flood of fishermen who come to catch its white bass, smallmouth and largemouth bass, walleye and muskellunge, and even sturgeon.

The **Merrimac ferry,** the last remaining vessel of a once-proud armada, provides a free shortcut, crossing the Wisconsin River between the Baraboo Hills and Devil's Lake in the north, and the village of Okee on the south bank of the river.

**Gibraltar Rock,** located off County Road V east of Okee, owes its steep limestone face to the power of the glaciers that melted before they could finish grinding down these hills. Its jutting rocks are trimmed with windswept pines that curl out into space, their branches and roots gnarled and arthritic from their lifelong fight with a stiff west wind. The south-facing slopes feature sandstone and dolomite outcroppings. Birch, hickory, and maple hills on the north slope face down the wind, their forest edge trimmed and planted with hay, corn, or alfalfa. The view from the top is classic Wisconsin: a landscape of white houses and red barns, a sea-green bog and, in the western distance, the azure hills of the Baraboo Range under an ever-changing sky. In a glacial pothole carved at Gibraltar's foot, a protected bog shelters pitcher plants and sphagnum moss.

Below Lake Wisconsin's dam lie the Castor and Pollux of Wisconsin River towns—Sauk City and Prairie du Sac. The twin cities, known administratively as Sauk Prairie, were once the site of the Sauk Indian encampment. The proximity to the river, and adjacent fertile farmland, made this area attractive to nineteenth-century settlers.

■ SAUK PRAIRIE

The houses of Sauk Prairie tell some interesting stories. The row of Queen Anne beauties overlooking the Wisconsin River along Highway 78—their turrets tall, their gables sharp, their columns upholding porches that wrap around the homes decorated with spindly trim and cut-shingle designs beneath bracketed roof lines—recall the heyday of logging, when great log rafts floated down the Wisconsin and fortunes were won and lost. Less flamboyant, but unique to this region, are the dolomite and limestone block-and-stack houses built by Swiss-German masons, who arrived in the early 1850s, attracted by promotional pamphlets. By alternating stacks of unfinished stone with one finished row of ashlar block, they ingeniously provided decoration while reducing the need for finished stone.

The wooded green space a few blocks off Water Street is **Freethinkers Park,** with a round bandstand in the center of the park and the Freie Gemeinde (Free-thinkers) Hall at its south end. The hall has served as a ceremonial center for the entire community—funerals, weddings, Sunday get-togethers, church dinners, school picnics—the sum and parcel of village social life. It has also served as the intellectual center for its namesake freethinkers, an offshoot of the Humanist movement at the University of Prague, and imported via German immigrants in the 1830s. According to **August Derleth** (1909-1971), a local novelist and chronicler of life along the Wisconsin River, the lecture fare at the hall was headier than the chautauqua lecture circuit. The Sauk Prairie Freethinkers' regular meetings to discuss their views on philosophy represented to Derleth the very substance of freedom of thought and small-town virtue.

The people and places in fictional "Sac Prairie" appear in dozens of Derleth's short novels and stories, illustrating the moods, joys, fears, strengths, and weaknesses of American small-town life. In *Walden West,* Derleth described the sad and somber underside of the psyche of the village residents, the once-bright beginnings of personal histories in large, friendly houses that overlooked the brooding river, later broken by the unfortunate and hard choices life deals through chance. Derleth's Sac Prairie is a place forever downriver from the source of wealth, where industry was life's own reward and expectation.

*The view from the top of Gibraltar Rock is best appreciated late on a summer afternoon as the sun's rays highlight distant corn fields.*

*Typical Wisconsin scenery in the Driftless area.*

# A PLACE FOR FREETHINKERS

*J*ust east of the house of my childhood, by a block, stood the Freethinkers' Park. It occupied an entire village block. It was bordered on the north by three very large clumps of lilacs, which flourished for years until a doltish caretaker let a leaf fire escape him and burn them down, and one of the stands—"the lemonade stand"—used for picnics; another of these stands, known as "the ice-cream stand," stood along the west line facing Lachmund's auxiliary lumber yard long the railroad tracks there. A trim round bandstand stood at the approximate center of the park, and along the sidewalk on the south line rose the great, barn-like structure of the *Freie Gemeind* Hall, in which the congregation held meetings, funerals, and the like.

It rose from a cozy basement room, used primarily for dinners, and soared upwards for more than two storeys, so that the main floor was a rather cavernous chamber, an acoustic marvel. Park and building were used for many years for the annual school picnic, the major event of the ending of each school year; they were host to all the children from both public and parochial schools, the mecca of a parade, of scores of aging people who came to sit on the benches in the June sunlight and reminisce of the old days, of the onetime *Gemuthlichkeit* which had made for such a mellow, casual way of life in Sac Prairie; and for one day therefore the park was colorful and gay with children and was then again deserted for another year.

The Hall, however, was far more in use. Though, with the inexorable thinning of the congregation with the passage of time because so many members were unmarried, the Freethinkers were declining in numbers and prestige, the Hall itself was used in the years of my childhood and youth for a variety of "doings" from visits of Casperle and his puppet shows—an event of huge importance for the children—to the annual Masquerade Ball. Yet it was not so much the special events which lent meaning to the cavernous old building as it was the regular meetings of the congregation, for, lacking a regular speaker after the initial speakers had passed on, the congregation was in the habit of asking speakers in. The Freethinkers had, in fact, set the cultural tone for Sac Prairie over many decades; they were an offshoot of the Humanist movement at the University of Prague, and were composed of dissident aristocrats or upperclass tradesmen from the German countries for the most part, most of them well educated, and they were not satisfied with the customary pap to be heard from the lecture platform.

I grew into the habit of attending their meetings—not regularly, not as regularly as in those years I went to Mass—but often enough to be enabled to reach out beyond the boundaries of Sac Prairie. Many times visiting members came from Milwaukee and Chicago —men like Leo Weissenborn, who was later to build a house for me and call it Place of Hawks, an architect who had studied in Paris and Rome, and had come back to Chicago only after years spent in the nation's capital, who could speak intimately of the *Little Review* and the Dill Pickle Club, of *Poetry* and the literary ascendance of Chicago during the days of Floyd Dell, Sherwood Anderson, Edgar Lee Masters, and others, and who supplemented at first hand the news of the creative arts I had in print through the mail . . .

*August W. Derleth. (State Historical Society of Wisconsin)*

Yet it was no one person, no one meeting of significance that mattered as much as the general atmosphere of the Park Hall and the Freethinkers' congregation and the ideals put into practise there. The very air in that great old building seemed to stand positively for freedom of thought, as were the Park Hall a repository for freedom itself, and the old building stood in the days of my youth as a tangible encouragement to think and act with complete freedom, respecting the rights and happiness of others.

—August W. Derleth, *Walden West,* 1961

A second-generation German boy, Derleth spent his childhood roaming the glacial end moraine of the Roxbury hills east of the river, and the worn sandstone teeth of the Ferry Bluff range downriver, and across the marshy sloughs and sand-bar islands that stand and reform with the river's annual flood. The woods, sloughs, marshes, and river gave sanctuary to the young Derleth, a contemporary of H. P. Lovecraft, who influenced his writing. Their tales were the infant steps toward the science fiction and horror-movie genre of the 1950s and 1960s. Derleth was also influenced by Edgar Allan Poe, and Derleth's stories reflect the spooky, worm-eaten tales of human decomposition produced by unmet hope, hunger, and affection.

### ■ ALONG THE RIVER

Each winter, when the open-water habitat in the sloughs and marshes of the Wisconsin River freezes over, bald eagles head downriver to fish the river at Sauk Prairie. The open water below the Wisconsin River Dam offers the eagles teeming fish and wildlife to support them each winter; the eagles respond with a voracious appetite and a spectacular mastery of aerial fish-hunting. The deep woods and bluffs below Sauk City and the Baraboo Hills afford plenty of roosting territory. Their numbers have increased in the years since the bald eagle became a protected species.

The lower Wisconsin is preserved for public hunting and recreation, along both the north and south banks, for 80 miles (128 km) from Sauk City to Prairie du Chien on the Mississippi. There are boat launches for anglers, and canoeing and primitive camping are available on the many islands of the river. Backroads and county trunk highways cut through scrub oak and pine windbreaks, and past farms and cottages, offering close-up views of the Wisconsin. The marshlands and timber stands are home to deer, pheasant, woodcock, turkey, and grouse. In summer and fall, the river's medium-paced flow belies an annual fall and spring torrent that carves and reshapes a new maze of sandbars and sloughs that feed and shelter owls, mink, raccoon, muskrat, deer, red-tail hawks, green and blue herons, sandhill cranes, and snowy egrets.

Heading down the Wisconsin River on Highway 78, you come to the glacial plain at **Mazomanie,** where Black Earth Creek runs into Blue Mounds Creek, which in turn flows into the Wisconsin River near the border of Iowa County. Petroglyphs left by prehistoric hunters in hope of invoking the help of spirits in their big-game hunting have been found on the walls of rock shelters in the hollows of these valleys.

*The Kickapoo Valley region provides an inviting environment for farmers and wildlife alike.*

Two fine old buildings—a log cabin and a double-square stone building (the Richard Thornber House)—stand sentinel on Highway 14 south of Mazomanie, an old city that boomed with the rail link from Madison to the Mississippi. As Mazomanie developed around the railroad, it attracted settlers from the nearby dry town of Dover (settled by members of the British temperance movement), and it wasn't long before the town went down the drain and disappeared.

One (presumably dry) Doverite, John F. Appleby, perfected a binding machine that began the mechanized farming revolution in America. Appleby's knotting baler allowed farmers to bale and stack sheaves of wheat rather than tying round sheaves by hand. The baler, working in common with the mechanized thresher, allowed large land parcels to be planted with wheat, where before only a few acres could be planted and harvested. Though the depleted soils around Mazomanie forced King Wheat west with the railroad in the 1860s, the town continued to prosper as the hub of a rich agricultural area.

A converted knitting mill serves as the local historical museum, a gateway to an historic business district lined with brick Italianate, utilitarian, and Victorian store fronts, many of which have made it into that exclusive club for buildings: the National Register of Historic Places.

On the trunk road north from Mazomanie sprawls the **Lower Wisconsin River State Wildlife Area.** The centerpiece of this stretch of river is **Ferry Bluff,** named for the river ferries which once plied the Wisconsin. Eagles find sanctuary hidden amid the three-lobed rocky prominence rising above the Wisconsin and crowned by cliffs dotted with opuntia cactus (prickly pear) and cedar. Hickory and oak forests reach up through the valleys to heights that provide hikers with spectacular views of the refuge, and of the Wisconsin River winding from Lake Wisconsin, through the Sauk narrows, and downstream into Iowa County. At the foot of Ferry Bluff, Honey Creek empties from deep in the hills of western Sauk County, past the village of Plain. The hardwood stand washed by the Honey Creek estuary is tapped as a sugar bush for maple sugar production. The nutrient-rich stream water feeding the marsh makes it an ideal habitat for fish, and an abundant amphibian and reptile population feeds generously on the small fry of walleye, perch, and panfish that breed in the marsh.

# ■ SPRING GREEN AND FRANK LLOYD WRIGHT

Downriver from Mazomanie, on the flood plain north of the Wisconsin River, is Spring Green, a small town with a world-wide association. Frank Lloyd Wright (1867-1959), one of the most famous and influential architects of the twentieth century, lived across the river in the Wyoming Valley for a few years at the very beginning of his life, and then later when he came here to live—first at Hillside Home (1903) and then at **Taliesin** (1911).

Wright was one of the most innovative architects of modern American history, discarding the conventional box shape for houses and replacing it with structures designed to fit both the landscape and the owners—"organic" designs. Wright was influenced by the simplicity of Japanese architecture, the ornament of Mayan temples, the Arts and Crafts Movement, and the innovative use of materials—like local stone, wood, and brick—that he believed would make the structure appear to spring naturally from the land around it. He also used new materials, like concrete, plywood, and masonite. His use of stained glass and banks of windows let natural light fill the interior, while the occupants could enjoy the view.

*A self-photographed portrait of Spring Green's most famous resident, Frank Lloyd Wright. (State Historical Society of Wisconsin)*

Wright's personal life was nearly as electrifying as his professional career. After he was born in Richland Center, his family lived briefly in Spring Green before moving to the East and then returning to Madison in 1878. As a young man, Wright attended classes at the University. His architectural career took him to Chicago and the drafting tables of Louis Sullivan. By the turn of the century he was at the height of his career with a wife, Catherine, and six children. In 1910, however, when Wright took a trip to Europe to promote his work, he went with the wife of a client, Mamah Cheney, and their affair destroyed his marriage. He returned to Chicago in scandal and retreated to his Hillside Home School in the Wyoming Valley, and built his famous home Taliesin (Welsh for "Shining Brow") for Mamah.

In 1914, while Wright was in Chicago, a housekeeper barricaded Mamah and her two children in a room at Taliesin and set the house on fire, killing them. The housekeeper then murdered all the servants who tried to escape, chopping them to death with an ax. Wright buried Mamah, obtained a divorce from Catherine, and took up with Miriam Noel for the next five years while he designed the Imperial Hotel in Tokyo. They married in 1923, but separated six months later. Soon thereafter, Wright met Olgivanna Hinzenberg, a divorcee with two children. The press hounded them until they married in 1928, when Wright was 60.

At a time when most men begin to retire, Wright produced his most important work. His best modernist works include Fallingwater House in Mill Run, Pennsylvania (1936); the Johnson Wax Headquarters in Racine (1936-49); the enormous home, Wingspread, built for Johnson Wax president, Herbert Johnson on Lake Michigan at Racine; and the Guggenheim Museum in New York (1943-59). Whether his 1957 design for a lakefront civic center in Madison should be built is still the subject of debate. Many of the Wright-designed homes in Wisconsin can only be seen from the street, but his legacy lives on in designs produced by the architectural school at Taliesin, which operates an active design service in Wisconsin and in Scottsdale, Arizona.

Wright died in 1959 in Arizona, but his body was driven back to his beloved Wyoming Valley for burial. His wife, Olgivanna, left instructions after her death in 1985 that Wright's body be exhumed and reburied next to her at Taliesin West in Arizona, in part because she disliked the controversy the locals raised over her early affair with Wright. So Wright, who spent so much of his life in Wisconsin, was removed from its soil, despite his specific request to spend his afterlife in the Badger State.

*Taliesin (Welsh for "Shining Brow") was built by Wright in 1911 as his home in Spring Green. His school of architecture is nearby.*

The Wright buildings are north of Spring Green at the junction of Highway 23 and City Road T. Tours are conducted daily May through October.

### ■ H O U S E   O N   T H E   R O C K

Another curious architectural monument of the Wyoming Valley is the **House on the Rock** on Highway 33, one of Wisconsin's top tourist attractions through no fault of the original owner, Alex Jordan, an artist with a penchant for collecting junk. The House on the Rock is balanced on a dolomite outcropping overlooking the Wyoming Valley, and is designed in a Japanese style, with Asian artifacts and furniture throughout its tiny upper level. As you descend into the bowels of the house, your feeling of claustrophobia will become ever more pronounced. You pass enormous wooden clocks from Germany, huge diesel engines that once powered ocean freighters, eerie orchestras (powered by hydraulic lines) playing classical music badly, and replicas of Main Streets that have been abandoned by their inhabitants. The tour descends through a maze of rooms in warehouse after warehouse, until you reach the basement, where a gigantic merry-go-round is careening almost out of control, its ceiling filled with hundreds of wooden maidens, their breasts pointing accusingly at the visitors, who hope that the next corner will produce an exit and fresh air. The tour is expensive and long, with no turning back once the hordes are funneled down the chute.

## ■ SOUTHWEST HIGHLANDS

South of the Wisconsin River and west of I-90, the land rises from flat glacial prairie into a rolling countryside characteristic of the Driftless highlands. Travelers bound southwest from Madison along Highway 18 will arrive at **Mount Horeb,** a tidy little town with antique shops bulging from behind its former opera house and storefronts. Craft shops are nestled next to the all-important coffee shop, where locals come and klatsch every day to monitor the comings and goings about town. In the valleys around Mount Horeb, stern-faced Norwegian men and women long ago built little homesteads and turned the oak and hickory hillsides into pasture and quarries. The sandy creek bottoms produced magnificent potatoes for making **lefse** (potato pancake), as well as tobacco. In one such valley in the shadow of Blue Mound, three miles (4.8 km) west of Mount Horeb, lies **Little Norway,** a collection of log and frame buildings—including a delicate log church

—which recreates a village typical of those that dotted the corners of this area more than a century ago.

Westward out of Mount Horeb leads The Trollway, the local moniker for Highway PD, called so in honor of the 15-foot-high (4.6-m) trolls carved into the stumps of oak trees that line the road. The Trollway leads to **Blue Mound State Park,** named for the 1,700-foot (518-m) mountain with views from the top that reach nearly 40 miles (64 km) in all directions. The park has camping facilities and hiking trails and is as much fun in winter as summer for those who like to ski cross-country.

South of Mount Horeb, the woods around New Glarus play host to the **Swiss Historical Village** (west of Highway 69 on County Road H), which preserves several homes built by Swiss settlers. The Swiss who came to New Glarus scouted the Midwest for many years before finding this wooded valley. They still celebrate annually the Heidi Festival and the William Tell Festival, both of which involve eating cheese and drinking beer from the New Glarus Brewery, among other activities.

From New Glarus, the **Sugar River State Trail** runs southeast to Monticello, Albany, and Brodhead along 23 miles (37 km) of level grade. From Monroe, south of New Glarus, the **Tri-County/Cheese Country Trail** runs to Mineral Point along an abandoned rail corridor. The 47-mile (75-km) trail is open to ATVs and horses from April to November, and to snowmobiles and cross-country skiing December to March. It is closed during deer-hunting season (usually about nine days in November).

The western and central area of this lower Driftless region was the first part of Wisconsin to be heavily settled by Americans, who staked their claims in lead. The Winnebago began mining for lead crystals centuries before near Potosi, but the large operations had to wait for the Americans' arrival. **Mining villages** sprang up with fanciful names like Hardscrabble, Fairplay, Hoof Noggle, Tail-Hole, Patch, and Nip and Tuck. Many survived only a few days or weeks, or until the vein petered out. Today, county trunks and backroads tracing the paths of the lead miners wind over hills and through narrow wooded valleys, past large piles of lead tailings, the waste product of the "badgers" digging for their fortunes. The boom lasted until the 1850s, although zinc mines operated in the area until 1965.

One town that is a survivor of this era is **Dodgeville,** 40 miles (64 km) west of Madison on Highway 18. It is named after Henry Dodge, an audacious bully who built a stockade here on Winnebago land, then took a leading role in the militia

(top) A phantasm of kitsch awaits the visitor to House on the Rock, one of the state's top tourist attractions south of Spring Green on Highway 33. The village on Mineral Point is known for its beautiful stone architecture.

that pursued Black Hawk. Later he served as governor of the newly created Wisconsin Territory (1836–1841) and as Wisconsin's first U.S. senator. The town's county courthouse, built in 1861, is the oldest still in use in the state. Nearby is vast **Governor Dodge State Park** whose bluffs and trails make a fine setting for a summer hike. **Military Ridge State Trail** runs nearby from Blue Mound, another wonderful state park with a great view.

The discovery of nearly pure veins of lead at the crotch of two tiny branches of the Pecatonica River led to the almost immediate blossoming of the village of **Mineral Point,** south of Dodgeville. Cornish and Irish miners began working the rich deposits in 1828. Mineral Point fared better than most of the small villages that sprang up in that period, and its beautiful stone architecture is best preserved at the adjacent historical area called Pendarvis. The village looks as if it were lifted from Cornwall, with stone buildings along the main and side streets quarried to access the rich lead deposits. Its fantastic stock of housing is numbered for identification with maps supplied by the local tourist information facility.

Another mining town, **Platteville,** now supports a branch campus of the University of Wisconsin (formerly a mining school) and a fascinating mining museum (405 East Main). Above ground you can ride in ore cars pulled by an old locomotive before you descend 90 steps into the mine. The largest town of the region, Platteville is very Yankee in flavor, with the oldest buildings sporting a Greek Revival look. The main street is well lined with taverns and restaurants that befit a Wisconsin college town, and the campus helps support a lively nightlife. Platteville also serves as the pre-season training grounds for the Chicago Bears.

Heading southwest of Platteville toward Dickeyville, the Little Platte and Blockhouse Creek snake along the bottomland below rounded, oak-covered hills. **Dickeyville** is the home of the Dickeyville Grotto, a remarkable roadside work of art built between 1925 and 1930 by a former pastor of the Holy Ghost Church, Father Mathias Wernerus. Whether religious devotion drove him to mortar millions of shells, stones, glass shards, pottery pieces, minerals, and crystals to form a series of religious shrines to God and Country, or whether it was a case of seemingly inexhaustible obsessive compulsion, his work is magnificent in the strangest sense of the word. For the rockhound, the grotto should be seen if only to enjoy its collection of geodes, convoluted sandstone, minerals, crystals, and stalactites. Wernerus achieved a great deal of color by using several shades of broken colored glass to highlight his mosaic work.

At the stagecoach stop of Hardscrabble, now called **Hazel Green** and located southeast of Dickeyville, are three inns—The Empire House, Wisconsin House, and Dewinter's—all built in the 1840s to accommodate the thousands of Southerners and immigrants hoping to strike lead. One immigrant was Father Samuel Mazzuchelli (1806–1864) who designed several churches in the area, including the sun-beaten and weathered Gothic St. Augustine Catholic Church, set at the top of the hill in nearby **New Diggins.**

**Shullsburg,** a few miles east, flourished when the lead was generous. Its mining museum, brick Main Street, and stone churches and schools illustrate the wealth that lead brought to the area, and its Fourth of July parade is a time capsule of small-town Americana.

## ■ LOWER MISSISSIPPI RIVER VALLEY

Along the lower Mississippi River from Cassville up to La Crosse, the marshy bottomlands are filled with life: cormorants diving for fish in the shallows, snowy egrets stalking their prey against a backdrop of green marsh grass and sweet flag, vultures carving lazy circles in the sky as hot air from the sun-baked bluffs lifts them. In the winter, bald eagles fish the ice-free waters below the locks that hold back the mighty Mississippi's flow. If you're not fortunate enough to have a boat available to you, it's worth traveling north up the backroads and getting out where possible to enjoy the area's great natural beauty.

The river town of **Cassville,** founded in the 1830s at the height of the lead boom, is located at the end of Highway 81 as it comes south from Lancaster, and at the beginning of Highway 133 as it moves up north toward Prairie du Chien. At Cassville, bluffs hang close on both sides of the river, and the tidy, redbrick Greek Revival homes and buildings mesh with Southern-style porches where the ferry crosses to Iowa. Cassville was one of the earliest cities in Wisconsin, and it served as a gateway for pioneers and miners. River traffic kept the money flowing during the 1800s. Its large churches and numerous redbrick homes are evidence of the wealth Cassville once enjoyed.

Cassville's most prominent citizen was Nelson Dewey, a Yankee from New York who came to Wisconsin's lead-mining region in order to ply his trade as a lawyer and claim a homestead on the newly opened Indian territory. He became

*The Dickeyville Grotto was built by Father Mathias Wernerus between 1925 and 1930 and consists of a collection of strange sculpture compiled from pottery pieces, glass shards, shells, minerals, and crystals.*

the state of Wisconsin's first governor in 1848, and presided over the first state legislature in Belmont. After retirement, he purchased a 2,000-acre tract of land on the Mississippi and called it Stonefield Village. There he built a beautiful home and barns and employed dozens of locals in his farm operations. Unfortunately, Dewey's wife found country life dull, and she took their son to live with her in Madison—action-packed by comparison. Dewey lost track of her and his son, and speculation in canal-building cost him Stonefield Village and his fortune. He died poor and sad in a rented room in Lancaster, Wisconsin, but you can still visit Stonefield Village at **Nelson Dewey State Park**, north of Cassville. The bluffs above the exquisitely maintained Dewey plantation offer camping and hiking.

**Wyalusing State Park**, near the confluence of the Wisconsin and Mississippi rivers, has a remarkable collection of effigy mounds that represent different phases of the mound-building cultures. The hiking trails that hug the bluff tops and wind down to the river provide terrific views of the big Wisconsin joining the much bigger Mississippi. Every winter more than 1,000 bald eagles gather here to fish the open Mississippi at the **Eagle Nature Preserve**, down river from Wyalusing State Park. There is nothing in the world like watching these majestic birds swooping down to catch a meal in their talons, their huge, strong wings returning them aloft to perch in the trees on the bluff. Take the local county highways for further bluff-top views of the Mississippi. Nearby is **Bagley**, an endearing river town with camping facilities close at hand.

One of Wisconsin's first permanent settlements, **Prairie du Chien** was initially an outpost for French voyageurs, who valued its strategic location near the mouth of the Wisconsin River, on a plain beneath the bluffs along the Mississippi River. The French were replaced by British fur traders, who were in turn pushed aside by the American Fur Trading Company. A beautiful Victorian mansion, **Villa Louis** (521 Villa Louis Road), was built here by Hercules Dousman on the site of a trappers' campground. The location also served as a fort for French and British soldiers, and later became Fort Crawford under American occupancy. The fishing is great and marina facilities are plentiful and readily accessible at Prairie du Chien. Catfish served in town restaurants are delicious, and you can taste the Big Muddy with every bite.

Traveling north along the river up Highway 35, you'll pass **Ferryville**. In this area, wild ginseng has been gathered as a means of supplementing farm income since the 1890s. Along the road from De Soto or Genoa there are spectacular views of the big, brown Mississippi flowing beneath high bluffs. Just north is **Victory,** the site of the defeat of Chief Black Hawk during the Black Hawk War. The Black Hawk War was a rout virtually from the moment it began, and the final slaughter took place at the mouth of the Bad Axe River. Black Hawk was captured, some women and children escaped to Iowa and safety, but hundreds were killed. (See the essay on Black Hawk in "HISTORY.")

## ■ KICKAPOO VALLEY

Before flowing into the Wisconsin River, the Kickapoo River meanders 130 miles (208 km) through the prettiest valley in Wisconsin's Driftless area. To see it, drive east from Prairie du Chien, then north on Highway 131; or drive east of La Crosse on Highway 33, turning south on 131 at the hamlet of Ontario. The countryside along Highway 33 is steeped in timelessness, and unadorned simplicity permeates the region. A great canoeing stream, the Kickapoo cuts through limestone and sandstone bluffs, and the wooded, fern-covered hillsides of the lower coulee region. (The lower coulees are narrow, generally V-shaped, as opposed to the broad, U-shaped valleys of the upper coulee, which is covered in the "UPPER COULEE COUNTRY" chapter.) On foggy days, the hills above the valleys are obscured, giving an unreal sense of enormous, primeval mountains. It is most beautiful in spring, when the apple orchards bloom in Gays Mills, and in fall, when the entire region is painted with the glow of summer past. Several wildlife refuges in the valley protect an extensive population of songbirds and waterfowl that enjoy the shallow meanders of the Kickapoo and its marshy perimeter.

A native tribe called the Kickapoo (or Kiwigapawa, the "wanderers") once lived here, but they moved south before American settlers arrived on the scene, ending up in Coahuila, Mexico, and leaving only their name. It was probably the sound of the name that inspired cartoonist Al Capp to place Dogpatch, Daisy Mae, and Lil' Abner along the Kickapoo. Unlike Capp's cartoon characters, the real residents of the Kickapoo keep their farms neat. Few brew mountain dew; virtually none wear torn polka-dot tops and one-strap suspenders.

The Kickapoo River rises near Wilton in Monroe County, dropping rapidly down to Ontario, where it snakes past **Wildcat Mountain State Park.** From the looming summit of Wildcat Mountain, the network of valleys cut by the Kickapoo and its tributaries can be seen spreading out below. Stream joins stream, and they veer and dodge south toward La Farge, Viola, and Readstown, all good bases for fishermen who wish to enjoy the quiet solitude of the region's 200 miles (320 km) of class-three trout streams.

Over the years, the Kickapoo has caused enough flooding to give homeowners pause at the idea of building near the flood plain. **Soldiers Grove**, downstream from Readstown, was moved after devastating floods on the Fourth of July in 1978. The village hired an architect to design a new town to replace the devastated Main Street. Besides building a commercial district on higher ground, town planners took the opportunity to build the only passive-solar-designed municipality in the United States, and now all the buildings capture 50 percent of their heat from the sun. Today, the Kickapoo runs harmlessly through the former downtown area, which now provides recreation instead of retail services.

Below Soldiers Grove, the Kickapoo cuts through the valley of **Gays Mills**, a village in the heart of Wisconsin's apple-growing region. The town was established in 1847 by James B. Gay, a newly arrived engineer from Indiana. By 1865, he had built a dam and a mill for lumber and flour milling, both of which prospered. When his health deteriorated, he convinced his brothers John and Thomas to help with his Kickapoo Valley enterprise, and their arrival gave Gays

*This quintessential American farmer resides in the dells of Vernon County, one of the most beautiful areas of the state.*

Mills its permanent identity. The small community supports grocery cooperatives, a natural-foods cafe, and annual festivals to promote the products of all the region's farmers. The apple orchards are a legacy of John Hays and Ben Twining, whose apples won highest honors at a national apple show in New York. Expanding upon a few dozen acres of orchards at the turn of the century, the pair planted the ridges surrounding Gays Mills with thousands of acres of orchards. From August through November, the continuous ripening of different varieties of fresh apples provides a kaleidoscope of different tastes, textures, scents, and colors. In spring, the fragrance of apple blossoms fills the entire valley, and the sight of a thousand acres of pink and white blossoms abuzz with honeybees is not soon forgotten.

From Gays Mills, the Kickapoo continues down through the state wildlife areas at Bell Center and at Wauzeka, where the Kickapoo joins the Wisconsin.

Though the Kickapoo is the centerpiece of the region, equally enchanting are the lateral highways that explore the ridges and valleys of the lower coulee region. One of the most beautiful of roads, Highway 33 tracks through eastern Vernon County en route from Baraboo to La Crosse. Eastern Vernon County is home to Wisconsin's largest Amish settlement; here you can purchase hickory furniture, maple syrup, quilts, rugs, cheese, and other produce. Farms advertise their wares on hand-lettered signs posted along the highways. The Amish do not conduct business

*An Amish quilt auction taking place near Amherst Junction. In recent years, many Amish have migrated to Wisconsin from Pennsylvania to escape creeping urbanization.*

on Sundays and visitors are not permitted to take their photographs. Their black-lacquered carriages and buggies are drawn by some of the best-groomed and most elegant horses you'll ever see, their manes and tails flowing as they trot along the shoulders of the highways. In spring and fall, large draft horses add picturesque power to the planting and harvest. Amish farms are easy to spot: no machines clutter up their yards, black lacquered wagons stand in the driveways instead of pick-up trucks, horses nibble hay in corrals, and the corn is tied up in sheaves.

Another beautiful road is Highway 61, from Viroqua to Coon Valley, by way of Westby. This is Norwegian country. **Viroqua's** remarkable Main Street features some lovely brick storefronts from the late 1800s and the turn of the century. The Viking motif is just one of the signs that tells you that *uff da* is the curse of preference when a *dammdesatan* (little devil) gets in your way. Farther north, in **Westby,** the signs that identify downtown buildings are decorated in Norwegian rosemaling, while scroll- and fret-work adorn the frame homes that are part of the artistic tradition of the locals. The farmers of Westby keep up with local news while nourishing themselves at Borgen's cafe, where coffee and nine kinds of pie accompany the conversation.

Four miles northwest of Coon Valley, the University of Wisconsin at La Crosse operates the **Norskedalen Bekkum Homestead and Thrune Center** from May through October. There you can see a pioneer Norwegian settlement that features log homes and buildings from the 1850s and later.

**Bicycling** is a particularly good way to see the hilly lands of the Kickapoo region. Bed-and-breakfast inns and other accommodations exist within manageable distance from one another, as do other such roadside attractions as cheese factories, orchards, and produce stands sufficiently stocked to sustain an occupying army. Nearly 100 miles (160 km) of trails follow former rail lines through the region—including the Elroy-Sparta bike trail, the 400 Trail from Baraboo (which parallels Highway 33), the La Crosse River Trail, and the Great River Trail that extends to Perrot State Park and Mount Trempealeau. (See "Bicycle Tours" in "Practical Information.")

# UPPER COULEE COUNTRY

THE UPPER COULEE COUNTRY is a distinct part of Wisconsin's Driftless area. The region is roughly bounded by the Mississippi on the west, and by Interstate 94 on the east; and it is not coincidence that such obvious landmarks should so closely define its edges. Roads, like rivers, tend to follow the course of least resistance, and the glacier-scoured lands on either side of the Driftless proved easier to negotiate than the hilly terrain of the Upper Coulees, both for rivers and road-builders.

Coulees are flat-floored valleys with steep walls, usually cut into plateaus, and usually ending in box canyons. They are a characteristic of much of the Driftless area north of the Wisconsin River, which is usually divided into Upper and Lower Coulee regions. Upper Coulee Country refers to the area roughly north of La Crosse and I-90, while the Lower Coulee lies to the south (and is covered in our "SOUTHWEST WISCONSIN" chapter).

The rivers that cut through the Upper Coulee drain the vast highlands of the North Woods, emptying into the Mississippi through a chain of bluffs stretching from La Crosse north to the St. Croix Valley. Driving along the wrinkled western bluffs above the Mississippi on a crisp, clear day, your eyes range upstream and downstream for miles. From each bluff-top plateau the sky grows wide, retreating with each descent into wooded valleys and stream beds. The mix of crop and woodland, so lush and green in summer's heat, forms a crazy-quilt patchwork of color each autumn, growing leaner through December, when tree skeletons silhouette against the winter snow, but glowing silver-green as life and vitality return in spring. Incoming cold fronts shake rain from the thundering and lightning-split cloud masses that cavort across the spring and summer skies.

There are many ways to see this region. Smaller highways heading south off I-94 to the Mississippi River lead through classic coulee country. Interstate 90 turns west at the southern boundary of the Upper Coulee region and heads to La Crosse. Here, the Great River Road (Highway 35) parallels the Mississippi River, traveling through small towns and river parks.

## ■ BACKROAD TRIP FROM OSSEO

The high plateaus and fertile river bottoms of the Upper Coulee attracted a variety of Europeans to the region. Highway 53 off I-94 leads to Osseo, a Norwegian town settled in 1857 in the midst of fertile farmland between the north and south forks of the Buffalo River. At **Norske Nook** restaurant farmers still stop in to gab with their buddies and scarf down slices of pie (more than 80 pies are made here daily *from scratch*) before returning home for the evening milking.

**West of Osseo on Highway 93** is the town of Eleva; about five miles (8 km) south, the road passes Chimney Rock, a tall sandstone pillar rising along the side of the road. Highway 93 continues to **Independence,** a Polish community. At the north end of the village is the red-brick **SS Piotra: Pawla (Saints Peter and Paul) Church,** one of the state's largest such edifices. Try Carolyn's Coffee Shop on Washington Street for a sample of the local community fare; its Sunday brunch attracts diners from across the region.

*Wisconsin's Norwegian influence is evident in the architecture of various chapels such as the Bjorklunden Chapel in Bailey's Harbor on the Door Peninsula.*

**Highway Q** east of Independence travels along the highlands overlooking the Trempealeau River and across an invisible cultural divide that separates the Polish community from the Norwegian town of **Whitehall.** The architecture changes from brick to frame, the religion from Roman Catholic to Lutheran. Citizens stand chatting on Main Street, men chew their favorite tobacco,

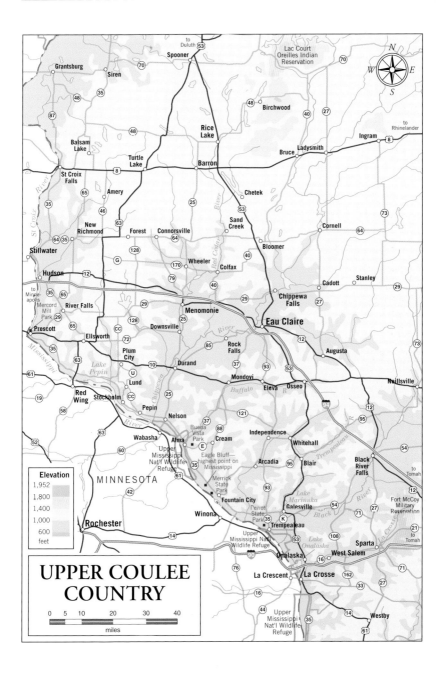

UPPER COULEE
COUNTRY

Elevation
1,952
1,800
1,400
1,000
600
feet

0  5  10    20      30      40
miles

and locals eat pie and coffee at the City Cafe. The cafe used to be a bowling alley, and it has the necessary "liar's table" in the back to keep the regular folk safe up front.

From Whitehall, Highway 53 heads south up the Trempealeau River Valley to **Blair,** a former mill town with a cheese factory. The Lutheran church on the western edge of town is a signal that Norwegians are close at hand. It's worth a moment to stop in and have some coffee and pie at Our Town Cafe on South Urberg, and contemplate the fate of one Hans Jacob Olson in 1889. Olson—a nasty drunk, and meaner sober—was an arsonist. After serving five years in prison for pyrotechnics, he returned home to his family. Less than pleased to see him again, they waited until he was asleep, then joined a mob of 40 to 50 citizens who were trying to convince him to leave the county. Olson refused to leave his house so his family and neighbors hanged him on a tree in his front yard until he passed out. Then they let him down. When he came to, they told him to leave and never come back. He refused again, so they hung him up again until he passed out. (He had a stout neck.) When he came to a second time, Olson laughed at the mob for being unable to kill him, so the mob hanged him a third time and did it right. The coroner's jury met the next day, headed up by the man that had hanged Olson, and no one was charged. The local district attorney, however, did find the guilty parties and the jury foreman, Olson's son, and Mrs. Olson were sentenced to life in prison. Thirty townspeople were charged for rioting in public.

The area has calmed down since. These days Amish farmers have taken over many of the area's farms, replacing tractors with horses, and fostering an air of peaceful simplicity and industry.

From Blair head south on Highway 53 along the Bear and Beaver Creek valleys. Hidden in a secret valley, locally reputed to be the site of the Garden of Eden, is the lovely town of **Galesville.** The brick and stone buildings of the main square are a reminder of a long gone era: tall glass storefronts, high-ceilinged cafes and stores, a small gazebo in the square. The river rushing from Lake Marinuka past the old mill and on to meet the Mississippi completes the picture. Coffee and food are fine at the Garden of Eatin' at Gale Street and the square, or at Jensen's Cafe. A more contemporary cuisine is available on the Mill Road at the Mill Road Cafe, which overlooks Beaver Creek.

Rising east of Galesville is **Decorah Mound,** named for the Winnebago chief who helped the American military capture Black Hawk at Bad Axe. Decorah sat atop that peak and saw his Winnebago warriors defeated by a band of Chippewa

## WINNEBAGO MEMORIES

*T*hat beautiful county where we were camping was at Black River Falls at the old depot in back of what is now G.W.'s general store. There was not a house around. We lived there in the spring of the year and my father fished. I suppose all of the Indians fished. There my father speared a big fish, an enormous fish, a sturgeon. When my father brought it home, carrying it over his shoulder, the tail dragged on the ground. He brought it back to where we were living. There I saw this big fish that looked like a man with a big fat belly, lying on his side with his belly protruding.

❖　❖　❖

In March we usually travelled to the Mississippi River close to La Crosse, sometimes even across the river . . . . My father, brother-in-law and brothers used to trap there for muskrats. When they killed the muskrats my mother used to save the bodies and hang them up there in great numbers. When there were a lot of muskrats then they used to roast them on a rack. . . . When they were cooled, the women packed them together and stored them for summer use.

In the spring when my father went trapping on the Mississippi and the weather became very pleasant my sister once said, "It is here that they dig yellow water lily roots." So, we all went out, my mother and sisters and everybody. When we got to a slough where the water lilies were very dense, they took off their shoes, put on old dresses and went wading into the water. They used their feet to hunt for the roots. They dug them out with their feet and then the roots floated up to the surface....They dried a great amount, flour sacks full. During the summer they sometimes cooked them with meat and they were really delicious.

❖　❖　❖

When I was small the Winnebago generally went to pick cranberries after they were through taking care of their gardens. We used to do that too. When we arrived at the marsh there were many Indians who camped together and they picked cranberries. The men used rakes and the women picked by hand.

❖　❖　❖

After cranberry time they went on the fall migration to hunt deer. That is what we always did, we went travelling to hunt deer. . . . They wrapped the deer in autumn leaves and carried the deer on their backs. As they were approaching you could see the red leaves moving along here and there, as they came home with the freshly killed deer. Just as soon as we arrived, the first day, they always brought home game. It was always this way. Sometimes they even used to bring in a bear.

—*Mountain Wolf Woman,* memoir of Indian life in the 1880s,
recorded by Nancy Oestreich Lurie, 1966

*An Indian woman gathers the bounty of the forest. (Murphy Library,
University of Wisconsin-La Crosse)*

*View of the Mississippi River in the Trempealeau area.*

in the early 1800s. When he saw his people killed, Decorah hid in a cave until he could escape to La Crosse. There he was befriended by settlers, whom he repaid by helping to cede much of the Winnebago tribal land to the federal government.

Highway 53 heads to La Crosse from Galesville, but it is best to find Highway K, which runs south from Highway 54, and head to **Trempealeau.** This is a fine river town, set in the shadow of two extraordinary mountains. Nicholas Perrot, the French explorer, once had a camp here because the mountain provided a vista north and south on the river. The area is preserved in one of the loveliest parks in Wisconsin, **Trempealeau National Wildlife Refuge,** noted for its stunning bluffs, a huge prairie on the side of one peak, and famous Trempealeau Mountain.

**Trempealeau Hotel** has fine food, Wisconsin beer, cheap lodging, and musical entertainment. The all-season restaurant, Ed Sullivan's Supper Club, provides a view of the Mississippi from its dining room. Try hiking up the 500-foot (800-km) -high Brady's Bluff to catch the sun setting over Trempealeau Mountain. It is as unforgettable a view as can be had in Wisconsin.

## ■ COULEE ROAD FROM MENOMONIE

Highway 25 provides one of the prettiest glimpses of the Upper Coulee region, cutting south from Menomonie, down the Red Cedar Valley, connecting with the broad Chippewa Valley, and meeting the Mississippi at the Beef Slough.

In 1846, Capt. William Wilson brought his family up the Red Cedar River to what is now **Menomonie** by keelboat, and began a logging operation that eventually grew to control 125,000 acres. Booming during the lumber era, the town grew silent once the supply of timber was exhausted. Today, visit **Mabel Tainter Hall**—a sandstone Romanesque confection at 205 Main Street, built in 1889 in memory of the daughter of Captain Tainter, a vice-president of the town's lumber company. Also of interest is **Wilson Place Museum**, the home of a lumber baron who began the largest white pine lumber company in the world, Knapp-Stout Lumber Company. James Stout founded the Stout Manual Training School here, devoted to training teachers in industrial and household arts. Now a part of the University of Wisconsin, it has an enrollment of over 7,000 students.

Highway 25 heads south of Menomonie on the east side of the **Red Cedar Valley**. Along the wide bottom of the Red Cedar River coulee, the **Red Cedar Bike Trail** parallels the river on a former rail corridor, curving past green fields and dairy farms. At **Downsville** is a small museum, **Empire in Pine**, packed with memorabilia of an earlier logging era. Downsville's redbrick creamery has been transformed into a fine restaurant and lodging called the Creamery. A former rooming house across from Empire in Pine, now T. J.'s Tavern, has an ancient, hand-crafted pine bar and backbar, salvaged from a riverfront tavern in Durand downriver. Highway 25 crosses the Red Cedar at Downsville and the view from this west side of the valley is highlighted by rounded bluffs to the west and the river gradually opening up into the yawning Chippewa Valley.

The Red Cedar Trail ends at the Chippewa River, but Highway 25 heads south along the Chippewa Valley, past the **Eau Galle Cheese Factory**, which is more than happy to give you a tour of the place and sell you some fresh cheese.

The road piggybacks on Highway 10 to cross the Chippewa and enters **Durand**, the Pepin County seat. The waterfront brick taverns and cafes are a lot tamer than when loggers ran wild here in the 1800s, and the Pepin County Courthouse and jail at 307 West Madison Street was built to help keep things in order. Try the Cafe Mozart or the Durand Cafe for a taste of life in this community, and then head south on Highway 25 past the **Tiffany State Wildlife Area.** The tall bluffs above the river are home to hawks and turkey vultures, and the thickly wooded hillsides have 100-year-old oak and hickory that have replaced the once-dominant white pine. The river bottom, open to seasonal hunting and hiking, is a summer home to tens of thousands of migratory birds, snowy egrets, great and little blue herons, swans, ducks, and geese. Coons, muskrats, fox, and deer thrive in the densely wooded flood plain.

The mouth of the Chippewa River forms a wide, swampy delta, and serves as a backwater estuary that blocks most of the Mississippi, forcing it along a fast-moving boat channel to the Minnesota side near Wabasha (a pretty river town). Highway 25 heads across this delta at **Nelson,** home of the **Nelson Cheese Factory,** which offers tours and fresh goods for sale.

## ■ TRAVELING TO LA CROSSE

Many people reach La Crosse by turning west with I-90 as it curves across west-central Wisconsin toward the Mississippi River and the state of Minnesota. Just

*A cheese factory producing pungent, semisoft Limburger cheese.*

off the Interstate is **Tomah,** a town known for its excellent cheese shops. Stock up on the usual: cheddar, Colby, bleu, Swiss, baby Swiss, and gouda and you're set for a picnic along the way. Highway 21, north of Tomah, passes the 60,000-acre military reservation at **Fort McCoy,** which serves a variety of combat-readiness functions for the army in association with Volk Airfield. Fort McCoy was used as temporary lodging for the convicts and institutionalized mentally ill that Castro sent to the United States from Cuba along with the Marielito refugees in 1979.

The fort has two recreation areas open to the public. **Ski Hill Recreation Area** for downhill and cross-county skiing, and **Squaw Lake Recreation Area,** where you can swim, camp, fish, and rent boats.

**Sparta** is the home of the greatest secret weapon in the art of roadside persuasion —the fiberglass effigy. A factory here makes them from huge molds—gigantic figures that appear all along Wisconsin's roadways: black angus cows, fiberglass fish, humongous gray mice nibbling blocks of cheese as large as a human head. Sparta is at the western end of the **Elroy-Sparta State Trail,** which connects to the La Crosse River Trail and the Great River Trail that together afford 75 miles (120 km) of biking.

Continuing west, Highway 16 arrives at **West Salem** in Green's Coulee (Valley). Here is the one-time home of Hamlin Garland (1860-1940), novelist, essayist,

## HOME FROM THE WAR

*Hamlin Garland (1860-1940) was born and raised on a farm in a place called Green's Coulee, a little valley along the La Crosse River in western Wisconsin. Here he describes the return of his father from the Civil War.*

*A*ll of this universe known to me in the year 1864 was bounded by the wooded hills of a little Wisconsin coulee, and its center was the cottage in which my mother was living alone—my father was in the war. As I project myself back into that mystical age, half lights cover most of the valley. The road before our doorstone begins and ends in vague obscurity—and Granma Green's house at the fork of the trail stands on the very edge of the world in a sinister region peopled with bears and other menacing creatures. Beyond this point all is darkness and terror.

It is Sunday afternoon and my mother and her three children, Frank, Harriet and I (all in our best dresses) are visiting the Widow Green, our nearest neighbor, a plump, jolly woman whom we greatly love. The house swarms with stalwart men and buxom women and we are all sitting around the table heaped with the remains of a harvest feast. The women are "telling fortunes" by means of tea grounds. Mrs. Green is the seeress. After shaking the cup with the grounds on the bottom, she turns it bottom side up in a saucer. Then whirling it three times to the right and three times to the left, she lifts it and silently studies the position of the leaves which cling to the sides of the cup, what time we all wait in breathless suspense for her first word.

"A soldier is coming to you!" she says to my mother. "See," and she points to the cup. We all crowd near, and I perceive a leaf with a stem sticking up from its body like a bayonet over a man's shoulder. "He is almost home," the widow goes on. Then with sudden dramatic turn she waves her hand toward the road, "Heavens and earth!" she cries. "There's Richard now!"

We all turn and look toward the road, and there, indeed, is a soldier with a musket on his back, wearily plodding his way up the low hill just north of the gate. He is too far away for mother to call, and besides I think she must be a little uncertain, for he did not so much as turn his head toward the house. Trembling with excitement she hurries little Frank into his wagon and telling Hattie to bring me, sets off up the road as fast as she can draw the baby's cart. It all seems a dream to me and I move dumbly, almost stupidly like one in a mist . . . .

We did not overtake the soldier, that is evident, for my next vision is that of a blue-coated figure leaning upon a fence, studying with intent gaze our empty cottage. I cannot, even now, precisely divine why he stood thus, sadly contemplating his silent home,—but so it was. His knapsack lay at his feet, his musket was propped against a post on whose top a cat was dreaming, unmindful of the warrior and his folded hands.

He did not hear us until we were close upon him, and even after he turned, my mother hesitated, so thin, so hollow-eyed, so changed was he. "Richard, is that you?" she quaveringly asked.

His worn face lighted up. His arms rose. "Yes, Belle! Here I am," he answered.

Nevertheless though he took my mother in his arms, I could not relate him to the father I had heard so much about.

—Hamlin Garland, *A Son of the Middle Border,* 1917

*A nineteenth-century scene reminiscent of the era author Hamlin Garland
described. (State Historical Society of Wisconsin)*

and short-story writer, whose subjects dealt sympathetically with the hardships of
frontier life, and particularly farm life. Garland moved on west with his family at
the age of eight, living the life of a farmer that he would later describe so realistically.
The second of a series of four autobiographical works, *A Son of the Middle Border*
was published in 1917 and described his life in the Upper Coulee Country in the
years following the Civil War. Garland returned to the Upper Coulee briefly in the
1890s, living in a two-story wooden house at 357 West Garland Street, now open
to the public.

# ■ LA CROSSE

La Crosse is the urban center of western Wisconsin. The Mississippi here is a big river, twice the size it is at Hastings (Minnesota) near the Twin Cities, after being joined by the St. Croix and La Crosse rivers. The city of La Crosse is built upon a plain backed by bluffs. To the north, the Mississippi widens behind a dam to form Lake Onalaska, while to the south, the river wends through the sloughs and islands of the Upper Mississippi National Wildlife and Fish Refuge. La Crosse offers a good stopover point for excursions up and down the Mississippi River, and deep into the coulees and plateaus that stretch inland for 100 miles (160 km) to the north and east.

The city's name comes from the French voyageurs' descriptions of a Siouan game, *le jeu de la crosse,* "the game of the hooked stick"—which we know as lacrosse. The Winnebago name for the La Crosse delta region was *Enookwasa-neenah,* "the river of the woman's breasts"—a reference to the sloping bluffs near the river's mouth. The plain of La Crosse became a terminus for the railroad in the 1850s, and with the barge and steamboat traffic made La Crosse an important shipping center. The first lumber mill opened in 1852 to saw the white pine logs

*La Crosse is one of the major lay-over points for Mississippi River barges.*

floated down the La Crosse and Black rivers. German, Norwegian, and Yankee emigration to this boomtown transformed La Crosse into Wisconsin's second largest manufacturing city, an entrepôt that built and distributed everything from agricultural machinery to riverboats.

The **G. Heileman Brewing Company** is an example of Wisconsin's German brewing heritage. Gottlieb Heileman arrived in La Crosse in 1852 and went to work for other brewers, rising to a partnership, and finally full ownership of his own brewery. Heileman's rise to national prominence as the nation's third largest brewer was accomplished partly by buying up strong regional labels. Wiedemann beer, brewed in Lexington, Kentucky, and the elixir of choice in the Ohio River Valley and Cincinnati, was sold to Heileman in 1967. By 1987, Blatz of Milwaukee, Grain Belt of Minneapolis, Lone Star of Texas, Rainier of Washington state, Carling Breweries of Baltimore and elsewhere, Schmidt of Philadelphia, and many others had come into the fold. Other factors, like the Anheuser-Busch strike of 1975 and the remarkable demise of Schlitz, opened new markets to Heileman—such as Chicago's, which was closely controlled and tenaciously held by Bud and Miller. Though the merger of Heileman with the Bond Corporation, owned by the Australian beer mogul Thomas Bond, nearly tossed Heileman into bankruptcy, a few divestitures of labels and Bond's exit have stabilized the La Crosse giant's financial position, and the beer still flows through the Old Style kraeusening tanks at the world's largest six-pack on 1111 South Third Street.

La Crosse also is home to the third largest campus in the **Wisconsin State University** system, which doubles as the summer home of the **New Orleans Saints,** part of the so-called Cheese Football League. Local history is presented at the **Hixon House,** an 1850s Italianate mansion on 429 North Seventh Street. The **Swarthout Museum,** at the corner of Ninth and Main streets, offers a walking tour of historic buildings, which include a number of **Prairie-style homes** designed by architect Percy Bentley, or his partner Otto Merman. There are several Prairie-style homes on Cass Street, South 17th Street, South 14th Street, and South 11th Street.

The **marinas of La Crosse** offer houseboats for rent if you would like to ply the ancient river and camp on the island campsites dedicated to fishing and bird-watching. The Mississippi flyway offers spectacular opportunities for viewing the hundreds of species of waterfowl and raptors that seasonally migrate past the bluffs above La Crosse. The Mississippi riverboat heritage continues in La Crosse with the cruises on the sternwheeler *La Crosse Queen,* a relic of a bygone era.

**Grandad Bluff,** rising 570 feet (174 m) above the La Crosse delta, offers a buzzard's-eye view of La Crosse and the complex system of sloughs and marshes that decorate this pinch-point of the Mississippi.

The people of La Crosse love to party, and **Octoberfest** is one of the important festivals along the Mississippi each autumn, just as the trees are reaching their peak color.

## ■ NORTH ALONG THE RIVER

The Great River Road (Highway 35) follows the Mississippi and St. Croix rivers from Dubuque, Iowa, (across from the southern-most point of Wisconsin) to Superior (at its northwest), past rolling countryside, rushing rivers, forested valleys, and hilltop farms. Whether driven or biked, this is one of the loveliest sections of Wisconsin to tour. The river towns set between the Mississippi River and its bluffs seem caught in the spell of the great river's charms.

The Mississippi guards its western face with towering bluffs carved by the glacial meltwater from four successive glacial ages. The river is the greatest of the North American flyways, and its marshy river bottoms are home to an enormous population of wildlife.

Wisconsin's best sunsets fall over the spectacular **hills of Trempealeau.** The French described this idiosyncratic range of stone peaks, carved by the Mississippi from the surrounding bluffs during the period of glacial retreat, as *trempe a l'eau,* (stepping in the water). They are now preserved in **Perrot State Park,** about a mile northwest of the town of Trempealeau.

German immigrants once cut caves into the limestone cliffs above Trempealeau to lager the beer brewed at the Trempealeau brewery. Riverboat crews would stop and sample it while staying at the Trempealeau Hotel on their way upriver. Fire ravaged the original site of the city of Trempealeau, and what wasn't burned was dragged to its present location. (For more on the town of Trempealeau, see the end of "Backroad Trip From Osseo," in this chapter.)

**Fountain City,** a center of Swiss-German settlement since the 1840s, is among the prettiest of riverside communities. The city is set picturesquely on terraced gardens, bolstered by stone walls. The Freemasons were prominent members of Fountain City, and their meeting hall on Second Street, on the second tier of the

*(following pages) The Mississippi River is wide and busy with river traffic between La Crosse and Prescott.*

city, maintains the original tin ceiling in fine condition, and as beautiful an oak bar as one can find along the Mississippi River. The building itself, like so many of Fountain City's masonry structures, is well built, with striking brick ornamentation, and its main door hints at the intrigue of the secret ceremonies that take place behind its silver-vaulted trim. The Fountain City Rock Garden is a multiple-tier garden of ceramic- and glass-studded figures guarded by two ceramic-studded pillars.

Behind Fountain City is **Eagle Bluff,** the highest point on the Mississippi. Its overlook can be reached by a gravel road off Highway 95, just north from Fountain City. From the heights, you can see upriver to the marshes and sloughs of the **Whitman Dam State Wildlife Area,** stretching from the mouth of the Waumandee River to Eagle Creek, roughly the boundaries of Merrick State Park. Downriver, the barge and boat traffic can be seen floating through Lock and Dam Number 5, and in the distance, across the river, is the Minnesota city of Winona.

The finest Mississippi view, however, is a few miles upriver from **Buena Vista Park,** donated by a local family to serve as the best picnic spot in the entire Midwest. The park is located above Alma on County Road E. Nearly 600 feet (183 m) below, the Mississippi flood rushes through Lock Number 4, while barges head north past the Buffalo River to Big Lake, the Chippewa delta, Lake Pepin, and the Twin Cities. In the 1850s, dozens of graceful paddlewheel steamboats passed this point hundreds of times each season, bringing immigrants to their New World homes. Burlington Northern trains still carry freight north to their Lake Superior railyard and south to the Gulf of Mexico. Turkey vultures ride the warm wind vectors rising off the plateau, giving picnickers an eye-to-eye view with one of Wisconsin's largest birds. The edge of the cliff has been polished by popularity, so be cautious in wet weather.

County Road E will take you to **Cream,** a crossroads community where the village hall is connected to a tavern and the two-step is the official dance on Friday and Saturday night.

Silt from the Chippewa River delta flowing into the Mississippi has dammed one of the river's widest stretches, known as **Lake Pepin.** The delta area is known as **Beef Slough,** christened such when an errant barge with bovine cargo ran aground, and the four-legged passengers escaped into the slough. The area is part of the **Upper Mississippi Wildlife Refuge,** which covers 200,000 acres and spans five states. A major migration route for birds, it's a fine place to watch magnificent tundra swans settling in to rest and feed during their spring flight north.

The shoreline of Lake Pepin forms three distinct terraces above the lake, serving as suitable beds for Highway 35, the Burlington Northern tracks, and the river towns, which often straddle one or more levels. At the middle of the Wisconsin side stands the **village of Pepin,** an old town with a modern harbor and a few new restaurants that have found acceptance among the day-trippers from the Twin Cities. Pepin was founded in the 1870s by Swedish and German immigrants. Whether they realize it or not, many readers might already know quite a lot about the lives of local pioneers through reading *The Little House in the Big Woods,* by Laura Ingalls Wilder (1867–1957), who was born in a log cabin about 10 miles (16 km) inland from Pepin (Highway CC) at the **Little House Wayside.** The present cabin is a replica. Revisionists claim that Wilder's daughter—who edited the manuscripts—embellished, structured, and "improved upon" the childhood recollections of her elderly mother; but that takes little away from the tales of pioneer Wisconsin that the senior Wilder evoked. The local museum in Pepin, housed in the old railroad depot at 306 Third Street, provides a good bit of information about Wilder and the history of the area.

**Stockholm,** a small settlement above Pepin, is home to an enterprising Swedish population. Of its famous immigrant sons, none was richer than Aleck Johnson,

*Barn raising has traditionally been a communal affair, as this turn-of-the-century portrait illustrates. (North Wood County Historical Society, Marshfield)*

who first found work on the riverboats of the Mississippi and after working the Manitoba Rail Line, promoted Minnesota's Red River Valley as a place for Swedes to emigrate. His A. E. Johnson Company served as emigration agent for the Scandinavian-American Line that brought tens of thousands of Norwegians and Swedes to the western prairies. Though he moved to New York and earned millions, he always returned to Stockholm, Wisconsin, to visit his sister. Descendants of the Swedish immigrants still live in the village, which has an active historical society—the Stockholm Institute—that chronicles its local histories from the former post office on Spring Street. Many of the older buildings have been transformed into antique and curio shops, but you still can get ice cream and pop at the corner market.

At the juncture of the St. Croix and the Mississippi rivers, at the top of the most delectable road trip in the Midwest, stands the city of **Prescott.** It might well have been the site of the Twin Cities had its original owner, Philander Prescott, not inflated the asking price of the land he owned. Prospective buyers instead chose to migrate upstream to St. Anthony Falls, which now separates St. Paul from Minneapolis. A stop at the Prescott bakery will convert you to fresh-baked bread from here on. Prescott has a river walk, inviting you to stroll along the Mississippi and to see the antique lift bridge rise to allow barges to pass through. **Mercord Mill Park** in Prescott looks over the St. Croix's fresh infusion of clean water into the Mississippi —which needs all the help it can get after passing through the Twin Cities.

*Celebrants indulge in a favorite Wisconsin pastime—polka dancing—during an Octoberfest event.*

# C E N T R A L   S A N D S

WHEN THE GREAT ICE AGE GLACIERS MELTED, the Baraboo Range and ice dams near Portage walled up a huge lake of glacial meltwater in the central part of the state. Slowly the Wisconsin River cut its present pathway through the barrier, draining off the water, and exposing a deposit of half-billion-year-old Precambrian sandstone. Today this is known as the Central Sands, a low-lying region of marsh lands and sandy clay soil at the heart of the state in the Wisconsin River Valley.

The Central Sands region embraces a wide range of landscapes, from ancient lake bottoms, flat as a pancake, to rolling countryside, sandy moraine, bog and steep, rocky buttes. Its eastern edge abuts a long chain of glacial moraines, separating the watersheds of the Wisconsin River and Lake Michigan, while its western edge cozies up to a rolling sand moraine cut through by the westward-flowing Black River and the coulees of western Wisconsin. Parts of the Central Sands are punctuated by isolated, dolomite-capped, sedimentary rock buttes, such as Roche-A-Cris, Mill Bluff, and Stand Rock, which once stood like islands above the surrounding glacial lake.

The Wisconsin River flows down the center, its long, steady pulse sculpting a meandering track from the granite highlands of Wausau and through the rock escarpments of the dalles, downstream. The sandy plains east of the river produce enough potatoes to make Wisconsin the third largest producer of spuds among American states. The landscape west of the river is dominated by forest, cranberry bogs, and marshland. Apart from the occasional dairy farm, with its silage, hay, and corn rotation, the major agricultural crops of the Central Sands are lumber, potatoes, and cranberries.

Although cheese-making abounds in surrounding areas of Wisconsin, the Central Sand counties are not exactly quiche and Brie country. A 50-cent cup of coffee is standard at the local cafe—no need to ask for espresso. This is friendly, down-home country, where strangers are somewhat unusual and drinking is considered good for your health. Bar culture is an important part of life in this area. In wintertime bars are where people gather to talk about football and fishing and drink beer, peppermint schnapps, and brandy. When snow is deep, some locals have taken to snowmobiling from bar to bar, and there are now severe penalties for unsafe snowmobile driving! A resort tavern on a hot weekend night will be *hopping*.

Some people here live their lives on farms or in the forests; some amidst the trailer parks, truck stops, and machine shops. German film director Werner Herzog chose this part of Wisconsin to update the story of German émigrés on the frontier in his 1976 film, *Strozek*.

## ■ ALDO LEOPOLD

A few miles from the Wisconsin River southeast of the Wisconsin Dells stands the most famous shack in the world of ecology, the **home of Aldo Leopold** (1886-1948), the University of Wisconsin professor of wildlife ecology who wrote *Sand County Almanac*. He wrote this classic text about living in harmony at the sandy edge of Sauk County, working out his ideas about the fragile relationship between man and the environment. He also died here, fighting a fire that threatened his stands of pine.

Aldo Leopold's foremost contribution to American life was the idea that wilderness was an asset to civilization. He was instrumental in the founding of the first National Wilderness Area, and always worked through his teaching and writing for the establishment of protected areas for waterfowl and wildlife. He was a founder of the Wilderness Society, and a director of the Audubon Society.

Aldo Leopold's shack—part home, part refuge, part laboratory—is off limits to the public. It still belongs to the Leopold family, who preserve their privacy. Anyone who wants to see the now well known countryside that Leopold loved and nurtured, however, should take a drive along the Levee Road (also called Rustic Road 49) on the south side of the Wisconsin River, down from the Wisconsin Dells.

Nearby stands another monument to conservation, the **International Crane Foundation,** home of dozens of crane species from across the globe. The Foundation hatches eggs taken from summer breeding grounds and from captive birds. The newborn chicks are fed with crane hand-puppets so they don't leap to the conclusion that humans are to be trusted. As the birds grow, staff members dress up as mother cranes to feed them, and to teach them how to feed in the wild. As juveniles, the cranes even learn their mating dance from staff members, who mimic the circular strut accompanied by a raising and lowering of graceful necks and percussive wing-snapping.

## NATURE LOVERS

*T*ake a look, first, at any duck marsh. A cordon of parked cars surrounds it. Crouched on each point of its reedy margin is some pillar of society, automatic ready, trigger finger itching to break, if need be, every law of commonwealth or commonweal to kill a duck. That he is already overfed in no way dampens his avidity for gathering meat from God.

Wandering in the near-by woods is another pillar, hunting rare ferns or new warblers. Because his kind of hunting seldom calls for theft or pillage, he disdains the killer. Yet, like as not, in his youth he was one.

At some near-by woods resort is still another nature-lover—the kind who writes bad verse on birchbark. Everywhere is the unspecialized motorist whose recreation is mileage, who has run the gamut of the National Parks in one summer, and now is headed for Mexico City and points south.

Lastly, there is the professional, striving through countless conservation organizations to give the nature-loving public what it wants, or make it want what he has to give. . . .

Why, it may be asked, should such a diversity of folk be bracketed in a single category? Because each, in his own way, is a hunter. And why does each call himself a conservationist? Because the wild things he hunts for have eluded his grasp, and he hopes by some necromancy of laws, appropriations, regional plans, reorganization of departments, or other form of mass-wishing to make them stay put.

—Aldo Leopold,
*A Sand County Almanac*, 1949

*Environmentalist Aldo Leopold about to embark on a bird-watching expedition. (State Historical Society of Wisconsin)*

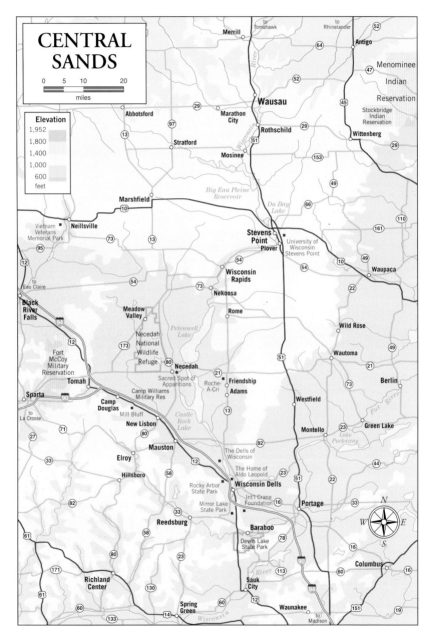

# CENTRAL SANDS

0 5 10 20
miles

**Elevation**

1,952
1,800
1,400
1,000
600
feet

The foundation has been single-handedly responsible for returning these graceful birds from the brink of extinction, not only in Wisconsin, but in Siberia, Japan, and China. The International Crane Foundation lies east of Highway 12 on Shady Lane, south of Wisconsin Dells.

## ■ WISCONSIN DELLS

West of Portage, Highway 16 cuts through a flat area, then rises through wooded, rolling hills to a slight plateau and the town of Wisconsin Dells, set above the river valley. Glacial melt carved the 100-foot (30-m) -high cliffs that rise above the water along a seven-mile (11-km) stretch of greenish-blue water. The cliffs are marked by horizontal bands of different hues: brown and buff, and pink and reds in sandstone layers cut by deep clefts. Whimsical sandstone formations along the way have been given names such as the Beehive and the Grand Piano.

What most visitors to the Dells see first off is a display of roadside kitsch run amok. Billboards advertise "duck boats," and the landscape is a welter of water slides, dog racing parks, and fudge shops. Family vacationers ride the river on amphibious assault vehicles, and flit through the air in mini-helicopters. Indian trading posts sell Wisconsin native crafts like basketry side-by-side with beadwork and rubber hatchets made in Asian sweatshops. Working the rides and manning the booths are a migrant crowd of college students and teenagers.

*A sandhill crane.*

A dam regulates river depth to reduce the possibility of flooding and produce a higher water level in the Dells, making its nooks and crannies visible to boat-loads of tourists. For boat tours of the upper and lower Dells visit the boat docks downtown in Wisconsin Dells; for Dells Duck Tours, call (608) 254-6080.

If the Dells has a king, it is Tommy Bartlett, whose water-ski shows became a featured attraction in the 1960s, and this success invented new attractions like Tommy Bartlett's Robot World, and Wisconsin Greyhound. To see Tommy Bartlett's Ski, Sky & Stage Show, and watch one to a dozen scantily-clad water skiers behind speedboats choreograph routines on skis, come to the bleachers along the river at 560 Wisconsin Dells Parkway.

The water slides at Noah's Ark, huge pools at the Family Land Tidal Wave, Waterworld, and other such attractions offer families the lure of chlorinated water spilling down twisting fiberglass slides, and pools that mimic ocean waves.

Two excellent state parks are worth enjoying. Eight miles (12.8 km) northwest of Baraboo off Highway 12 is **Mirror Lake State Park,** set in the midst of sandstone bluffs where Camel Creek goes into Mirror Lake. In summer, visitors can enjoy canoeing, swimming, camping, and fishing here; in winter, cross-country skiing.

**Rocky Arbor State Park** is the best place to see the original, untouched Dells configuration. It has some fine campsites, valued in summer for their cool, wooded location.

Because there is so much to do in this area, it might be worth calling the Wisconsin Dells Visitor and Convention Bureau at (608) 254-INFO and asking for their guide to the area.

■ WINNEBAGO INFLUENCE

Despite the fact that Wisconsin Dells is an artificial wonderland of sorts, a trip on the river will once again remind you of the real beauty of the place, as well as its history. The thick woods and sheltered valleys of the Dells blunt the harsh winter wind, a good reason why nomadic hunters sought shelter here 10,000 years ago. In recent centuries, the carved-rock valleys became home to several bands of the Winnebago, some of whom moved there following the treaties of the 1830s. Though the Winnebago were sent west to reservations, where many died, many tribe members filtered back. Though they never received land in trade for the treaties, some Winnebago did get land through Wisconsin's homestead laws, broadened under the 1870 Indian Homestead Act. Unfortunately, many Winnebago lost their homestead land when property taxes were not paid by local tax "agents" who defrauded the Indians and later bought the land at tax auctions. Despite disease, diaspora, and disenfranchisement, the Winnebago kept a foothold at their tribal base in the Wisconsin Dells.

**Winnebago dances** are performed at **Stand Rock**—a tall stone column next to a cliff on the river, three miles (4.8 km) north of the Dells. Winnebago children participate in powwows that feature dancing, and some kids participate in the Stand Rock performances. Tribal events occur each spring and fall, when dances and competitions are held to exercise some friendly rivalry, and to re-unite the different clans and far-flung families of the tribe.

These dances became an important means to entice tourist money to the Dells. The Winnebago's annual canoe parade through the Dells, with the Winnebago dressed up in colorful clothing, has been a part of the entertainment milieu since

*An Indian harvesting wild rice. Wisconsin is one of America's leading producers of this tasty but expensive grain. (Milwaukee Public Museum)*

the turn of the century. In their best light, these performances have introduced strangers to native Winnebago life, legends, customs, and spiritualism, and have also brought in public and monetary support for maintaining traditional tribal ceremonies and beliefs. The Winnebago sell traditional crafts, particularly basketry, at the **Trading Post.**

In recent years, the Winnebago have taken advantage of the Indian Gaming Act of 1988; **Ho Chunk Bingo Parlor** is located on Highway 12 in nearby Baraboo; here too is the **Golden Nickel Casino.** Call (608) 355-7777 .

### ■ HOPS AND HISTORY

The **town of Wisconsin Dells,** set on a bluff above the river, was first named Kilbourn City, and the area around it, during the late 1850s and 1860s, was a center for growing and drying hops. Hops—a botanical relative of marijuana and an important flavoring ingredient in beer—boomed as a regional crop during the early 1860s, when bug infestations in the eastern crop jacked up the dried herb's price. As hops is a perennial, farmers only had to plant it once, and the viney crop would proliferate abundantly year to year, climbing tepees of tamarack. But if growing hops was easy, harvesting them was labor-intensive, and trains brought in

*"Home of the Earth" powwow at Lac Court Oreilles Indian Reservation. Wisconsin Dells area also hosts several such events.*

carloads of hops pickers. The boom went bust, however, when hops lice destroyed the Wisconsin plantings, and new hop fields in Washington state provided superior hops at lower prices.

Signs of the hops era in the Central Sands remain in the silos of the oldest farmsteads, where the lowest eight feet (2.4 m) or so are made of fieldstone or cutstone, which once served as kilns to dry hops cones.

Determined to develop the economy along new lines, townsfolk renamed Kilbourn City Wisconsin Dells in 1931, thinking the name might entice more tourists. The area had been a popular attraction since the 1880s, with visitors plying the river in small steamboats. In the late 1940s and 1950s, when family theme parks like Disneyland and Six Flags began to catch on, the Dells started providing tours of the Wisconsin River in "Ducks," amphibious landing craft. Billboards that read "Ride the Ducks" studded the highways. During the 1950s and 1960s, aquatic ballet star Tommy Bartlett and a bevy of blondes in bathing suits water-skied along in the channels of the Wisconsin, powered by Evinrude and Mercury Marine. When the Winnebago tribe began to festoon its dancers with brightly colored costumes at their tribal dances at Stand Rock, the Dells' fame as a tourist attraction was clinched. Huge billboards proclaimed the Dells as

*Summer vacationers "ride the wave," one of many diversions available at Wisconsin Dells.*

a family entertainment center—with a combination of natural beauty, "exotic" native dancing, and water-skiing. Soon the Dells basked in a multi-million-dollar economic miracle.

## ■ ROCHE-A-CRIS

On Highway 13 north of the Dells, the road leads to Adams and Friendship, the twin cities of the Central Sands. Nearby, a sand and limestone butte, **Roche-A-Cris** juts up nearly 300 feet (90 m) from the surrounding forests of jack, red, and white pine. Honed and whittled over millennia by wind and water erosion, this castellated butte now serves as a remarkable vantage point from which careful climbers ascend a rock-step trail (watch for rattlesnakes!) to scan the marsh- and forest-covered countryside spreading for miles around. The southern face of Roche-A-Cris has been carved with figures of animals and grooved geometric designs, etched by the prehistoric residents of Wisconsin. The grooves in particular appear to have been made not only for sharpening stone tools, but for finishing and polishing, a step that went beyond mere utility, and which suggests concern with aesthetic effect. When you consider the rigors of Stone Age life, and the difficulties of producing even the most utilitarian of hand-made material comforts from stone, bone, sinew, leather, and bark, the fact that these craftsmen also valued aesthetics suggests a very high degree of sophistication.

## ■ NECEDAH

Necedah, west of the Wisconsin River at the junction of Highways 21 and 80, is a pretty town with a certain charm that makes you want to stop there for lunch. Its fame rests on its visionary history. On November 12, 1949, a little east of town, Mary Ann Van Hoof received the first of several visions of the Virgin Mary. The site is marked with a shrine, called the **Sacred Spot of Apparitions,** and is open to all visitors. Mrs. Van Hoof received a second visit the following April 7, when her cross began to glow and she heard a voice telling her to pray hard. On May 28 and 29, in a grove of ash trees, the Virgin Mary again appeared, this time to warn Mrs. Van Hoof, "Wake up America! The enemy of God is creeping all over America." The Virgin returned five more time that year. In 1951 and 1952, from Holy

Thursday through Easter Sunday, Mrs. Van Hoof received the stigmata, and relived the suffering of Jesus Christ. Van Hoof's visions warned that God does not approve of Pentecostal and charismatic faiths, weapons of Satan that drew the faithful away from the sacrifice of the Crucifixion. Van Hoof was warned that 30,000 communists had infiltrated Catholic and Protestant churches in order to destroy them. Similar erosions of human standards were prophesied, such as women becoming immodest and posing naked, and the destruction of future white generations if they would abort their own children. Similar admonitions were fielded that warned against euthanasia for the retarded and the elderly by people who would set themselves up as God.

The shrine contains several statuary tableaus depicting the Last Supper (The First Mass), Christ's Passion, and St. Joan of Arc. Lincoln, Washington, and Jesus Christ are also pictured, flying the American flags at half-mast to signal their abhorrence of abortion. There are plans to build an enormous church at the spot where the Virgin indicates, once the faithful's prayers, penance, and sacrifices have been answered. The gift shop at the shrine offers a wide variety of pamphlets and anti-abortion material, as well as reproductions of artwork created by a local nun that depicts religious themes. The Vatican has refused to acknowledge this visitation of the Virgin Mary, and most Roman Catholics are skeptical that Van Hoof's visions were divine.

Visitors to this area who prefer military to spiritual experiences, or anyone with a penchant for watching high-explosive, rocket-propelled, computer-guided missiles destroy static hunks of rusting vehicles, should take a trip to the **Hardwood Firing Range.** It's northeast of Necedah, right below the Central Necedah National Wildlife Refuge.

## ■ CASTLE ROCK AND PETENWELL LAKES

To prevent flooding, dams were built across the narrows of the Wisconsin River near Necedah, forming the Castle Rock and Petenwell lakes. The shores of these shallow lakes, Wisconsin's largest reservoirs, sustain a culture of supper clubs, summer cabins, bait shops, and resorts, from which boats are launched every minute of the day in quest of bass, perch, and game fish. Private campgrounds in dozens of private, county, and state campgrounds are often set on lakefronts amidst original scrub oak and pine forest and glacial sand dunes.

**Castle Rock Flowage** is named for a geological landmark on the river below the dam. The stump-filled backwaters provide a good place for fish, but underwater stumps are a bit of a hazard for boaters. Water quality has improved since industries in the area were forced to clean up effluents in the 1960s. Still, fish are often tested for PCB and Dioxin contamination, and for mercury (carp are probably not safe for human consumption). The most intense fishing in the area occurs at **Petenwell Dam** in March and April. There are numerous boat launch sites along the west bank of the river below the Petenwell Dam, and one on Highway 21 at a park on the east side of the river. It's possible to rent boats and buy bait and tackle just north of the Highway Z bridge over Klein Creek. For excellent maps and locations, call the Wisconsin River Power Company; (715) 422-3073.

**Petenwell Flowage,** just above Castle Rock, is a big body of water covering 23,000 acres. Its walleyes have been notorious for smelling bad and tasting worse due to pollutants. Today, they're back to being safe to eat, as are the muskies and smallmouth bass. (Nevertheless, it's best to check around locally.) Numerous public lands off Highway Z on the eastern shore are available to fishermen and boatmen, including Strongs Prairie Flats, Brown Deer Road, Adams County Park, Apache Lane, and Devil's Elbow. For information on resorts and campgrounds, call the Juneau County Visitor's Bureau; (608) 847-7838. A free map of Petenwell, with landings, is available from the Castle Rock-Petenwell Lakes Association; (608) 847-5359.

## ■ ROME AND PLAINFIELD

Twenty miles (32 km) north of Roche-A-Cris, on the east side of the river at the crossroads of Highway 13 with County Road D, is village of **Rome.** It might well be the home of the prime-time TV program "Picket Fences"—although a Jefferson County village may also be the model for the show. (Neither seems too impressed by the notoriety.) But neither fulfills the scope of the screenwriter's imagination.

The genius of Alfred Hitchcock turned a modest frame house into the archetypal rural symbol of horror in *Psycho,* but it was a quiet, shy outdoorsman named Ed Gein who brought the real horror of the heartland to life in the early 1950s. Investigating a murder at Gein's farm near **Plainfield** (east of Highway-51 on

*View from the top of Roche-A-Cris, east of Castle Rock and Petenwell*
*reservoirs in Adams County.*

Highway 73), officers found the farmer wearing a vest made of a woman's tanned skin around the house. Locals soon began to speculate that Gein's tangy "venison" sausages had been made from bodies exhumed from local graveyards. Unlike the Anthony Perkins character in Hitchcock's movie version of the story, Gein did not run a small motel, nor did his mastery of taxidermy encompass birds, but apparently Gein's mother had warned him of the danger of women, and his simple devotion to her drove him to gruesome ends. Local folks try to forget the shock of the discoveries; queries about Gein usually lead to silence and perturbed looks. The Gein house was burned down, and the family grave marker stolen. Gein died in the 1980s at the Mendota Mental Health Institute, once the State Hospital for the Insane, and he was buried in an unmarked grave next to his mother. (The author of the *Psycho* screenplay was Milwaukee writer Robert Bloch.)

## ■ SWAMPS AND CRANBERRY BOGS

What is sometimes known as "the Great Swamp of Wisconsin" sprawls to the west of the Wisconsin River and north of Necedah, straddling the Little Yellow River in an area about one-third as big as Rhode Island. This vast marshland provides homes to hundreds of species and sustains migrating flocks of songbirds and waterfowl. Many acres are preserved in the **Necedah National Wildlife Refuge**, and the **Wood County, Sandhill, and Meadow Valley state wildlife areas**. Other acres are cultivated for the state's biggest bog-water crop, the cranberry.

Wisconsin grows more than a third of the nation's crop of cranberries, only slightly less than Massachusetts, making it the second largest producer among states. The Cranmoor region of Wood County has thousands of acres of cranberry bogs, sculpted into a network of levees and canals. Sluice gates permit adjustment of water levels on the canals, which are flooded in autumn for the cranberry harvest, when giant aquatic tractors and pickers gather the tart, ruby-red berries as they float on the surface, sending them to be sauced for Thanksgiving dinner tables, or squeezed into juice. The enormous pickers that cull the cranberries are distant relatives of the graceful wooden combs of times past. Work in the bogs has always been hard; temperatures at nightfall are usually 20 to 30 degrees lower than in surrounding areas. Workers often must jump over ice-covered ditches, and if they miss they go in over their heads.

# ■ NEKOOSA AND WISCONSIN RAPIDS

Nekoosa and Wisconsin Rapids, both located on the west bank of the river on Highway 34, started life as lumber-mill towns before converting to paper mills in the 1860s. Today, they are the southernmost paper-milling towns in the vast reach of pulpwood forest that reaches down the Wisconsin River from Rhinelander. The paper industry requires huge factories with specialized equipment, millions of gallons of water, and millions of trees for pulpwood—scrub pines, poplar, pine, spruce, and hemlock—which are cut, ground, shredded, soaked, treated, and re-knit into products that relieve our most intimare and unspoken functions, wrap our dearest gifts, and record our loftiest ideas. If you'd like to visit one of these mills, try Consolidated Papers in downtown Wisconsin Rapids and ask about their tours; (715) 422-3789.

There's a price to pay for all this paper luxury. Milling is a dirty process that takes a toll on the rivers that relieve its waste. Toxins, like dioxins, and wood pulp sludge defy rapid oxidation from aquatic bacteria, and kill microscopic flora and fauna. Through state supervision and regulation, the industry has reduced its pollution of state waters, and the Wisconsin River is so much the better for these efforts.

# ■ STEVENS POINT

The heart of the Central Sands is Stevens Point, a riverside city northeast of Wisconsin Rapids, whose citizens keep busy with paper production, environmental studies, insurance, and breweries. Founded as a trading post in 1838, it was flooded with emigrants from Poland in the 1850s—so many that entire communities from Poland transplanted themselves into this piney "paradise." Work was available in the mills along the river and up in the frozen logging camps each winter. Good timber was too sparse to sustain the lumber industry, but the abundant scrub forest prompted the switch to papermaking. As land was cleared, the sandy soils were planted with potatoes by pioneer farmers, many of them Polish. The brick Roman Catholic churches and bathtub grottoes are popular evidence that this Polish community is thriving still. Roadside grottoes can still be found, their brick foundations and windowed enclosures protecting the Virgin Mary from the cruel vagaries of the Wisconsin weather whipping the surrounding farm fields.

More than 60 buildings are included in the city's **Mathias Mitchell Public Square,** a large historic district. Pick up one of the easily available guides for a walking tour of this area. The city is also graced by **The Green Circle,** a 24-mile (39-km) nature trail connecting the parks and nature areas.

**Sentryworld Sports Center,** at 601 N. Michigan Avenue, is owned by Sentry Insurance, one of several giant Wisconsin-based insurers. This recreational preserve was built for its employees, but its tennis and world-class golf course are open to the public.

The **University of Wisconsin at Stevens Point,** with its 9,000 students, gives the city a collegiate atmosphere. The school specializes in health sciences and environmental management; its College of Natural Resources is the second largest in the United States. Adjacent to campus, the **Schmeeckle Reserve** is a 200-acre wooded reserve serving as an outdoor research and teaching laboratory, and providing practical understanding of the environment in a natural setting. You can hike the grounds in summer, and ski there in winter. The **Schmeeckle Reserve's Wisconsin Conservation Hall of Fame** pays tribute to John Muir, Aldo Leopold, and other environmental icons, including its namesake, Professor Fred Schmeeckle, father of the academic major in conservation.

*A winter blizzard buries a farm in a scene all too common throughout the state.*

*Harvesting cranberries near Nekoosa. This region is second only to Massachusetts in cranberry production.*

The most popular product in Stevens Point is made at the **Stevens Point Brewery,** 2617 Water Street, which has brewed a variety of beers since 1857. Recently sold to an out-of-state concern, Point is famous for selling its product only within 50 miles of the brewery, prompting billboards along U.S. 51 on the edge of town to state, "When you're out of Point you're out of town." Stumbling upon a cache of "blue bullets" in a tavern cooler, or a barrel of Point on tap, is like finding an oasis in a desert on a hot day.

About 10 miles (16 km) north of Stevens Point is **Lake DuBay,** formed by a dam on the Wisconsin River. Its inlets and back bays make it a good spot to fish. Fishermen drift among stumps, snags, and flooded timber along the shore. Fish in these brown waters are abundant and safe to eat, and include walleye, northerns, muskies, panfish, crappies, and trophy northern pike. There are boats for rent, a boat landing, and camping available at the DuBay County Park on Highway E at the southwest end of the lake.

## ■ NORTHWEST CORNER

In the northwest corner of the sand counties, along the **Black River,** dairy farms begin to appear and the land begins to rise on the west into the Clark County forests.

**Neillsville** is an older town on the Black River, located west of Stevens Point on Highway 10. Its dozens of brick homes and downtown scarcely seem to have changed since the late 1800s. The 1897 **Jail Museum** at 215 E. Fifth Street and the **Tufts Museum** at 26 Hewett provide a glimpse of the variety of nineteenth-century lifestyles, when logging was king.

West of Neillsville, the Wisconsin **Vietnam Veterans' Memorial Park** (Highway 10) honors the service personnel who fought and died in Vietnam. A life-size bronze statue depicts four members of a platoon aiding one of their wounded buddies, as their bronze ponchos whip in an unseen wind; their isolation and vulnerability are frozen as they search for help on this high ridge at the northern edge of the Central Sands.

## ■ AUGUSTA

Among the red sandstone hills of this rolling moraine, near Augusta in Eau Claire County, a pocket of Amish and Mennonite farmers and craftspeople have settled in recent years. Wisconsin farms are generally well kept and tidy, but Amish farms are even more so. During your travels, watch out for the black, horse-drawn carriages and the gentle, hard-working people who drive them.

Many of the Amish and Mennonites have moved here from Pennsylvania, where development pressures threaten their simple way of life. Selling off the Pennsylvania farms, they move to Wisconsin, where land prices are lower. They buy farms too small and poor for modern farming, which requires a variety of gas- and electric-powered equipment to produce on a competitive scale. With their simple lifestyles and rejection of modern equipment, the Amish do not want or need to compete with the outside world. Their homemade signs offer well-made goods and foods. These are the places to buy your Amish goods, here on these back roads and county trunk highways, rather than in the Amish specialty shops that spring up in the tourist towns and main streets of larger cities. The money goes directly to the Amish, and the prices are better, as is the freshness of produce and quality of crafted items.

## WISCONSIN BRATWURST

Bratwurst, or "lean meat sausage," is usually pale in color and made from veal and pork. For this recipe you'll need:

| | |
|---|---|
| 10 bratwurst | 1 tablespoon vegetable oil. |
| 2 cups beer | 2 tablespoons brown sugar |
| 2 large onions chopped | 2 tablespoons cider vinegar |

Grill bratwurst over coals for 10 minutes.

Sauté onions in vegetable oil until translucent. In a large pot add sautéed onions to beer, brown sugar, and cider vinegar.

Add cooked bratwurst to pot and simmer with beer mixture for 15 minutes. Serve bratwurst on a hot bun with hot mustard.

❖   ❖   ❖

## DOOR COUNTY CHERRY CHEESECAKE
### *W*ITH CHOCOLATE TOPPING

| | |
|---|---|
| 4 eight-ounce packages of Neufchâtel cheese | $1/4$ teaspoon salt |
| | 4 large eggs, beaten |
| $1/4$ cup flour, sifted | 1 stick butter, melted |
| 1 cup sugar | 1 cup sour cream |
| 1 $1/2$ teaspoons vanilla | $3/4$ cup Door County cherries, pitted |

Combine cheese, flour, sugar, vanilla, and salt in bowl. Cream ingredients. Add following ingredients separately: eggs, melted butter, sour cream, and cherries, blending well with each ingredient. Pour into 10-inch spring-form pan, bake in water bath at 325 degrees for 1 hour and 15 minutes. Cool; flip over pan and turn cheesecake onto serving plate.

*T*opping:

| | |
|---|---|
| 2 ounces butter | $3/4$ teaspoon light karo syrup |
| 2 ounces dark semi-sweet chocolate | |

Directions: melt butter, chocolate, and karo syrup together. Spread over top and sides of cheesecake. Chill; serve when firm.

# NORTHERN WISCONSIN

THE NORTHERN REGION OF WISCONSIN is dominated by the North Woods—and its endless pine forests, thousands of lakes, and crystal-clear streams. Clear-cut logging created farmland in the southern counties, and there is a small belt of farming in the basin south of Lake Superior. Along the Lake Superior shoreline fishing towns and beach resort communities exist, but for the most part, forests, lakes, marsh, and hills prevail.

Water, granite, and timber are the defining elements of the North Woods. Water and granite are legacies of the Ice Age, when glaciers gouged out Lake Superior—the northern boundary of Wisconsin and the largest freshwater lake in the world—as well as thousands of much smaller lakes. Glaciers also scraped the tops off an old mountain range, leaving behind a well-polished, gently rolling highland of granite. This granite basement is rich in mineral wealth: iron in the Gogebic Range in Iron County, copper and zinc at Crandon, gold and zinc at Ladysmith, and even kimberlite, a diamond-bearing ore. But it is the heavy forests

of the northern third of Wisconsin that have most affected its human history. The American era in Wisconsin was built on the back of the great trees themselves, as lumbermen pushed farther and farther north, felling the timber and floating it south to the river mills.

## ■ LUMBERJACK LEGENDS

The lumberjack remains the mythic figure of the North Woods: Paul Bunyan, the lumberjack titan, felled the forests with his gigantic blue ox, Babe, and his merry band of woodsmen—Big Ole, Chris Crosshaul, Axel Axelson, Happy Olson, Hels Helsen, and Shot Gunderson.

The legend of the lumber camp and the romantic, manly vision it inspires is the stuff of fiction. Its reality was much harsher, more brutal, and most lumberjacks only lasted a winter or two. In the lumber camps each winter, life was harsh and cold. Talking was forbidden at mealtime, partly to discourage organizing labor unions, partly to discourage fights. In place of talk was the warble of the Norwegian

*Wisconsin's North Woods consist almost entirely of second-growth forests due to massive timber clearing in the nineteenth century.*

"hardanger" fiddle, Irish reels and jigs, and the never-ending inanity of "My name is Yon Yonson, I come from Wisconsin" ditties. The lumber camps ran all winter, with sawyers working the woods and teams of oxen dragging the logs to frozen rivers where the spring thaw would carry them downstream. An engraved hammer stamped the lumber company's mark on each log so sawmills would know which lumber teams to pay. Saturday night, lumberjacks went to backwoods towns for a night of drinking, fighting, whoring, and gambling.

The first ax hit the white pine at the mouth of the Chippewa River in the 1820s; by 1900 the woods had been cut down. Life on these cut-over wastelands created by logging could be dangerous. Millions of acres of stumps and smoldering fires from loggers burning scrap produced occasional flash fires. These conditions, along with a serious drought, ignited the **Peshtigo fire** on October 8, 1871, the same day the Great Fire broke out in Chicago. Fanned by high winds, it burned for days in the drought-stricken, tinder-dry woods of eastern Wisconsin, killing more than 1,200 people. At Peshtigo, where 600 people died within minutes, only a small wooden cross in the cemetery remained unburned. The firestorm barely missed Marinette, and destroyed Menominee, Michigan, burning a swath 40 miles (64 km) long and 10 miles (16 km) wide in four hours. After the

*A log sled loaded with 16,860 board feet of timber—in addition to some Price County youngsters, ca.1900. (State Historical Society of Wisconsin)*

fires had been put out above ground, they smoldered under the rich, pine-needle-strewn soil, tunneling back to the surface to burst into flame days or weeks later. Dangerous conditions persisted until autumn rains soaked the area.

Along the southern edge of the woods and across the north-central section of Wisconsin, the stumps of the great pine forest were cleared by farmers. A **farm belt** soon began to reach from the St. Croix River east to Antigo. In some parts of this area, now prime dairy country, great granite boulders lie like huge red, pink, and speckled eggs hatched by the glaciers that ground them. In spots, jagged clefts reach out from beneath sandy banks, stone shoulders of an underground giant that stretches beneath the entire North Woods.

## ■ LUMBER TOWNS AND EAU CLAIRE

Logs chopped in the North Woods were floated down rivers to mill towns where they were processed into lumber and sold to settlers needing new frame houses and barns, furniture and tools. Life in these young towns—Eau Claire and Chippewa Falls on the Chippewa River, Menomonie on the Red Cedar, and

*Cooks and fiddlers pose for a group portrait in a loggers' dining hall in turn-of-the-century Barron County. (State Historical Society of Wisconsin)*

*A painting, purportedly of Eau Claire, at a time when the riverine city was booming as a gateway to the riches of northern Wisconsin. (Photo by Mike Long)*

Wausau on the Wisconsin—was often little easier than in the lumberjack camps. Mill workers labored long hours in unheated and dangerous sheds. Amputations were common, as men were dragged into gears by the long, leather belts that connected the machines to the steam engines. Child labor was endemic. Boiler explosions or fires destroyed many mills. In town after town, it was common to see a new mill being built next to the ashes of the old mill.

One of the most important of these early lumber towns was **Eau Claire,** located at the southern extremity of the North Woods, just north of I-94 as it curves west toward Minnesota. It was named "Clear Water" by French explorers and fur traders traveling down the brown Chippewa River, who noticed the waters become clear here at the junction with the Eau Claire River. By 1870, this was the shipping point for logs from the Chippewa Valley, and within 20 years the town was operating 20 sawmills. At the same time, cleared forest land was being claimed by wheat farmers, and by 1875, Eau Claire was shipping out 300,000 bushels of wheat a year from surrounding Eau Claire County. By the early 1900s, dairy farming became an important part of the area's economy, and the town added creameries and cheese-making to its industries. Since that time, its citizens have produced cigars, Presto logs, paper products, and tires.

Eau Claire's **campus of the University of Wisconsin** is one of the state's most beautiful; and proximity to the Chippewa and Eau Claire rivers make this area a wonderful spot for kayaking and canoeing. Sites of interest (near each other) are the **Paul Bunyan Logging Camp in Carson Park**, the one-room **Sunnyview School,** and the 1860 **Lars Anderson Log Home.** Exhibits at the **Chippewa Valley Museum** on Carson Park Drive explain early Woodland cultures, the fur trade, and farm life.

## ■ ALONG THE ST. CROIX RIVER

The St. Croix River runs along Wisconsin's western boundary with Minnesota, until it joins the Mississippi River. The St. Croix is probably the finest canoeing stream in the north, with rapids big enough to startle and challenge the expert as well as long stretches of placid flow to enchant the novice. The St. Croix is protected as a National Scenic Riverway on both the Wisconsin and Minnesota sides—and many state and county parks take up where the federal government leaves off—so the banks remain lovely and largely undeveloped, home to thriving populations of

*The St. Croix River meanders between Minnesota and Wisconsin before flowing into the Mississippi near the town of Prescott.*

wildlife. Access to the river is possible on the hundreds of local roads along the river's length between Hudson on I-94 and Danbury about 90 miles (144 km) to the north.

The source of the St. Croix is a tamarack bog around upper St. Croix Lake, about 25 miles (40 km) south of Lake Superior, which forms part of the northern boundary of Wisconsin. From its birth in the bogs and lakes of the north, the pristine St. Croix tumbles down rock-filled, cliff-edged clefts, joining with rivers from the east and west: such as the Clam River, which flows from the St. Croix Reservation around Clam Lake (just east of Siren on Highway 35); and the Wood River, which drains the picturesque wetlands of the Crex Meadows wildlife refuge north of Grantsburg (west of Siren on the St. Croix). At St. Croix Falls, glacial meltwater long ago scored potholes big enough to hide in, and the **St. Croix Dalles** (part of the Interstate State Park, south on Highway 35 off Highway 8) is about the prettiest gorge in Wisconsin. The water-worn contours of the granite highlight the trails that wind on cliffs above the Dalles. Curious formations have been carved from the 200-foot (61-m) cliffs above the rushing stream, including the stern profile of the Old Man of the Dalles. The Chippewa venerated the Old Man as a protector who once destroyed the canoes of a war party of Sioux.

## ■ LAKES AND STREAMS

Thousands of lakes dot the North Woods in an arc which runs roughly east of the St. Croix, up to Chequamegon National Forest. There, the number of lakes thins out, then explodes once more in hundreds of tiny lakes further east, from the Lac Du Flambeau Indian Reservation east toward Nicolet National Forest. In between are some of the finest trout streams in Wisconsin, not to mention in the country. This is a paradise for vacationers, who come to enjoy both country conviviality and nature's solitude, boating and fishing on the rivers and lakes.

By day come all variety of anglers—from the solitary child with a pole and worms to spoon-bending muskie maniacs and walleye warriors. On chill spring nights, hundreds of fishermen wait, with waders and nets stretched across streams, to harvest smelt. On freshly thawed northern lakes, Chippewa fishermen stand in boats, spears poised, their torches attracting fish to the surface of the lakes. On summer nights, the loons weave their lonesome cry amid the moonlit pines and shimmering surface of the lakes.

At most resort lakes a "live bait" shop is the cultural center of the area, the repository of local gossip and fishing wisdom. The supper club has replaced the cook shanty of the logging camp, and the heaping helpings of food are usually reasonably priced. Lakeside resorts range from a few little cabins and a trailer; to motels rooms with furniture made from branches and 3-D lake scenes in plastic frames; to the classic old log lodges, with glassy-eyed buck deer proudly holding up a dusty rack of antlers over the stone fireplace. These provide a taste of the authentic flavor of the North Woods, and their fireplaces add the tang of wood smoke to the night air while the haunting chorus of loons serenades a moonlight-dappled lake. The fresh smell of pine rises as the sun warms the forest by day, and the lakes shimmer like giant tear drops, clear and fresh, amid thick forests and gravel hills.

## ■ HAYWARD AND VICINITY

The lakelands east of the St. Croix River and north of Chippewa Falls form the heart of a recreational area that includes the Lac Court Oreilles Reservation. This band of Chippewa was named by the French for their practice of cutting the exterior cartilage around their ears, and leaving little cups of cartilage on either side of their head.

Hayward (located at the intersection of Highways 63 and 77) was once one of the state's toughest logging towns. It's mellowed; today you can buy espresso a few doors down from the bait shop.

The **Freshwater Fishing Hall of Fame** provides the closest thing to worship of graven images since Moses melted the golden calf. An enormous four-story-high muskie looms above the treetops surrounded by other equally grandiose fiberglass statues. Visitors can stand inside the jaws of this giant fish. The Hall of Fame is located on Hall of Fame Drive; (715) 634-4440.

Lumberjacks are just part of the show at the **Scheer's Lumberjack Show:** powerful men in T-shirts and blue jeans, armed with chain saws, doing fierce battle with logs. You can find these "jacks" at City B, Lumberjack Bowl; (715) 634-5010.

Just north of Hayward on Highway 63, the swish of waxed skis on fresh snow fills the woods around Cable. **The Birkebeiner,** the biggest and most important cross-country ski race in North America, threads through 59 miles (94 km) of pine and hardwood hills and valleys across this lake-dotted region. The trail is set on the edge of the **Chequamegon National Forest,** which stretches from the granite highlands of Bayfield County south to Medford. The woods also support a fat-tire, off-road bicycle race each summer, and more trails are being developed for people who like to ride their bikes in the woods.

Spoon-bending devotees of northern pike should head east from Spooner (on

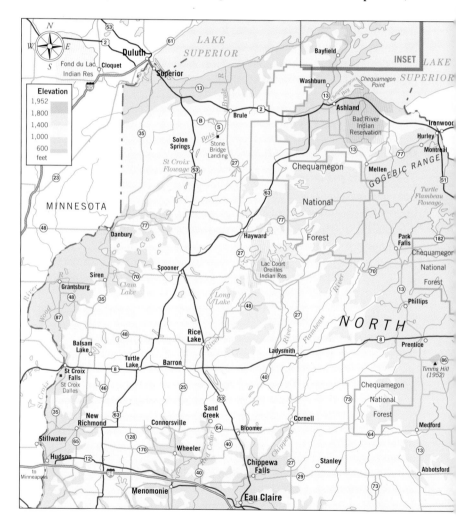

Highway 53/63) to **Long Lake.** The Pioneer on Long Lake resort can set you up with camping and housekeeping cottages while you dip your lures in this pristine lake, or enjoy July's classic wood-boat show or the sailing regatta in August. In wintertime, vacationers at Long Lake carve holes in the ice for the February Fishing Contest or enjoy cross-country skiing at the north end of the lake.

# ■ LAKE SUPERIOR

*Gitche Gumee* is the Chippewa name for Lake Superior. The poet Henry Wadsworth Longfellow borrowed it for his long narrative poem, *Song of Hiawatha:*

> *B*y the shore of Gitche Gumee,
> By the shining Big-Sea-Water,
> Stood the wigwam of Nokomis,
> Daughter of the Moon, Nokomis.
> Dark behind it rose the forest,
> Rose the black and gloomy pine trees,
> Rose the firs with cones upon them;
> Bright before it beat the water,
> Beat the clear and sunny water,
> Be at the shining Big-Sea-Water.

Today few American children know *Hiawatha;* more have probably heard the song by Canadian singer Gordon Lightfoot, "The Wreck of the Edmund Fitzgerald," wherein he sings about the fate of the ore boat SS *Edmund Fitzgerald.* In November of 1975, the boat left the town of Superior in a storm, was swamped by three-story "box waves," and sank with the loss of the entire crew.

Superior is an awesome body of water with great fishing in its depths, danger in its storm-tossed waves, and beauty in the rock caves and sand beaches carved at its margins. The largest fresh-water lake in the world, it is 1,302 feet deep (397 m) at its deepest point. Along Superior's shore, snow covers the ground 140 days per year, compared to 85 days in southern Wisconsin. In some winters, the lake freezes over, and some daredevil will drive across it to Canada.

# ■ CITY OF SUPERIOR

The Burlington Northern Railroad begins and ends in the estuary at the city of Superior, joined to neighboring Duluth, Minnesota, by two bridges across their common harbor, St. Louis Bay. The bridges often look like graceful ribbons of steel cutting through the fog rolling off the hills above Duluth. Beneath the bridges flow huge ore boats and freighters bound for ports around the world. From both cities roll the rail lines that bring the goods and materials harborside from the interior of Wisconsin and Minnesota, and which carry back the cargoes in return. The rail yards are a train buff's dream.

The secure shipyards at Superior blossomed during World War II. Nearly 50,000 workers worked night and day as men and women riveted steel plate to ship skeletons to keep the lifeline open to England and to support the war in the Pacific. In the peace that came with victory, the jobs and boatyards slowly rusted away. Today 28 miles (45 km) of shoreline in this area are dominated by grain elevators, shipyards, warehouses, and docks connected to the Burlington Northern Freight yards on the city's western waterfront.

**Fairlawn Mansion and Museum** at 906 East Second Avenue is a lovely Queen Anne structure built for Martin Pattison, a lumber baron and mayor. The building, restored to its Victorian splendor, now houses exhibits on Great Lakes shipping, regional Native American history, and nineteenth-century fashions.

Barker's Island, two miles (3 km) east on Highway 53, has sightseeing boats at Vista Fleets that tour Superior Harbor; (715) 394-6846.

Protecting St. Louis Bay from the full force of Lake Superior, the sandbar known as **Minnesota Point** stretches almost all the way across the bay. Restaurants, resorts, hotels, marinas, and a seaplane base are located there.

A narrow gap, allowing ships to enter and exit St. Louis Bay, separates Minnesota Point from nearby Wisconsin Point. **Wisconsin Point,** accessible south of Superior on Highway 53 off Moccasin Mike Road, is a preserve, a sandy band of trees and grass that looks much as it did a few thousand years ago. The lighthouse at the end of Wisconsin Point can become isolated when storms punish the bay and swell the lake with 30-foot (9-m) waves; in calm weather, the point is a pleasant picnic spot to enjoy the sandy beach and the lake.

## ■ BOIS BRULE

The coast between Superior and Bayfield, drained by nearly 50 creeks and streams, is one of the loneliest stretches in the state, and lake fog rolls in each night to blanket the landscape. The deep snowfalls recorded here each winter are caused by frigid Canadian air hitting the moist air above Lake Superior. In the deep of a winter night the icy wastes of Superior are lit by the northern lights, and the crack and boom of the ice echoes up the highlands. These are the sights and sounds the

Chippewa called old Winneboujou, the blacksmith, pounding away on his copper forge in the Smoky Mountains, 20 miles (32 km) south of the lake. Winneboujou was stern and industrious. When his own grandmother disobeyed his command, he turned her into a beaver, and her grandchildren are still trying to dam the streams of the north to this very day.

**Bois Brule,** Wisconsin's premier trout stream, drains into Lake Superior after a long journey from its headwaters near Solon Springs. Trout fishing on the Brule River is perhaps the finest in Wisconsin, and the entire length of the river is protected as a state park. One of the best-known resorts is Brule River Classics, which can set you up in log cabins at different spots along the Brule. For more information call (715) 372-8153.

If you want **to canoe or kayak** from near the source of the river down toward Lake Superior, take Highway 53 south of Superior to Solon Springs and put in at Stones Bridge Landing on Highway S. (Needless to say, this is not an adventure for amateurs, and its important to check water conditions locally and to ask for advice.) The first stretch of the Brule flows past the private boathouse and footbridge

*The city of Superior is the busiest port on Lake Superior, shipping tons of minerals and grains towards the St. Lawrence River and eventually the Atlantic Ocean. (Photo by Jerry Stebbins.)*

*Ice caves form every winter along the Lake Superior shoreline. Some winters are long and cold enough to enable daredevils to drive across the lake to Canada.*

at **Cedar Island** (in the middle of the stream), where President Calvin Coolidge spent the summer in 1928. You drift past the world's tallest white pine on the banks above, then flow into faster water and enter **The Falls**, which are the first serious rapids you will encounter before the river widens into Big Lake. Stay in your canoe past the **Wildcat Rapids** before you drop into **Luscious Lake** and slip under the Winneboujou Club bridge, where can land your canoe at Winneboujou and Highway B.

Many canoe trips end here: the rapids north of this point can be really hairy, and skillful paddlers only need apply. If you can make it through the Halls Rapids and the treacherous Little Joe Rapids, there is a DNR campground on the east side of the river, about two miles (3 km) south of Brule.

North of the town of Brule (at the intersection of U.S. 2 and Highway 27) is the **Meadows**, a flat, meandering stretch of water. The **Copper Range bridge and campground** is a good place to put in before testing your mettle on the boiling stretch of rapids before you reach Highway 13. From there the river settles down, though a few rapids remain, and the river widens as you approach Lake Superior.

## ■ BAYFIELD PENINSULA

The Bayfield Peninsula, which forms a wedge in the southern shoreline of Lake Superior, is lined by lonely strands, its forested heights sloping down to the lakeshore, and its highlands of thick forest offering a rare glimpse of pristine, primeval woods. Certainly, there are a few farms, some cabins, and a sprinkling of small villages on the Superior shore, but this great northern region once rife with lumberjacks is now cloaked in graceful solitude.

**Red Cliff Indian Reservation** hugs the end of the peninsula where Highway 13 curves south. If you're interested in native crafts stop at the **Buffalo Art Center**. The nearby town of Bayfield is one of several places in the northern Wisconsin where street signs warn of bear crossings. The bear population is rather high in this sparsely populated forest, and occasionally bears swim from the mainland to the islands in the Apostles chain. Because disgruntled bears already on the Apostle Islands tend to swim on to the next island, the last island in the chain, Stockton Island, is now over-populated with bears.

**Bayfield** itself is a quaint village set around a fine, deep-water harbor. A number of its fine Victorian mansions have been converted into bed and breakfasts, and there are several small restaurants here, making this a good base for exploring the Apostle Islands. **Apostle Islands National Lakeshore Visitor Center** will give you information about the ferries into the islands, hiking trails, and camping facilities. In town visit the **Booth Cooperage** at One Washington Avenue, a factory-museum where you can watch woodworkers make barrels. The local delicacy? Whitefish livers.

■ A P O S T L E   I S L A N D S

Wisconsin's northernmost point is the Apostle Islands. Their rock cliffs, carved caves, red-gravel beaches, and mixed woodlands are spread over 22 islands in Lake Superior's Chequamegon Bay. There are six lighthouses on the islands, four of which are open to the public. The fishing around the Apostles is fantastic, with huge lake trout, pike, and perch thickest in **Chequamegon Bay** and the channels between the islands. The 21 islands under the jurisdiction of the Apostle Islands National Shoreline are not accessible by car. The visitors center in Bayfield provides information on sight-seeing excursions. Call (715) 779-3397.

Madeline Island has year-round residents (some of Wisconsin's hardiest) at the small village of La Pointe, bolstered by an influx of summer visitors who arrive on ferries to stay in vacation homes and camp at the state and national parks that span the island. Madeline Island ferries can be reached at (715) 747-2051. In winter, once the ice is frozen thick, a road is marked with discarded Christmas trees, and you can drive on the ice back and forth from Bayfield to Madeline Island. The eastern edge of Madeline Island is part of the reservation of the Bad River band of Chippewa. The Bad River band operates a commercial fishing operation on the lake, and harvests wild rice on their reservation, as well as operates one of the ubiquitous casino, bingo hall, smoke shop complexes that dot the reservations. Camping is available at Big Bay State Park.

The Chippewa arrived in the Apostles at the end of the fifteenth century. Within a few generations a large community lived in this safe haven, fishing in the channels and venturing into the rich lands of the Sioux on the mainland. They named the region *Shaugawaumikong*—The Place of the Soft Beaver Dam, which the French later decided was spelled, Chequamegon.

As the population grew, so too did the influence and strength of a renegade group of shamans. This enclave of medicine men began to demand an annual tribute of a young woman (as have shamans since time began), so they could sacrifice her to ensure successful fishing. Legend has it that one year when a shaman paddled away from Madeline Island with a beautiful maiden, her lover followed her to the shaman lair on Devil's Island. When he arrived, he saw his love being murdered, then roasted and eaten as a rite of sacrifice. Returning to Madeline Island, he convinced a war party to descend on the shamans, kill them, and destroy their lodges. The warriors did so, but when they returned to Madeline Island the spirits of the young, slaughtered women invaded their dreams. These experiences were so powerful that the Chippewa abandoned Madeline Island and descended on the bands of Sioux that lived on the mainland. Eerie sounds still come from the deep, wave-cut caves of Devil's Island, and depending on your inclination, you can attribute them to the cries of the sacrificed maidens or the hiss and squeal of air escaping from fissures in the rock.

After the Chippewa exodus, the islands were deserted until the French arrived in the early 1600s. French explorer Pierre Esprit Radisson and his companion Groseilliers built a primitive fort on a spit of land across the mouth of Chequamegon Bay in 1659, and in 1693 a camp at La Pointe. The Chippewa returned to the islands and remained there until the 1854 Treaty of La Pointe forced their removal to mainland reservations.

*Smoked fish, in this case chubs, are a Superior shoreline specialty. (Photo by Medford Taylor)*

*The lighthouse complex on Devil's Island, one of the outermost islands in the Apostle chain. (Photo by Jerry Stebbins)*

■ ASHLAND

The city of Ashland is set on a flat plain that curves in a semi-circle around the southern end of Chequamegon Bay—an expanse of water that is frozen solid from December through April. All winter, the windows of the town look out on an icy world, but when the ice breaks, life changes dramatically. Ships come into view on the lake, and life picks up speed once again.

The town first secured its importance when it became a stop on the railroad in 1877; after that its sawmills boomed, and it became a center for brownstone quarrying companies. In the course of its developing prosperity, Ashland also reached for culture, and has always had a reputation for having fine local musical groups.

Today it is the home of **Northland College**, well known for its environmental studies program at the **Sigurd Olson Environmental Institute**. If you come through town in the evening, visit the former depot of the Soo Line Railroad on Third Avenue, which now houses a restaurant and a nightclub. Daytime, walk out

*Ladies of the Ashland Community Theatre prepare for a performance sometime in the nineteenth century. (Ashland Historical Society)*

*Ashland founder Aspah Whittlesey dressed in his traveling clothes. He snowshoed to Chippewa Falls to catch the train to take his seat in the state legislature. (Ashland Historical Society)*

on the town's enormous concrete dock (off Water Street). The largest concrete structure of its kind in the United States, it stretches 1,800 feet (549 km) out into the lake.

# ■ IRON COUNTY

East of Bayfield Peninsula and south of the Lake Superior shoreline is Iron County, named after a vein of ore that stretches across the Wisconsin-Michigan border through the Penokee and Gogebic ranges. After a pocket of nearly pure ore was discovered here in the 1880s, an Iron Rush brought in thousands of speculators and miners, though few struck any fortune. Mining and logging together sparked the economy in this region, bringing mixed benefits to **Hurley,** located on the Wisconsin-Michigan border and the Montreal River, at the intersection of Highways 2, 77, and 51.

It was once said that "the four toughest places on earth were Cumberland, Hayward, Hurley, and Hell," and that Hurley was the toughest. Miners and loggers, rank from a week up on the Gogebic Range, gnawing bark and iron, would swoop

*Gogebic Range miners in 1886 looking ready for the bars of Hurley. (State Historical Society of Wisconsin)*

*A round fieldstone barn in Iron County. Round barns can be found throughout the state.*

across the Montreal River from Upper Michigan and drink till they puked. Those that fought the hardest and didn't get rolled would stumble through the high, plank gates of stockades where prostitutes were kept for their purchase, and where many women were murdered.

During Prohibition, the streets of Hurley were lined with nearly 200 saloons, disguised as soft-drink parlors, with secret doors that led to casinos where silver dollars served as chips. Gangster John Dillinger stayed at a lodge in the woods called Little Bohemia, near Manitowish Waters. The restaurant still boasts about the bullet holes in its wall from a gunfight between Dillinger and the FBI.

Today, the shadowy men that ruled Hurley are long gone, and the tame taverns and striptease bars offer only a glimmer of the notoriety that Hurley once reeked. The wildest time of year is deer season, when men head up north to drink, shoot, and maybe even hunt.

Just west of Hurley on Highway 77, the village of **Montreal** stands quiet, which seems appropriate given the number of men that died digging and mining for iron in a mine that once was the world's deepest. At its height, 600 miners working two shifts entered 40-man cages for the half-mile trip underground to drive huge

# BURLY HURLEY

*Edna Ferber upset many of the residents of the northern logging town of Hurley when her work of fiction,* Come and Get It, *was published in 1934. The story takes place in a town she calls Iron Ridge which, in fact, was a thinly vieled version of Hurley. It was meant to be representative of the many hard-scrabble North Woods mining and lumber towns that existed in Wisconsin during the latter half of the nineteenth century and through the 1930s, when Chicago gangsters came to establish "country resorts" and gaming rackets in and around these same small towns.*

A sordid enough town, Iron Ridge, with all its vices and crudeness of the mining camps of an earlier day, but with few of their romantic qualities. Lumber and iron were hard masters to serve. A cold, hard country of timber and ore. None of the allure of gold, the swaggering brilliance of the California and Colorado gold fields. Long bitter winters up here, and summers brief but fiercely hot. It was like parts of Russia, this northern climate. A rich and wildly beautiful country, already seared and ravaged by Hewitt and his ilk. They hacked and tore and gouged and schemed and took and took and never replaced. There was no end to this richness. Thousands of miles of it, and no one to stop them.

Silver Street was lined up one side and down the other with one- and two-story false-front wooden saloons. It was the loggers' and miners' paradise. The Stockholm House, Joe's Place, Moose Saloon, the Gayety Parlor, Swedish Home, Jack's Place. Crazy plank sidewalks wandered up and down. Encircling the town were the hills and ridges that had once been green velvety slopes, tree shades. Now the rigs and shafts of the iron mines stalked upon them with never a tree or blade of grass to be seen. They had found iron on the Ridge before loggers came to despoil the forests beyond town. It was as though Nature, hearing the dreaded footsteps of the white man, had attempted to hide the treasures concealed in her bosom by tricking herself out with furebelows. She had decked herself with plumes of pine and balsam. She had scented herself with the pungent resin. But they had found the metal and had torn at her to get it. Now the hills all about were bleeding from a thousand wounds.

Suddenly in the '70s, the town swarmed with engineers and prospectors and rich men from the middle West and even the East, for they had hoped to find precious copper and silver and perhaps even gold in these ridges and hills, as well as

> the baser metal, iron ore. So they dug and blasted and drilled but nothing more precious than iron rewarded them. The timber lands—hundreds of thousands of acres of timber—went unsought until Jed Hewitt and the other paper-mill men from the New England coast came along and saw that their gold lay beneath the bark of the century-old pine forests.
>
> —Edna Ferber, *Come and Get It*, 1934

pneumatic drills into bedrock. Dynamite blasted the pockets of low-grade iron ore. Carried up from the depths, the ore was loaded on rail cars and sent west to Ashland.

If logging denuded the forest, mining operations blasted the countryside. The scars and stubble have overgrown and healed somewhat in recent decades, as mixed forest begins to rise over the hardscrabble.

## ■ LAC DU FLAMBEAU AREA

South of Hurley lies the Chippewa reservation of Lac du Flambeau or "Lake of the Torches." It was named thus by French explorers after they watched the Chippewa head out on the lake at night holding torches of birchbark and pine pitch. Their lights lured fish to the surface, where they could spear them.

In recent years, there has been controversy over spearfishing. Whites have claimed that over-fishing, in particular night fishing, has depleted the fish stock radically, and that the special privileges the Chippewa enjoy is unfair. At boat landings protesters shouted insults at Chippewa fishermen, and they drove power boats close to the Chippewa boats to try to upset them. Confrontations attracted outsiders to support each of the sides in the conflict, until county sheriff's deputies had to guard the boat landings to prevent scuffles and provocations from flaring into small riots.

Claims of the white protesters were filed in a Madison courthouse, hundreds of miles south of the lakes. Their claims were denied, and Wisconsin courts guaranteed the Chippewa native treaty rights to fish, hunt, and gather for personal and tribal use. Since the 1992 decision, the lakes of the Lac du Flambeau have become quieter, though some locals still complain that the Indians have ruined the fishing.

Monster muskies lurk in **Fence Lake** on the Lac du Flambeau Reservation. This huge lake is well stocked by the Lac du Flambeau tribe fishery, and the fish are well fed by the clean water. The Fence Lake Resort on Frying Pan Road is a good place to find out how the denizens of the Lac du Flambeau chain are biting, and they can set you up with cabins, camping, and bait, and feed you when you boat home. You can also try **Tomahawk Lake** and the **Turtle Flambeau Flowage** for muskie and walleye that will wrestle you for their very lives.

Southeast of Lac du Flambeau on Highway 17 lies the paper-making and brewing center of **Rhinelander**. It was here that the hodag, a leathery horned beast, was first sighted and captured in the nearby swamps. The hodag was displayed in the Milwaukee Museum for many years following its capture, but a fire in a coal chute destroyed the exhibit. There are still some who disbelieve in the hodag—but you won't find anyone who admits to that in Rhinelander.

*Ice fishing is a popular way to while away the long winter months.*

(top) Pat at Pat's Bait Shop in Sayner in the heart of the Lac du Flambeau fishing region. (above) In addition to the "hodag" of Rhinelander is the monster muskie of Hayward which can be found at the Fishing Hall of Fame.

# ■ WAUSAU

An industrial and commercial center flanking the Wisconsin River, Wausau is located due south of the Lac du Flambeau area on Highway 51. Originally called Big Bull Falls, the town boasted a population of 1,500 people in 1850 and 14 operating sawmills. It was Walter McIndoe, a lumberman, who suggested the town be given the more poetic name, "Wausau," an Indian word for "far away." Now an important center of the insurance industry, the city is also near one of the world's leading ginseng-producing areas. The folks at **Hsu's Ginseng Garden** five miles (8 km) north of Wausau, can tell you about this root crop, a valuable medicinal herb popular in the Orient.

If you come into town in summer, remember this city hosts the annual **World Kayaking Championships and "Log Jam" Festival.** Both attract thousands of spectators. **Wausau Insurance Companies** offers tours by appointment; 2000 Westwood Drive; (715) 842-6591.

Just south of town on Highway 51 (on the way to Stevens Point) is one of the oldest geological formations on earth, **Rib Mountain.** An enormous granite hogsback, three miles (5 km) long and a mile (1.6 km) wide, it is a remnant of a mountain range that once occupied all of Wisconsin. Hiking trails lead to various observation points where a vast expanse of glistening green plain can be seen below. Be sure to stop at this lovely state park and bring a picnic.

*Marathon County is still one of the world's leading ginseng producing areas, the valuable root fetching upwards of $100,000 per quarter acre when harvested every few years. (Marathon County Historical Museum)*

# PRACTICAL INFORMATION

## ■ AREA CODES

Wisconsin has three telephone area codes: 414 serves eastern and southeastern Wisconsin including Green Bay, Milwaukee, Racine, and Kenosha; 608 serves southwestern Wisconsin including Beloit, Janesville, Portage, Madison, La Crosse, and Prairie du Chien; and 715 serves all of northern Wisconsin including Ashland, Eau Claire, Hudson, Marinette, Rhinelander, Stevens Point, and Wausau.

## ■ TRANSPORTATION

### BY AIR

Major airports at Chicago (Ill.), Dubuque (Iowa), Duluth (Minn.), Green Bay, La Crosse, Madison, Milwaukee, and Minneapolis (Minn.) provide easy air access to Wisconsin, and commuter and charter flights can be made to smaller airports.

### BY CAR

Wisconsin highways are well maintained in winter and under repair in the summer. The Department of Transportation has a road condition hotline at (800) 762-3947. Winter driving can be treacherous, so pack a survival kit with shovel, blankets, warm clothes, some high-energy food, and water in case you get stuck in a remote area. If stranded, stay with your car and run the engine sparingly; local road crews maintain the roads and will likely find you soon enough and pull you out. Leaving your car and heading out on your own can be dangerous during storms when wind chills dip to threatening levels.

### BY RAIL

AMTRAK, (800) 872-7245, serves Wisconsin from Chicago and Minneapolis, with stops in Kenosha, Racine, Milwaukee, Columbus, Portage, Wisconsin Dells, and La Crosse.

### BY BUS

Badger Coaches, (608) 255-6771, has a shuttle from Milwaukee to Madison several times a day. Van Galder, (800) 747-0994, also has shuttles several times a day. Greyhound/Trailways, (800) 231-2222, links the major Wisconsin cities on its east-west route between Chicago and Minneapolis, as well as providing service to the major cities from hubs within the state.

## ■ SEASONS AND CLIMATE

In January and February be prepared to dress in layered clothing that will withstand -20°F at night and 10°F by day. It is wise to cover exposed skin during windy conditions to prevent frostbite, as wind chills can exceed -20°F. The temperature begins to moderate starting in late March, but wind and rain require waterproof gear. The temperature varies from 15°F at night to 45°F by day. Pleasant weather begins to arrive in April and May, 40°F night and 65°F by day, but be prepared for rain. June, July, and August are sometimes hot and muggy, sometimes chilly ranging from 55°F–70°F night, 85°F day, so be prepared to dress in light clothing, (pop-up thunderstorms can require some rain gear). September has a few rare hot days, but by October, light sweaters, jackets, and rain gear will be necessary as the general temperature heads south (35°F night and 55°F by day). November and December can be dark, occasionally warm, but on the brink of frigid, so dress in layers, prepare for snow, and think warm thoughts as the mercury drops to 10°F at night and stays below 32°F by day.

| CITY | FAHRENHEIT TEMPERATURE | | | ANNUAL PRECIPITATION | |
|---|---|---|---|---|---|
| | Jan. Avg. High/Low | July Avg. High/Low | Record High/Low | Average Rain | Average Snow |
| Eau Claire | 22  4 | 82  60 | 111  -40 | 32.86" | 38" |
| Green Bay | 24  8 | 79  60 | 104  -36 | 27.97" | 42" |
| La Crosse | 28  5 | 85  62 | 108  -43 | 31.76" | 33" |
| Madison | 26  7 | 83  61 | 107  -40 | 30.60" | 36" |
| Milwaukee | 30  11 | 79  62 | 105  -25 | 29.64" | 48" |
| Superior | 16  -2 | 74  55 | 105  -35 | 26.75" | 60" |
| Wausau | 21  5 | 77  58 | 107  -40 | 31.06" | 44" |

# ■ ACCOMMODATIONS

The Wisconsin Innkeepers Association and Wisconsin Bed and Breakfast Homes and Historic Houses Association both publish free booklets which include some of Wisconsin's most beautiful homes and small hotels. Bed and breakfasts do not always allow children or pets, so call ahead for inquiries or reservations. These publications are available from the Wisconsin Division of Tourism, 123 West Washington Ave., Madison, 53703; (800) 432-8747, or (608) 266-2161.

### *Prices*
B (Budget): up to $45;  M (Medium): $45 to $65;  L (Luxury): $65 to $95;
LL (Extra-luxurious): $95 and above

## ALBANY
**Albany Guest House,** 405 South Mill St.; (608) 862-3636. Farm home across from Sugar River east of Driftless area. **M**

**Oak Hill Manor Bed & Breakfast,** 401 E. Main St.; (608) 862-1400. Large, brick manor house near Sugar River Trail. **B-M**

## ALMA
**Hillcrest Motel,** Hwy. 35N Great River Rd.; (608) 685-3511. Overlooking the Mississippi, beneath the bluffs of Alma. **B**

**Sherman House,** 301 S. Main St.; (608) 685-4929 (seasonal). Above the locks and beneath the bluffs in Alma. **B–M**

APPLETON

**The Queen Anne,** 837 E. College Ave.; (414) 739-7966. On ridge above the Fox River, close to downtown. Restored and furnished with period antiques. Full breakfast included. **M**

ASHLAND

**Hotel Chequamegon,** 101 W. Lake Shore Drive (Hwy. 2); (715) 682-9095. New version of Grand Hotel with a view of the bay and lake. **M–L**

BAILEY'S HARBOR

**Bailey's Harbor Yacht Club & Resort,** 8115 Ridges Rd.; (414) 839-2336/(800) 927-2492. Swimming, dining, tennis, fishing, kid's activities, boating, and more on the Michigan shore. **L–LL**

**Potter's Door Inn,** 9528 Hwy. 57; (414) 839-2003. A historic log cabin on 40 acres of forest and meadows. Full breakfast included. **M–L**

BARABOO

**Barrister's House,** 226 9th Ave.; (608) 356-3344. A Victorian home in the city of Baraboo. **M**

**Gollmar Guest House Bed & Breakfast,** 422 3rd St.; (608) 356-9432. A Victorian circus home in the heart of circus town. Original furniture and woodwork; full breakfast included. **M**

BAYFIELD

**Bayfield Inn,** 20 Rittenhouse Ave.; (715) 779-3363. Mansion high above Bayfield. **L–LL**

**Baywood Place,** 20 N. Third St.; (715) 779-3690. A charming 1930s-style house on the hill above Bayfield Harbor and Chequamegon Bay. Remodeled rooms; full breakfast included. **B–M**

**Old Rittenhouse Inn,** 301 Rittenhouse Ave.; (715) 779-5111. 21 rooms in three elegant historic homes. 20 have fireplaces. Full and continental breakfasts. **L–LL**

## BRULE

**Brule River Classics,** P.O. Box 306; (715) 374-3178. Log cabins along the Brule for fly-fishing fanatics; Wisconsin's premier trout stream. **M–L**

**Twin Gables Motel and Restaurant,** Hwys. 2 and 27; (715) 372-4831. For the fly-fishing devotee on a budget. **B**

## CEDARBURG

**Stagecoach Inn B&B,** W61N520 Washington Ave.; (414) 375-0208. Thirteen rooms in restored stone building in one of Wisconsin's loveliest towns. **M–L**

**Washington House Inn,** W62N573 Washington Ave.; (414) 375-3550, (800) 554-4717. Historic hotel in picturesque Cedarburg. **M–LL**

## DELAVAN

**Allyn House Mansion Inn,** 511 E. Walworth Ave.; (414) 728-9090. Queen Anne mansion, in the center of Delavan's historic district. **B–M**

**Lakeside Manor Inn,** 1809 South Shore Dr.; (414) 728-2043. Victorian home overlooking Lake Delavan. Honeymoon suite and fireside parlor. **M–L**

## EAGLE RIVER

**The Inn at Pinewood,** 1800 Silver Forest Lane; (715) 479-4114. A delightful bed and breakfast in a modern log lodge. Eight rooms, all with private baths; some with whirlpools and fireplaces. Lake activities; full breakfast included. **M–LL**

## EAU CLAIRE

**Apple Tree Inn,** 6700 Hwy. 53 S.; (715) 836-9599, (800) 347-9598. 4 rooms, each with whirlpool, fireplace, and private bath. **M–LL**

**Exel Inn of Eau Claire,** 2305 Craig Rd.; (715) 834-3193, (800) 356-8013. Budget accommodations in Eau Claire. **B**

**Otter Creek Inn,** 2536 Hwy. 12; (715) 832-2945. Nestled on a wooded acre, this inn features Victorian decor, double jacuzzis, and breakfast in bed. **M–LL**

## EGG HARBOR

**Alpine Inn & Cottages,** 7715 Alpine Rd., County G; (414) 863-3000. Full-service resort on Green Bay. **M–L**

**Landing Resort,** Box 17, 7741 Egg Harbor Rd.; (414) 868-3282. Resort overlooking Green Bay. **M–LL**

### EPHRAIM

**French Country Inn,** 3052 Spruce Lane; (414) 854-4001. 1912 Door County inn, close to the bay and state parks in the pretty village of Ephraim. **M–L**

**Trollhaugen Lodge & Motel,** Hwy. 42 N.; (414) 854-2713. Convenient lodging near state parks and Ephraim. **B–M**

### FISH CREEK

**Whistling Swan,** 4192 Main St.; (414) 868-3442, (414) 868-2466. An elegant B&B with 7 rooms. Turn-of-the-century furnishings and modern conveniences. **L–LL**

**White Gull Inn,** 4225 Main St.; (414) 868-3517. One of Wisconsin's finest inns; private baths and fireplaces. **M–LL**

### GREEN LAKE

**Heidel House Resort/Conference Center,** 643 Illinois Ave.; (800) 444-2812, (414) 294-3344. Posh Resort on Green Lake. **L–LL**

**Oakwood Lodge,** 365 Lake St.; (414) 294-6580. An elegant "cottage" on Wisconsin's deepest lake. Families welcome. Full breakfast included. **B–L**

### HAYWARD

**Herman's Landing,** Hwy. CC at Bridge; (715) 462-3626. Fishing cultural center, bait shop, cabins, restaurant, and bar in the heart of the Chippewa flowage. **B–L**

**Lumberman's Mansion Inn,** 4th and Kansas Ave.; (715) 634-3012. Stick-built, 1887, Queen Anne Mansion overlooking Hayward Lake. Winter and summer fishing, skiing, boating, and lumberjacking. **M–L**

**Ross's Teal Lake Lodge,** Hwy. 7NC; (715) 462-3631. Large resort with cabins and lodge on quiet Teal Lake (no waterskiers) in Chequamegon Forest. **M–L**

**Spider Lake Lodge,** Rte. 1, Box 1335C; (715) 462-3793. Historic log lodge from the 1920s with modern amenities, close to Cable. **M–LL**

### HUDSON

**Phipps Inn,** 1005 3rd St.; (715) 386-0800, Queen Anne Victorian above St. Croix Valley, across from Octagon House. Six double rooms. **L–LL**

## IOLA

**Taylor House Bed & Breakfast,** 210 E. Iola St.; (715) 445-2204. A trim Queen Anne built with Scandinavian skill in this little Norse town. **B–M**

## KENOSHA

**Black Swan Inn,** 6003 7th Ave.; (414) 656-0207, 694-7700. Greek Revival home with widow's walk to scan the lake for boats arriving at Kenosha harbor; their yacht is available to sail Lake Michigan. **B–L**

**Manor House,** 6536 3rd Ave.; (414) 658-0014. Georgian mansion and sculpted gardens overlooking Lake Michigan. Four double rooms with baths. **LL**

## KEWAUNEE

**Duval House Bed & Breakfast,** 815 Milwaukee Rd. (Hwy. 42); (414) 388-0501. Elegant Italian Victorian, with nifty parquet floor, parlor, and trim. **B–M**

**The Gables,** 821 Dodge St.; (414) 388-0220. A charming shingled and gabled Victorian close to Lake Michigan beach. Full breakfast included. **M**

## LAC DU FLAMBEAU

**Fence Lake Lodge,** 12919 Frying Pan Camp Lane; (715) 588-3255. Two restaurants, cottages, boating, and the trophy muskies and walleye of Fence Lake await your lures. **B–M**

**Thomsen's Thunderbird Hill Resort,** 2181 Hwy. D; (715) 588-7284 summer, (414) 775-4612 winter. Fishing, swimming, and boating from cottages on the Lac du Flambeau chain. **M**

## LA CROSSE

**Guest House Motel,** 810 S. 4th St.; (608) 784-8840, (800) 274-6873. Budget digs in downtown La Crosse. **B–M**

**Martindale House,** 237 S. 10th St.; (608) 782-4224. Italianate Victorian from the early lumber years at La Crosse. 4 double rooms with baths; 4-course breakfast included. **M–L**

**Wilderness Escapes,** Box 39; (608) 625-4346. Cabins in isolated locations in rustic Kickapoo Valley, located under cliffs and overlooking coulee valleys. **B–L**

## LAKE GENEVA

**End of the Line,** 301 Town Line Rd.; (414) 248-7245, (800) 747-7245, Converted cabooses and rail cars fixed up for fancy lodging. Prices are seasonal. **L–LL**

**T. C. Smith Historic Inn,** 865 Main St.; (414) 248-1097. Glorious mansion with view of Lake Geneva. Tiffany chandeliers, period courtyard gardens, and waterfall gazebo; full breakfast included. **M–LL**

## LAKE MILLS

**Fargo Mansion Inn,** 406 Mulberry St.; (414) 648-3654, Historic Queen Anne, with turret, wraparound porch, and stick-built entryway in this 1880s resort city, west of Aztalan State Park. Full breakfast included. **M–LL**

## LAND O' LAKES

**Sunrise Lodge,** 5894 West Shore Dr.; (715) 547-3684, (800) 221-9689. Full-service resort on west shore of Lac Vieux Desert, 1/2 mile from the source of the Wisconsin River. **B–M**

## MADELINE ISLAND

**Island Inn on Madeline Island,** Box 93, La Pointe; (715) 747-6315, (800) 822-6315. Luxury condos and cottages on Madeline Island. **LL**

**Madeline Island Motel,** Box 51, La Pointe; (715) 747-3000. Moderate accommodations on Madeline Island. **M**

## MADISON

**Collins House,** 704 E. Gorham St.; (608) 255-4230. Prairie-style home on Lake Mendota. Features handmade quilts, and Arts-and-Crafts furniture; full breakfasts included. **M–L**

**Edgewater,** 666 Wisconsin Ave.; (608) 256-9071. One of Madison's most elegant hotels. 143 rooms, most with views of Lake Mendota. Lakeside activities and entertainment available. **M–LL**

**Ivy Inn,** 2355 University Ave.; (608) 233-9717. Access to west campus, stadium, and University Hospitals. There's even a vegetarian Sunday Brunch. **M**

**Mansion Hill Inn,** 424 N. Pinckney St.; (608) 255-3999. Elegant bed and breakfast in sandstone, Italianate mansion on Old Mansion Hill, with top-notch renovation and 11 sumptuous rooms. **L–LL**

**Memorial Union,** 801 Langdon St.; (608) 262-1583, Rooms on campus at lakeshore; libraries, Archives, and State St. **B–M**

MILWAUKEE

**Astor Hotel,** 924 E. Juneau Ave.; (414) 257-4220, (800) 558-0200. Best deal on the east side, near Lake Michigan. Older hotel with its charm intact. **M–L**

**B&B of Milwaukee, Inc.,** (414) 242-9680, provides lists and reservations service for almost 30 bed and breakfast inns in and around Milwaukee.

**Grand Milwaukee Hotel,** 4747 S. Howell Ave.; (414) 481-8000, (800) 558-3862. Near Mitchell Field Airport. Movie theater, health club, meeting rooms, and ballrooms available. **M–LL**

**Marc Plaza,** 509 W. Wisconsin Ave.; (414) 271-7250. Built in 1927, with a marble and wood-trim lobby, plus two restaurants, it's the largest hotel in downtown Milwaukee. **M–LL**

**Marie's Bed and Breakfast,** 346 E. Wilson St., Bayview; (414) 483-1512. A handsome Victorian home in the historic Bay View district. Furnished with antiques; full breakfast included. **M–L**

**Ogden House,** 2237 N. Lake Dr.; (414) 272-2740. Set above Lake Michigan in historic district of lakefront mansions. **L**

**The Pfister Hotel,** 424 E. Wisconsin Ave.; (414) 273-8222. A grand Old Hotel built in 1893, and done up to the nines. The English Room is a top-notch restaurant, and the hotel features a night club and two other restaurants. **M–LL**

**Wyndham Milwaukee Center,** 139 E. Kilbourn; (414) 276-8686. Elegant addition to the theater district with an Italian marble lobby and large rooms. In-house health facilities and restaurant available. **L–LL**

MINOCQUA

**Pine Hill Resort,** 8544 Hower Rd., Dept. M; (715) 356-3418, Cottages and recreation on the Minocqua chain of lakes, on an 80-acre parcel on Lake Kawaguesaga. **B–L**

MONROE

**Alphorn Inn,** 250 N. 18th Ave.; (608) 325-4138, (800) 448-1805. Budget lodging in the Swiss cheese capital of Wisconsin. **B**

**Victorian Garden Bed & Breakfast,** 1720 16th St.; (608) 328-1720. A Queen Anne home in a district of historic homes. Charming suites. **B–LL**

## MOUNT HOREB

**The Dahle House,** 200 N. Second St.; (608) 437-8894. A Victorian Gothic mansion built by Norwegian craftsmen, near Trollway and Mustard Museum. **M–L**

**The Karakahl Inn,** 1405 Business 18/151; (608) 437-5545. On the Trollway in the antique center of Mt.Horeb, near Little Norway and Blue Mound. **M–L**

## OSCEOLA

**St. Croix River Inn,** 305 River St.; (715) 294-4248, (800) 645-8820. A plush, stone home on the St. Croix, appointed with comfort in mind. **LL**

## ONTARIO

**The Inn at Wildcat Mountain,** P.O. Box 113, Hwy. 33; (608) 337-4352. A Greek Revival home built by local ginseng farmer in the Kickapoo Valley. **B–M**

## PLYMOUTH

**Yankee Hill Bed and Breakfast,** 405 Collins St.; (414) 892-2222. Lodging in two adjacent historic landmark homes. **M–L**

## PRAIRIE DU CHIEN

**Neumann House,** 121 N. Michigan St.; (608) 326-8104. Close to the Mississippi waterfront in historic Prairie du Chien. Full breakfast included. **M**

## PRESCOTT

**The Oak Street Inn,** 506 Oak St.; (715) 262-4110. An 1850s home with interior trim identical to Villa Louis. Full breakfast included. **M–L**

## RACINE

**Mansards On-the-Lake,** 827 Lake Ave.; (414) 632-1135. Second Empire house overlooking Lake Michigan. Walking distance from beach and zoo. Continental breakfast included. **M**

## ST. CROIX FALLS

**Wild River Motel and Marina,** 517 N. Hamilton; (715) 483-9343. On the St. Croix River above the falls. Great for waterskiers, anglers, and canoers. **B–L**

## ST. GERMAIN

**St. Germain Bed & Breakfast Resort,** 6255 Hwy. 70 East, P.O. Box 6; (715) 479-8007. Summer and winter recreation nearby to this log cabin resort. **M–L**

**St. Germain Lodge,** 8679 Big St. Germain Dr.; (715) 542-3433. A lodge in the heart of Vilas County and the lake district. **M–L**

## SOLON SPRINGS

**St. Croix Inn,** Lake and 5th St., P.O. Box 291; (715) 378-4444. A year-round resort on Lake St. Croix, south of the tamarack nexus joining the Bois Brule and the St. Croix Rivers. **M**

## SPRING GREEN

**Spring Valley Inn,** Hwys. 14 and C; (608) 588-7828. Taliesen design, with a tasty restaurant and good beer. South of the Wisconsin River. **B–L**

**The Usonian Inn,** E5116 Hwy. 14; (608) 588-2323. Frank Lloyd Wright's Usonian home design applied to a nifty motel. **B**

## STAR LAKE

**North Star Lodge and Resort on Star Lake,** 7919 Hwy. K; (715) 542-3600. Formerly the 100-year-old Walheim grand hotel, a fishing resort and cottages on Star Lake. Log and frame construction, shared bath—ancient, and wonderful. **B**

**Whippoorwill Inn,** 7919 Hwy. K; (715) 542-3333. Hand-built modern cabin for skiers and anglers. Two-night minimum stay on weekends. **M–L**

## STURGEON BAY

**Inn at Cedar Crossing,** 336 Louisiana St.; (414) 743-4249. Renovated inn in historic downtown Sturgeon Bay; plush suites upstairs and, tasty cuisine, and Wisconsin beer on the main floor. **L–LL**

**Whitefish Bay Farm,** 3831 Clark Lake Rd.; (414) 743-1560. Turn-of-the-century foursquare farm house on eighty acres of orchards, north of Sturgeon Bay near Whitefish Dunes State Park. **M–L**

## THREE LAKES

**Country House,** 7265 Chicken in the Woods Rd.; (715) 546-2012. A small place to base your summer and winter fun in the Nicolet Forest around Three Lakes. **M**

TREMPEALEAU
**Trempealeau Hotel,** 150 Main St.; (608) 534-6898 (seasonal). Rooms in an 1871 hotel with views of the Mississippi, good food, beer, and music. Down the road from Perrot State Park. **B**

VIROQUA
**Eckhart-Dyson House,** 217 E. Jefferson St.; (608) 637-8644. A grand, historic mansion with period decor in bedrooms ranging from 1895–1935. **M–L**
**Viroqua Heritage Inn,** 220 E. Jefferson St.; (608) 637-3306. An elegant Victorian mansion with original furnishings. Murder Mystery Weekends available. Full breakfast included. **M–L**

WATERTOWN
**Brandt Quirk Manor,** 410 S. 4th St.; (414) 261-7917. A 1857 brick, wing-and-gable mansion furnished with period antiques. Full breakfast included. **M–L**
**Karlshuegel Inn,** 749 N. Church St., Hwy. 26N; (414) 261-3980. Stucco and stick-built, hilltop mansion on 7.5 acres above Rock River. Site of Carl Schurz home and America's first kindergarden. **M–L**

WAUPACA
**Crystal River Bed & Breakfast,** E1369 Rural Rd.; (715) 258-5333. An 1853 farmhouse along the banks of the Crystal River. Romantic bedrooms with queen-sized beds and fireplaces. **M–L**

WAUSAU
**Rosenberry Inn,** 511 Franklin St.; (715) 842-5733. Prairie-style home with a combination of spas, suites, and fireplaces; adjacent 1862 home with luxury suites. **M–L**
**Stewart Inn,** 521 Grant St.; (715) 848-2864. Prairie-style home by George Maher above rapids on the Wisconsin. **M–L**

WISCONSIN DELLS
**Historic Bennett House,** 825 Oak St.; (608) 254-2500. Home of 1800s photographer L. L. Bennett, with a white picket fence, tucked away from the frenzy of the downtown Dells. **M–L**

# ■ RESTAURANTS

Some restaurants do not accept credit cards, some are closed out of season, and some close Mondays, so call first or bring enough cash to cover your bill, just in case. Most local cafes and supper clubs provide adequate and even fine food, but the following selections offer something a little different.

### Prices
B (Budget): $10 or less;  M (Median): $10 to $20;  E (Expensive): over $20

## ASHLAND
**The Depot.** 400 3rd St.; (715) 682-4200. Great fish and supper club fare in a beautifully renovated train depot which also houses a top-notch, historical museum. **M–E**

**Golden Glow Cafe.** 519 Main St. W.; (715) 682-2838. A favorite for the locals. **B**

**Fifields.** 101 Lake Shore Dr. W.; (715) 682-9095. Located in the Hotel Chequamegon above Lake Superior and Chequamegon Bay. **M–E**

## BAILEY'S HARBOR
**The Common House.** 8041 Main St.; (414) 839-2708. Extensive menu on lakeside village at Bailey's Harbor. **M-E**

## BARABOO
**Alpine Cafe.** 117 4th St.; (608) 356-4046. A great old cafe off the main square in Baraboo. **B**

**Susie's.** 146 4th Ave.; (608) 356-9911. New Wisconsin and international cuisine a few doors down from Al Ringling Theater. **B–M**

## BAYFIELD
**Greunke's Restaurant.** 17 N. 1st St.; (715) 779-5480. The traditional fish boil and fresh fish in downtown Bayfield. **M**

**Old Rittenhouse Inn.** 301 Rittenhouse Ave.; (715) 779-5111. Multi-course, haute cuisine with views of Lake Superior and the Apostle Islands. **E**

**Pier Plaza.** 13 Front St.; (715) 779-3330. Local cafe with fresh baked goods and fresh fish. **B–M**

## BERLIN
**Café Schatzi.** 118 W. Huron St.; (414) 361-1201. Contemporary European cafe with authentic German food, soups, sandwiches, and salads. **B–M**

## CEDARBURG
**Barth's at the Bridge.** N58W6194 Hwy. 57; (414) 377-0660. Well-known supper club next to Milwaukee River and across from Cedarburg Mill. **M**

## CHIPPEWA FALLS
**Coyote Joe's.** 860 Woodward Ave. and Hwy. 124; (715) 726-2288. Southwestern style Mexican food, with a coyote story to boot. **B**

**Olson's Ice Cream Parlor and Deli.** 611 N. Bridge St.; (715) 723-4331. Tasty sandwiches made with fresh bread, and delicious ice cream. **B**

## DELAVAN
**Stephen's Casual Dining.** 214 Walworth Ave.; (414) 728-9143. Contemporary supper club with classic American fare and Wisconsin specialties. **M**

## DOWNSVILLE
**The Creamery.** 1 Creamery Rd.; (715) 664-8354. Contemporary twist on regional cuisine offered at this renovated brick creamery in the Red Cedar Valley. **M–E**

## EAGLE
**Kettle Moraine Inn.** 201 Grove St.; (414) 594-2121. Food and lodging at tavern in heart of southern kettle moraine. **B–M**

## EAU CLAIRE
**Camaraderie Bar-Restaurant.** 442 Water St.; (715) 834-5411. Beer garden in a renovated commercial building on the waterfront. **B**

**Fanny Hill Inn and Dinner Theatre.** 3919 Crescent Ave.; (715) 836-8184. An elegant restaurant and comedy dinner theater with award-winning continental cuisine. One of the best restaurants in the state. **M-E**

**Grandma's Spare Room.** 2159 Brackett Ave.; (715) 832-9298. Homemade soups, sandwiches, and specials. **B–M**

**EGG HARBOR**

**Landmark Restaurant.** 7643 Hillside Rd.; (414) 868-3205. Perched on a bluff overlooking Green Bay, the Landmark Restaurant and Resort offers spectacular views and great food. **M–E**

**Village Cafe.** 7918 Hwy. 42; (414) 868-3342. Popular local cafe. Specializes in fish boil. May need reservations. **B–M**

**ELLISON BAY**

**Viking Restaurant.** 12029 Hwy. 42; (414) 854-2998. Famous fish boil and other treats from the depths of Lake Michigan. Also serves breakfasts that will set you straight. **B–M**

**FISH CREEK**

**Bayside Tavern.** 4160 Main St.; (414) 868-3441. Tavern fare, salads, chili, and lake perch fish fry on Fridays. **B**

**The Cookery.** Hwy. 42; (414) 868-4417. Hearty breakfasts include homemade pastries and lunch fare features delicious whitefish chowder. **B–M**

**White Gull Inn.** 4225 Main St.; (414) 868-3517. Classic cuisine and fish boils in a rustic, candlelit setting.  **M–E**

**FORT ATKINSON**

**Black Hawk Restaurant and Tavern.** 9 Milwaukee Ave. W.; (414) 563-3152, Supper club food in former hotel, and garden setting in season. **B–M**

**Cafe Carpe.** 18 S. Water St. W.; (414) 563-9391. Wide range of specials, regional beers, and on weekends, acoustic music. **B**

**GALESVILLE**

**Jensen's Cafe.** 112 E. Gale Ave.; (608) 582-2411. Careful clutter, history, and great cafe food on the square. **B**

**Mill Road Cafe.** 219 Mill Rd.; (608) 582-4438. Charming cafe overlooking Beaver Creek. Fare includes vegetarian entrees, homemade breads, and desserts. **B–M**

**GREEN BAY**

**Caffé Espresso.** 119 S. Washington St.; (414) 432-9733. Italian espresso and other specials. **B**

**La Bonne Femme.** 123 S. Washington, City Center; (414) 432-2897. Romantic setting and fine country-French cuisine. **M–E**

**Los Bandidos.** 1258 Main; (414) 432-9462, and 2335 W. Mason; (414) 494-4905. Family-run Mexican restaurants west and east of Green Bay. **B–M**

**Marique's.** 1517 University Ave.; (414) 432-9871. Lake perch served with fresh rye bread topped with a slice of onion. Ah . . . the real thing! **B–M**

**Two Women Cafe.** 1105 Main St.; (414) 432-9358. Fresh food, soups, vegetarian cuisine, and whole-grain breads. **B–M**

**Zimmani's.** 333 Main St. (Regency Center); (414) 436-2340. Italian restaurant and delicatessan in a colorful tiled setting. **B–M**

GREEN LAKE

**Boathouse Lounge & Eatery.** 643 Illinois Ave.; (414) 294-3344. The more casual of two restaurants on the beautiful grounds of the Heidel House compound. **M**

**Carver's on the Lake.** N5529 Hwy. A; (414) 294-6931. Replete with spectacular views and a fireplace, Carver's offers fine, continental cuisine. **M–E**

**Heidel House's Grey Rock Mansion Restaurant.** 643 Illinois Ave.; (414) 294-3344. A celebrated resort overlooking Green Lake. **M–E**

HAYWARD

**Herman's Landing.** Hwy. CC at Bridge; (715) 462-3626. Fishing cultural center, bait shop, restaurant, and bar in the heart of the Chippewa flowage. **B**

**Moose Cafe.** 106 N. Dakota Ave.; (715) 634-8449. Traditional cafe food, specials, and breakfasts fit for ten lumberjacks or one fisherman. **B–M**

HAZELHURST

**Jacobi's.** 9820 Cedar Falls Rd.; (715) 356-5591. Jacobi's takes an innovative approach to traditional fare. One of the best restaurants in the state. **M–E**

HOLY HILL (HUBERTUS)

**Old Monastery Inn.** 1525 Carmel Rd.; (414) 673-3540. Delicious soups, sandwiches, specials, and sinful sweets on the grounds of Holy Hill, Wisconsin's most important Roman Catholic Shrine. **B**

**KENOSHA**

**Mangia.** 5717 Sheridan Rd.; (414) 652-4285. Excellent Italian food and pizza served with delicious breads baked in a wood-fired oven. **B–M**

**KOHLER**

**Immigrant at the American Club.** Highland Dr.; (414) 457-8888. The Owners Association of Major League Baseball held a tight-lipped meeting here in 1993 because the service is the American equivalent of a Swiss hotelier. **E**

**LA CROSSE**

**Alpine Inn.** W5717 Bliss Rd., Hwy. F; (608) 784-8470. Tavern fare at entrance to Grand-Dad's Bluff with outdoor beer garden. **B**

**Freighthouse.** 107 Vine; (608) 784-6211. Steaks and seafood in this traditional eatery. **M**

**Piggy's.** 328 S. Front St.; (608) 784-4877. Barbequed beef, pork, chicken, turkey, and ribs on hickory fire in this oak-trimmed restaurant filled with beautiful antiques. Voted one of the best restaurants in Wisconsin by a number of restaurants across the country. **M–E**

**MADISON**

**Antonio's.** 1109 S. Park St.; (608) 251-1412. Home-style Italian food near the old Italian neighborhood on Madison's south side. **B–M**

**The Avenue Bar.** 1128 E. Washington Ave.; (608) 257-6877. The best downtown supper club, fish boil, sandwiches, and tavern. **B–M**

**Badger Candy Kitchen.** 7 W. Main St.; (608) 255-3538. The last luncheonette on Capitol Square, and the best hand-dipped chocolate in Badgerland. **B**

**Dotty Dumpling's Dowry.** 116 N. Fairchild; (608) 255-3175. Award-winning burgers and eclectic decor. **B**

**El Charro Cocina Mexicana.** 600 Williamson St.; (608) 255-1828. Popular, family-owned Mexican restaurant. Cheerful and friendly atmosphere.

**Hide-Away Bar.** 118 S. Pinckney; (608) 257-1521. Tavern off Capitol Square that caters to statehouse crowd, sandwiches and specials. **B**

**Memorial Union.** 800 Langdon. Grilled brats outside in summer, fast-food and cafeteria year-round. Views of Lake Mendota and free music Friday and Saturday nights. **B**

**New Orleans Take-Out.** 1920 Fordem Ave.; (608) 241-6655. Madison's most delicious creole cooking. **B**

**Shanghai Minnies.** 608 University Ave.; (608) 256-0022. Chinese food, fast, plentiful servings in the style of Pei Mei of Taiwan. **B**

**Smoky's Club.** 3005 University Ave.; (608) 233-2120. Madison's best steak joint, no reservations, prepare to wait at the bar for a meal worth remembering. **M–E**

**Sunporch.** 2701 University Ave.; (608) 231-1111. Cheerful restaurant and bakery offering Wisconsin specialities and international fare; breakfast and lunch cafeteria style, carry-out. Jazz on Sundays. **B–M**

**Wilson St. Grill.** 217 S. Hamilton; (608) 251-3500. Wisconsin foods in open setting, perfect for lunches and light suppers just off the Square. **B–M**

MANITOWOC

**Berner's Old Fashioned Ice Cream Parlor.** 1662 Jefferson St. Home of the first ice - cream sundae, located in the historic Washington House Museum.

**Sally's Drive-In.** 2705 South 10th St.; (414) 683-9301. Spotless drive-in, nice food and service at the south edge of town. **B**

MENOMONIE

**Acoustic Cafe.** Broadway and Main; (715) 235-1115. Real coffee for the needy. Sandwiches, music, and late hours for the college set. A block from Mable Tainter Hall. **B**

MILWAUKEE

**Boder's on the River.** 11919 N. River Rd., Mequon; (414) 242-0335. Make reservations for lunch or dinner and peruse the lakefront mansion. Voted Milwaukee's favorite fine dining restaurant. **M–E**

**Chip and Py's.** 1340 W. Town Square Rd.; (414) 241-9589. Weekend jazz, and an eclectic menu of tasty food makes this a popular suburban restaurant in a contemporary, stylish setting. **M–E**

**Coffee Trader,** 2625 Downer Ave.; (414) 332-9690. Where to cop some cappucino amid the bookstalls and specialty shops, a few blocks west of Lake Dr. **B**

**La Casita Mexican Cafe.** 2014 N. Farwell; (414) 277-1177. Southwest-style cuisine and an outdoor patio. **M–E**

**John Ernst.** 600 E. Ogden at Jackson; (414) 273-1828. The oldest of the three mainstays of German food in Milwaukee. **M**

**Grenadier's.** 747 N. Broadway; (414) 276-0747. Reservations and jackets. Elegant American and Continental food. **M-E**

**Italian Community Center.** 631 E. Chicago St.; (414) 223-2180. A wonderful taste of Italy, and bocce courts on the lakefront. **B–M**

**Jake's Delicatessen.** 1634 W. North; (414) 562-1272. An original deli that still is in its prime. **B**

**The King and I.** 823 N. 2d St.; (414) 276-4181. Thai cuisine, with a great lunch buffet. **B–M**

**Lone Star Texas Barbecue.** 19990 W. Greenfield, Waukesha; (414) 821-1511. The best texas-style barbecue in Wisconsin. **M–E**

**Mader's German Restaurant** 1037 N. Old World St.; (414) 271-3377. One of three reasons that Milwaukee is famous for German food. **M–E**

**Milwaukee Turner Hall, Bar and Restaurant.** 1034 N. 4th St.; (414) 273-5598. A traditional spot for Friday fish fries at Turner Hall, built for tumbling, and rented for weddings, anniversaries, parties, and wakes. **B**

**Old Town Serbian.** 522 W. Lincoln; (414) 672-0206. In a world with so few, Milwaukee has two excellent Serbian restaurants, and Old Town has music on weekends. **M–E**

**Oriental Drugstore Lunch Counter,** 2230 N. Farwell. Swivel stools, sandwich grill, and soda fountain at the authentic and opulent Oriental Theater. **B**

**Perkins FamRestaurant.** 2001 W. Atkinson; (414) 447-6660. A landmark of family-style, southern cooking in Milwaukee for 50 years. **B**

**Karl Ratzch's Restaurant.** 320 E. Mason St.; (414) 276-2720. One of the three pillars of Milwaukee's German cuisine, decorated with antlers, porcelain, glass, and other artifacts of German kitsch. **M–E**

**Sanford.** 1547 N. Jackson St.; (414) 276-9608. Fine Italian cuisine and traditional foods served with verve and creativity in a former grocery store on the near North side. **M-E**

**Serb Memorial Hall.** 5105 W. Oklahoma Ave.; (414) 545-6030. The cultural heart of the Serbian community on the southwest side of Milwaukee, famous for weddings and fish fries. **B–M**

## MINERAL POINT

**Chesterfield Inn.** 20 Commerce St.; (608) 987-3682. Old inn set beside a land-scaped sandstone bluff which offers cool summer dining. (seasonal). **M**

## MINOCQUA

**Bosacki's Boat House.** Hwy. 51; (715) 356-5292. Classic supper club on the water at the island center of the Minocqua chain of lakes. **M**

## MOUNT HOREB

**Moen Creek Restaurant.** 3223 Hwy. JG; (608) 437-4141. Inspired farmhouse cuisine makes this old Norwegian farmhouse come alive, and one of the loveliest settings for a Wisconsin dinner. **M–E**

## MUKWONAGO

**Heaven City Restaurant.** S91W27850 National Ave.; (414) 363-5191. Wisconsin foods with a distinctive culinary twist, live jazz on weekends in this 1920s-decorated interior in this lake city southwest of Milwaukee. **M-E**

## NEW GLARUS

**New Glarus Bakery & Tea Room.** 534 First St.; (608) 527-2916. The breads are the best, especially the ryes, but Christmas Stollen is their specialty. **B**

**New Glarus Hotel Restaurant.** 100 6th Ave.; (608) 527-5244, (800) 72-SWISS. Schnitzel cooked by chefs transplanted from the Swiss hotelier schools, polka music every weekend, and Swiss Italian pizza in the basement. **M**

**Puempl's Tavern.** 18 6th St.; (608) 527-2045. Watch the feet of the men in the murals on the wall as you walk past the ancient bar of this 100-year-old tavern. **B**

## OSSEO

**The Norske Nook.** 207 W. 7th St.; (715) 597-3069 (closed Sunday). Famous for its pies and waitresses in the Norwegian town of Osseo. **B**

## PEPIN

**Harbor View Cafe.** First and Main Sts.; (715) 442-3898. Fish, European cuisine, soups and fresh breads across street from Lake Pepin. **M–E** (cash/check)

## RACINE

**Corner House.** 1521 Washington Ave.; (414) 637-1295. Place for prime rib, steaks, delicious standards, and drinks. **M–E**

**The Great Wall.** 6025 Washington Ave.; (414) 886-9700. One of Wisconsin's best Chinese restaurants. **B-M**

**Infusimo's.** 3225 Rapids Dr. (Restaurant); (414) 633-3173; 3301 Washington (Carry-out), (414) 634-2722. Carry-out pizza and Italian food on the south side, and the northside location provides restaurant service at one of Racine's favorite Italian eateries. **B–M**

**Larsen Bakery.** 3311 Washington Ave. (Hwy. 20); (414) 633-4298. Features kringle, and they will ship it to you. **B–M**

**Lehmann's Bakery.** 2210 16th St.; (414) 632-4636. Kringle. **B**

**Main St. Bistro.** 240 Main; (414) 637-4340. New Wisconsin cuisine and grill. **B-M**

**Mexico Lindo.** 2217 Racine; (414) 632-8161. Family-owned restaurant on the south side. **B**

**O & H Danish Bakery.** 1841 Douglas Ave.; (414) 637-8895. Great kringle, and they will ship it to you, too. **B–M**

## SISTER BAY

**Al Johnson Swedish Restaurant and Butik.** 702–712 Bayshore Dr.; (414) 854-2626. Fish boils outside and goats on the sod roof belie the Scandinavian roots of Door county. **B–M**

## SPRING GREEN

**Spring Valley Inn.** Hwys. 14 and C; (608) 588-7828. A pleasant setting, just a few miles from Taliesen and the Wyoming Valley of Frank Lloyd Wright. **B–M**

## SUPERIOR

**China Inn.** 15 Belknap St.; (715) 392-3434. Szechuan, Cantonese, and Hong Kong styles to carry out. **B-M**

**Diane's Restaurant.** 403 Belknap St.; (715) 392-2862. Fresh baked goods, food to go, and home-cooked, 24-hour breakfast. **B**

**The Library.** 1410 Tower Ave.; (715) 392-4821. Fish, ribs, chops, salad bar, everything you'd want after two months on a Great Lakes freighter. **B–M**

**Old Town Bar and Restaurant.** 2215 Harbor View Parkway, Hwys. 2 and 53; (715) 398-7792. Supper club and take-out in a tavern by the bay. **B–M**

STEVENS POINT
**The Wooden Chair.** Main St.; (715) 341-1133. Breakfast and lunch cafe with fresh-cooked food. B

STURGEON BAY
**Del Santo's Restaurant.** 341½ N. 3rd Ave.; (414) 743-6100. Pizza, pasta, and other fresh-cooked entrees that complement the beers of the Cherryland Brewery on site at the converted rail depot. B–M
**The Inn at Cedar Crossing.** 336 Louisiana St.; (414) 743-4249. Renovated inn with plush suites, fine pastries, tasty cuisine, and variety of Wisconsin beer. M–E
**The Nautical Inn.** 230 Michigan St.; (414) 743-9910. Steaks, fish, and supper club fare accompanied by live jazz. B–M

WASHBURN
**Sandie's Log Cabin.** Hwy. 13, 905 W. Bayfield; (715) 373-5728. Fish fresh from the lake, real soups, North Woods breakfasts, and other specials; overlooking Chequamegon Bay. B–M

WAUNAKEE
**The Hofbrau Haus.** 107 Baker; (608) 849-5626. German food supper club, tavern, and wedding hall, with the tenderest veal you will ever eat. B–M

WESTBY
**Borgen's Cafe and Bakery.** 109 S. Main St.; (608) 634-3516. The writing on the wall is Norwegian, the cafe food is good, and the baked goods would do any Norwegian grandmother proud. The men sit in the back of the cafe and speak Norwegian. B

# ■ SELECTED BREWERIES

**Appleton Brewing Company,** 1004 S. Olde Oneida St., Appleton; (414) 735-0507.
**Brewmaster's Pub, Ltd.,** 4017 80th St., Kenosha; (414) 694-9050.
**Briess Industries, Inc.,** 158 E. Main St., Chilton; (414) 849-7711.
**Capital Brewery Company, Inc.,** 7734 Terrace Ave., Middleton; (608) 836-7100.

Cherryland Brewing Company, 341 N. 3rd Ave., Sturgeon Bay; (414) 743-1945.

G. Heileman Brewing Company, Inc., 1111 S. 3rd St., La Crosse; (608) 782-2337.

Joseph Huber Brewing Company, Inc., 1208 14th Ave., Monroe; (608) 325-3191.

Lakefront Brewing Company, 818A E. Chambers St., Milwaukee; (414) 372-8800.

Jacob Leinenkugel Brewing Company, 1-3 Jefferson Ave. (Highway 124 N.), Chippewa Falls; (715) 723-5557.

Miller Brewing Company, 4251 W. State St., Milwaukee; (414) 931-2337.

New Glarus Brewing Company, Hwy. 69, New Glarus; (608) 527-5850.

Pabst Brewing Company, 915 W. Juneau Ave., Milwaukee; (414) 223-3709.

Sprecher Brewing Company, Inc., 730 W. Oregon St., Milwaukee; (414) 272-2337.

Steven's Point Brewery, 2617 Water St., Stevens Point; (715) 344-9310.

Water Street Brewery, 1101 N. Water St., Milwaukee; (414) 272-1195.


## ■ CHEESE FACTORIES

Wisconsin residents are called Cheeseheads for a reason: there are over 200 cheese factories in the state, making about 100 kinds of cheese. Whether you like Brie, Swiss, beer, cheddar, monterey jack, baby Swiss, Neufchâtel, jarlsberg, mozzarella, parmesan, romano, string cheese, cheese curds, or cream cheese, it's made in Wisconsin, a paradise for cheese-lovers. The state even offers refuge to the last limburger cheese factory in the United States—in the town of Monroe.

The following list of towns with cheese factories that offer tours and/or sell cheese is only a small sampling of what awaits the inveterate cheese taster in Wisconsin.

**Adell.** Beechwood: N1598W Highway A, Adell; (414) 994-9306

**Auburndale.** Wiskerchen: 5710 E. Highway H; (715) 652-2333

**Boscobel.** Mid-America Dairymen: Highway 133 N; (608) 375-5466

**Bristol.** Merkt: 19241 83rd St.; (414) 857-2316

**Comstock.** Crystal Lakes: Highway 63; (715) 822-2437

**Durand.** Eau Galle: HC 63 Box 43, Highway 25; (715) 283-4276

**Fremont.** Union Star: 7742 State Rd. 110; (414) 836-2804

**Granton.** Lynn Dairy: W1929 U.S. Highway 10; (715) 238-7129

**Jackson.** Bieri's Cheese Factory: 3271 City P; (414) 677-3227

**La Valle.** Carr Valley: S3797 Highway G; (608) 986-2781

**Marion.** Dupont: N10140 Highway 110; (715) 754-5424

**Milladore.** Maple Grove: 10498 Mayflower Rd.; (715) 652-2214

**Monroe.** Chalet Cheese: N4858 Highway N; (608) 325-4343

**Nelson.** Nelson: Highway 35; (715) 673-4725

**Newburg Corners.** Newburg Corners: W1437 Highway 33; (608) 452-3636

**Plain.** Cedar Grove: Valley View Rd., R1; (608) 546-5284

**Rudolph.** Wisconsin Dairy: Highways 34 and C; (715) 435-3144

**Somerset.** Bass Lake: 5948 Valley View Trail; (715) 549-6617

**Theresa.** Widmer's: 214 W. Henni St.; (414) 488-2503

**Thorp.** Cloverleaf: W10911 Highway N, Stanley; (715) 669-3145

**Twin Grove.** Prairie Hill: N3948 Twin Grove Rd.; (608) 325-2918

## ■ MUSEUMS

### APPLETON

**Houdini Historical Center,** 220 E. College Ave.; (414) 735-9370. Home to a great collection of Houdini memorabilia.

### BARABOO

**Circus World Museum,** 426 Water St.; (608) 356-0800. Circus acts in summer and collection of circus wagons, posters, and circus artifacts. One of the great circus museums of the world. Fee.

**International Crane Foundation,** Shady Lane Rd. (east of 12); (608) 356-9462. Research and recovery center for wild cranes, saving several crane species from extinction. Fee.

## CEDARBURG

**Cedar Creek Settlement,** Hwy. 57 and Hwy. 143; (414) 377-8020. The Old Wittenberg Mill, and several German homes of the 1840s and 1850s that have been preserved. The Cedar Creek Winery is now located in the mill and tours are available for a fee.

## EAU CLAIRE

**Chippewa Valley Museum,** Carson Park; (715) 834-7871. Call for hours. History of the Ojibwa Indians. Admission fee.

## FORT ATKINSON

**Hoard Historical Museum and Dairy Shrine,** 407 Merchants Ave. (US 12); (414) 563-7769. Call for hours. The history of dairying in Wisconsin. Free.

## GREEN BAY

**Green Bay Packer Hall of Fame,** 855 Lombardi Ave.; (414) 499-4281. The Curly Lambeau years, the Lombardi years, everything a Bears fan could hate. Fee.

**National Railroad Museum,** 2285 S. Broadway; (414) 437-7623 (May 1–Oct. 15). A train buff's dream—75 locomotives and train rides. Admission Fee.

## HARTFORD

**Hartford Heritage Auto Museum,** 147 North Rural St.; (414) 673-7999. Antique car collection in the home of the Kissel car factory. Admission fee.

## LAC DU FLAMBEAU

**Lac du Flambeau Chippewa Museum and Cultural Center,** P.O. Box 804; (715) 588-3333. The Lac du Flambeau band of Chippewa holds powwows during the year that are open to the public. Admission fee.

## MADELINE ISLAND

**Madeline Island Historical Museum,** Ferry landing, La Pointe; (715) 747-2415. Memorial Day–First Weekend in September, 9–5. Exhibits and memorabilia of the Chippewa encampment, French fur trade, and early maritime life on Madeline Island. Admission fee.

## MADISON

**Elvehjem Museum of Art,** 800 University Ave.; (608) 263-2246. Call for hours. Collections of Russion icons, and of Egyptian, Greek, and Roman sculpture, coins, and ceramics. Free.

**Geology Museum,** 1215 W. Dayton; (608) 262-2399. Dinosaur and mastodon skeletons, extensive and exhaustive collection of semi-precious stones, minerals, fossils, and crystals, and also something about the glaciers. Free.

**Madison Children's Museum,** 100 State St.; (608) 256-6445. Open Tuesday–Saturday 10–5, Sunday 1–5. Hands-on museum for kids. Admission fee (first Sunday of month is free).

**State Historical Society,** 30 North Carroll St.; (608) 264-6588. Closed Mondays. Excellent presentation of Wisconsin's Native American artifacts, and quarterly exhibits.

**Wisconsin State Historical Society Library, Archives, and Iconographic Collections,** 816 State St.; (608) 264-6534 (circulation desk). The shreds and artifacts, papers and portraits of the people who lived in Wisconsin, with a great collection on Civil Rights, Abolitionism, small press publications, film, and photographs.

## MANITOWOC

**Manitowoc Maritime Museum,** 75 Maritime Dr.; (414) 684-0218. Manitowoc was a Great Lakes boat building center for more than 150 years, and built submarines during World War II; you can tour a submarine. Admission fee.

**Rahr-West Art Museum,** Park St. at North Eighth; (414) 683-4501. Magnificent Queen Anne mansion in Lake Michigan port city of Manitowoc with collection of contemporary American art and Victorian antiques. Free.

## MILWAUKEE

**American Geographical Society Collection, Golda Meir Library,** University of Wisconsin, Milwaukee, 2311 E. Hartford Ave.; (414) 229-6282. One of the finest map, atlas, and chart collections in the U.S. Free

**Brooks Stevens Automotive Museum,** 10325 Port Washington Rd.; (414) 241-4185. Open daily, 1–5; closed holidays. Brooks Stevens was the designer of the Streamline and Moderne period, responsible for a variety of hallmark industrial and graphic art designs, like the Oscar Mayer Weinermobile. Admission fee.

**Charles Allis Art Museum,** 1801 N. Prospect Ave.; (414) 278-8295. Call for hours. Exhibits include Chinese porcelains and Winslow Homer landscapes. Free.

**Discovery World Museum of Science, Economics and Technology,** 818 W. Wisconsin Ave; (414) 765-9966. Call for hours. Hands-on science exhibits that are geared to students of all ages, and has particularly good exhibits to describe those pesky technological phenomena to inquiring young minds. Admissio fee.

**Milwaukee Art Museum** (War Memorial), 750 N. Lincoln Memorial Dr.; (414) 224-3200. Famous for its German Expressionists. Admission fee (but free to Milwaukee County residents).

**Milwaukee County Historical Center,** 910 N. Old World 3rd St.; (414) 273-8288. Call for hours. Collections of firefighting equipment, toys, women's clothing, and a genealogical research library. Free.

**Milwaukee Public Museum,** 800 W. Wells St.; (414) 278-2702. Monday, noon–8; Tuesday–Sunday, 9–5. One of the four largest natural history collections in the United States, and an excellent collection of Native American artifacts presented in a cultural context from the Paleolithic era to modern native culture. Other featured exhibits include a rain forest and life-size dinosaurs. Admission fee.

**Pabst Mansion,** 2000 W. Wisconsin Ave. (414) 931-0808. Call for hours. The flagship of the Pabst family, built by Captain Frederick Pabst, with carved wood, stained glass, and ironwork. Pretty at Christmas. Admission fee.

### OSHKOSH

**EAA Air Adventure Museum,** Hwys. 41 and 44; (414) 426-4818. More than 80 aircraft on display and aeronautical memorabilia from 100 years of flight. Admission fee.

**Oshkosh Public Museum,** 1331 Algoma Blvd.; (414) 731-1598. An English-style mansion, with a very good collection of meteorites. A nineteenth-century railway station and fire station on grounds. Admission free.

### PORTAGE

**Old Indian Agency House,** Agency House Rd.; (608) 742-6362. Early home to American Indian agents on the Wisconsin frontier. Admission fee.

## RACINE

**Johnson Wax Administration Building**, 14th and Franklin Sts; (414) 631-2154 (Reservations requested). Wright's masterwork industrial design. Free.

## SHEBOYGAN

**Artspace: A Gallery of the John Michael Kohler Arts Center**, Woodlake Complex; (414) 452-8602. Touring exhibitions and a large collection of Wisconsin and American contemporary artists. Free.

**John Michael Kohler Arts Center**, 6th and New York Aves; (414) 458-6144. Fine small museum with five galleries that exhibit contemporary American art, in J. Kohler's Italianate mansion built in 1882. Free.

**Kohler Design Center**, 101 Upper Rd.; (414) 457-3699. If you ever thought of putting in a new bathroom . . . and a ceramic art gallery featuring pieces by artists invited to use Kohler's industrial plant and foundry to produce art. Free.

## SPRING GREEN

**Taliesen**, Hwys. 23 and C (3 miles south of Spring Green); (608) 588-2511. The Frank Lloyd Wright Home, the Hillside Farm, and the Taliesen School of Architecture.

## STURGEON BAY

**Door County Historical Museum**, 18 N. 4th St.; (414) 743-5809. Equal portions of antique fire-fighting equipment, Native American artifacts, the fur trade, early settlement, and orchards of Door County.

## WATERTOWN

**The Octagon House and First Kindergarten**, 919 Charles St.; (414) 261-2796. Admission fee.

## WAUSAU

**Marathon County Historical Museum**, 403 McIndoe St.; (715) 848-6143. Traces the development of the region's lumber industry.

# ■ NATIONAL AND STATE PARKS

There are 45 state parks in Wisconsin, five official recreational areas, 10 State forests, 16 state trails, and each county has parks and occasionally forest land set aside for enjoying the outdoors. Call (608) 266-2181 for information, or write to the DNR Bureau of Parks and Recreation, P.O. Box 7921, Madison, WI 53707-7921 for the *Traveler's Guide to Wisconsin State Parks & Forests* (which costs $10.95 or $8.95 with purchase of annual park admission sticker). They also offer free information about biking, boating, canoeing, hiking, horseback riding, maps, park admission stickers, pets, snowmobiling information, trails, and accommodations for people with physical disabilities.

## ■ NATIONAL PARKS

The federal government has huge tracts of Wisconsin set aside as part of its national forest system, and there also are designated wildlife preserves. Information about the National Park Service in Wisconsin can be obtained by calling (608) 264-5610, or by writing to the National Park Service National Trails Office, 700 Ray O Vac Dr., Madison, WI 53711. Following is a list of National Parks.

**Apostle Islands National Lakeshore;** (715) 779-3397

**Chequamegon National Forest;** (715) 762-2461

**Nicolet National Forest;** (715) 362-3415

**St. Croix National Scenic Riverway;** (608) 264-5610

**Ice Age National Scenic Trail** in Wisconsin is 1,000 miles long and can be hiked; (414) 691-2226, or (608) 251-5550.

## ■ STATE PARKS

CENTRAL

**Buckhorn** (Castle Rock Lake) Necedah; (608) 565-2789

**Hartman Creek,** (Chain O' Lakes) Waupaca; (715) 258-2372

**Roche-A-Cris,** Friendship, (608) 339-6881

FOX VALLEY

**Heritage Hill,** (Fox River) Green Bay; (414) 448-5150

**High Cliff,** (Lake Winnebago) Menasha; (414) 9489-1106

## NORTHERN
**Amicon Falls,** Superior; (715) 399-8073
**Big Bay** (Madeline Island) Bayfield; (715) 779-3346
**Copper Falls,** Mellen; (715) 274-5123
**Pattison Falls,** Superior; (715) 399-8073

## DOOR PENINSULA
**Newport,** (Lake Michigan) Ellison Bay; (414) 854-2500
**Peninsula,** (Green Bay) Fish Creek; (414) 868-3258
**Potawatomi,** (Green Bay) Sturgeon Bay; (414) 746-2890/2891
**Rock Island** (Lake Michigan) Washington Island; (414) 847-2235
**Whitefish Dunes,** (Lake Michigan) Sturgeon Bay; (414) 823-2400

## SOUTHEAST
**Aztalan,** Lake Mills; (414) 648-8774
**Big Foot Beach,** Lake Geneva; (414) 248-2528
**Bong Recreation Area,** Kansasville; (414) 878-5600
**Harrington Beach,** (Lake Michigan) Belgium; (414) 285-3015
**Kohler-Andrae,** (Lake Michigan) Sheboygan; (414) 452-3457
**Lake Kegonsa,** Stoughton; (609) 873-9695

## SOUTHWEST
**Blue Mound,** Blue Mound; (608) 437-5711
**Browntown-Cadiz Springs,** Monroe; (608) 966-3777 (summer)
**Devil's Lake,** Baraboo; (608) 356-8301/6618 (campsites)
**Governor Nelson,** (Lake Mendota) Waunakee; (608) 831-3005
**Mirror Lake,** (Wisconsin Dells) Baraboo; (608) 254-2333
**New Glarus Woods,** Monroe; (608) 527-2335
**Rocky Arbor,** (Wisconsin Dells) Baraboo; (608) 254-2333
**Wildcat Mountain,** (Kickapoo River) Ontario; (608) 337-4775
**Yellowstone Lake,** Blanchardville; (608) 523-4427

UPPER COULEE COUNTRY
**Brunet Island,** (Chippewa River) Cornell; (715) 239-6888
**Hoffman Hills,** Menomonie; (715) 232-2631
**Interstate,** St. Croix Falls; (715) 483-3747
**Kinnickinnic,** River Falls; (715) 425-1129
**Lake Wissota,** Chippewa Falls; (715) 382-4574
**Merrick,** (Mississippi River) Fountain City; (608) 687-4936
**Perrot,** (Mississippi River) Trempealeau; (608) 534-6409

## ■ STATE FORESTS

**Black River,** Black River Falls; (715) 284-1400/4103
**Brule River,** Brule; (715) 372-4866
**Flambeau River,** Winter; (715) 332-5271
**Governor Knowles,** Grantsburg; (715) 463-2898
**Havenwoods,** Milwaukee; (414) 527-0232
**Kettle-Moraine Northern Unit,** Campbellsport; (414) 626-2116
**Kettle Moraine Southern Unit,** Eagle; (414) 594-2135/2136
**Lapham Peak/Kettle Moraine,** Delafield; (414) 646-3025
**Northern Highland-American Legion,** (Vilas County) Woodruff; (715) 356-5211
**Point Beach,** (Lake Michigan Shore) Two Rivers; (414) 794-7480

## ■ FISHING

Those planning to fish or hunt in Wisconsin should remember two important rules: buy a license and always remove weeds and bilge water before entering another body of water to prevent spread of zebra mussel and purple loosestrife. Fishing licenses are available locally and through the state Department of Natural Resources (DNR), which can answer all your fishing questions at (608) 266-2621, and (608) 273-5955 for Dane, Green, Rock, and Jefferson counties.

If you use a motorboat for fishing, that boat must be licensed in Wisconsin, or in another state if used less than 60 days in Wisconsin. Each boat must be equipped with a personal flotation device for each rider. Lights and sound signals are required for use at night. Contact a district DNR office with all your boating questions: Lake Michigan District, (414) 492-5800; North Central District, (715) 362-5800; Northwest District, (715) 635-2101; Southeast District, (414) 263-8500; Southern District (608) 275-3266; Western District, (715) 839-3700. There are more than 150 trout streams offering hundreds of miles of cold-water trout fishing for brown and brook trout in Wisconsin but the Bois Brule is the most famous. A call to the Department of Natural Resources will get you a booklet and map of all the trout streams in Wisconsin and the daily bag limits; call (608) 266-2621. Remember, Wisconsin is surrounded by water, cut by rivers, and has 15,000 lakes, so safety on the water can save your life, and observation of boating rules (no drinking) can prevent fines and keep you out of jail. An excellent resource is *Fish Wisconsin* by Dan Small.

# ■ BICYCLE TOURS

Wisconsin maintains several excellent bike trails for a small daily fee paid in boxes at each trail. A short list follows, but other loops and bike trails around Wisconsin make use of back roads and county highways. Some state parks permit off-road bicycling. For information call (800) 354-BIKE.

**Bearskin State Park Trail:** North Woods near Minocqua (18 miles); (715) 385-2727.

**Elroy-Sparta Trail:** Travel a scenic abandoned rail line through tunnels in the heart of the Driftless area (33 miles); (608) 337-4775.

**400 Trail:** Connecting Elroy to Reedsburg along Baraboo River (22 miles); (608) 275-3214.

**Glacial Drumlin State Trail:** From Waukesha, past Lapham Peak, through Kettle Moraine (47 miles); (608) 873-9695.

**Great River Bike Trail:** Perrot State Park to La Crosse River Trail (22.5 miles); (608) 534-6409.

**La Crosse River Trail:** Access to Elroy Sparta Trail and Trempealeau State Park (23 miles); (608) 337-4775.

**Military Ridge State Trail:** Fitchburg past Blue Mound to Governor Dodge State Park near Dodgeville (40 miles); (608) 935-2315.

**Pecatonica State Trail:** 10 miles along Pecatonica River in Lafayette County; (608) 523-4427.

**Red Cedar State Trail:** Lovely scenery in Upper Coulee valley (15 miles); (715) 232-1242.

**Sugar River Trail:** Between New Glarus and Brodhead, traces the eastern edge of the Driftless area along the Sugar River (24 miles); (608) 325-4844.

## ■ SELECTED BOAT TOURS AND FERRIES

**Apostle Islands:** Apostle Islands Cruise Service, Bayfield; (715) 779-3925, (800) 323-7619. Tours of the inner Apostle Islands, fishing charters, and water taxi service for campers to the outlying islands, especially Devil's Island.

**Cassville:** Cassville Car Ferry, Cassville; (608) 725-5180. One of few remaining ferries to Iowa, saves 30-mile drive to bridges at Dubuque or Prairie du Chien.

**Chain O' Lakes:** Chief Waupaca Sternwheeler Cruise; (715) 258-2866. Memorial Day to Labor Day. Narrated cruise on the Chain O' Lakes, and evening cruises of 11 lakes. Dinner and brunch cruises available Memorial Day to Labor Day.

**Door County:** Washington Island Ferry Line, from Northport to Washington Island; Lollipop Boat tours, from Sturgeon Bay; C. G. Richter Passenger Cruise, through Death's Door to Washington Island, from Gil's Rock; Island Clipper, ferry service from Gil's Rock to Washington Island.

**Manitowoc:** Michigan-Wisconsin Car Ferry Service, open all year-round to Ludington, Michigan. P.O. Box 708 Ludington, MI 49431, (800) 841-4243; Manitowoc office (414) 684-0888. May–October.

**Milwaukee:** Michigan-Wisconsin Car Ferry Service, open all year-round to Ludington, Michigan. P.O. Box 708 Ludington, MI 49431, (800) 841-4243; Manitowoc office (414) 684-0888. May–October.

**Minocqua:** Wilderness Cruises on the Willow flowage, music, and dinner cruises too; (715) 453-3310, (800) 472-1516.

**Wisconsin Dells:** Dells Boat Tours explores the sculpted sandstone of the upper and lower dells of the Wisconsin; Wisconsin Ducks: sightsee the Dells overland and through the water in amphibious landing craft; Olson Boat Line: boat tours of the upper and lower dells of the Wisconsin. Riverview Boat Line: the Dells and cliffs. Follow the signs that say "Ride the Ducks."

## ■ TRAIN TOURS

**East Troy Electric Railroad,** 2002 Church St., East Troy; (414) 642-3262. Open Memorial Day–September.

**National Railroad Museum,** 2285 South Broadway, Green Bay; (414) 435-7245. May–November.

**North Freedom Mid-Continent Railway Museum,** Walnut St., North Freedom; (608) 522-4261. Summer runs and special winter runs on the Snow Train. Mid-May–Labor Day.

## ■ FESTIVALS AND EVENTS

JANUARY
**Polar Bear Swim,** Sheboygan (414) 457-5148
**Empire 130 Dog Sled Race,** Solon Springs (800) 942-5313
**Epiphany Concert and Bavarian Dinner,** Holy Hill, Hubertus (414) 628-1838

FEBRUARY
**Mid-Continent Railway Snow Train,** North Freedom (800) 22-DELLS

MARCH
**St. Patrick's Day,** La Crosse, Oshkosh, Milwaukee
**Maple Sugar'n Open House,** Riveredge Nature Center, Newburg (414) 675-6888

APRIL
**Annual Smelt Fry,** Port Washington (414) 284-9069
**Turkey Hunting Festival,** Boscobel (608) 375-2672

MAY
**Cinco de Mayo,** Milwaukee (414) 278-2700
**Sytennde Mai, Norwegian Independence Day,** Stoughton, Viroqua, Westby
**Swiss Polka Fest,** New Glarus (608) 527-2095

JUNE
**Canal Days,** Portage (608) 742-6242
**Railroad Heritage Days,** Superior (715) 394-5712
**Heidi Festival,** New Glarus, (608) 527-2095
**Bavarian Folkfest,** Milwaukee (414) 462-9147
**Summerfest,** Milwaukee (800)-837-FEST

JULY
**Old Car Show,** Iola (715) 588-3303
**Circus Train Loading,** Baraboo (414) 273-7877
**The Great Circus Parade,** Milwaukee (414) 273-7877
**Honor the Earth Pow-Wow,** Lac du Flambeau (715) 634-2100
**Festa Italiana,** Milwaukee (414) 223-2180
**Lumberjack World Championships,** Hayward (715) 634-2484
**Experimental Aircraft Association Fly-In,** Oshkosh (414) 426-4800

AUGUST
**Menominee Pow-Wow,** Keshena (715) 799-5114
**Wisconsin State Fair,** West Allis/Milwaukee (800) 844-FAIR
**Great River Jazz Festival,** La Crosse (608) 788-1876
**Sweet Corn Festival,** Sun Prairie (608) 837-4547
**Irish Fest,** Milwaukee, (414) 476-3378
**Mexican Fiesta,** Milwaukee (414) 383-7066
**Serbian Days,** Milwaukee (414) 545-4080

SEPTEMBER
**Wisconsin State Cow Chip Throw,** Prairie du Sac (608) 643-4317
**Great Green Bay Kickoff,** Green Bay (414) 494-9507
**Wilhelm Tell Festival,** New Glarus (608) 527-2095
**Indian Summer,** Milwaukee (414) 383-7425
**Old Town Water Street Celebration,** Eau Claire (715) 835-1540
**Bavarian Oktoberfest,** Old Heidelberg Park, Milwaukee (414) 462-9147
**Cheese Days,** Monroe (608) 325-7771
**Apple Festival,** Gays Mills (608) 735-4810

OCTOBER
**Octoberfest,** La Crosse (608) 784-3378
**Fall Flyaway,** Horicon (800) 937-9123
**Apple Festival,** Bayfield (715) 779-3335
**Mid-Continent Steam Train Autumn Color Tours,** North Freedom (800) 22-DELLS
**Pumpkin Patch Festival,** Egg Harbor (414) 868-3717

NOVEMBER
**Danish Jule Fest,** Kenosha (414) 657-9781
**Christmas at the Octagon House,** Watertown (414) 261-2796

**DECEMBER**
Winterfest, Milwaukee (800) 837-FEST
Festival of Trees, Cedarburg (414) 271-4704


## ■ INFORMATION NUMBERS

**Attractions:** (800) 432-TRIP

**Chambers of Commerce:** Appleton (414) 734-3358, Bayfield (800) 472-6338, Door County (800) 52-RELAX, Eau Claire (800) 344-FUNN, Green Bay (800) 236-EXPO, Hidden Valleys (SW) (608) 725-5867, Indianhead Country (NW) (800) 826-6966; La Crosse (800) 658-9770, Madison (800) 373-MDSN, Milwaukee (800) 231-0903, Minocqua (800)44-NORTH, Rhinelander (715) 362-7464, Southeast Wisconsin (414) 324-4431, Spring Green (800) 588-2042, Stevens Point (715) 344-2556, Wausau (800) 236-WSAU, Wisconsin Dells (800) 22-DELLS

**Department of Natural Resources:** Biking (608) 266-2621, Camping (608) 266-2181; Fishing, Hunting, Boating (608) 266-2161; Mobility Impaired, (608) 266-2181

**Department of Transportation:** Aeronautical charts (608) 266-3351, Airport Directory (608) 246-3265, County Maps (608) 246-3265; Road conditions (800) ROAD-WIS

**Division of Tourism:** (800) 432-TRIP; Snowmobile Trails Map, (800) 372-2737

**National Weather Service:** Green Bay (414) 494-2363; La Crosse (608) 784-1930, Madison (608) 249-6645, Milwaukee (414) 744-8000, Superior (715) 392-7421

**Sports:** Green Bay Packers (414) 494-2351, Milwaukee Brewers (414) 933-1818, Milwaukee Bucks (414) 227-0500, UW-Madison Athletics (608) 262-1440

**State Historical Society of Wisconsin:** 816 State Street, Madison, 53706, (608) 262-1368

# RECOMMENDED READING

## ■ ARCHITECTURE

Brooks, H. Allen. *The Prairie School: Frank Lloyd Wright and his Midwest Contemporaries.* New York: W. W. Norton and Co., 1972.

Garber, Randy (ed). *Built in Milwaukee: An Architectural View of the City.* Milwaukee: City of Milwaukee, 1981.

Visser, Kristin. *Frank Lloyd Wright & the Prairie School in Wisconsin: An Architectural Touring Guide.* Madison, Wis.: Prairie Oak Press, 1992.

Zimmerman, H. Russell. *The Heritage Guidebook: Landmarks and Historical Sites in Southeastern Wisconsin.* Milwaukee: Harry W. Schwartz, 1989.

## ■ COUNTY AND REGIONAL HISTORIES

Goc, Michael J. *Land Rich Enough: An Illustrated History of Oshkosh and Winnebago County.* Northridge, Calif.: Windsor Publications, 1988.

Heib, Jane. *An Illustrated History of Eau Claire.* Northridge, Calif.: Windsor Publications, Inc., 1988.

Hildebrand, Janice. *Sheboygan County: 150 Years of Progress.* Northridge, Calif.: Windsor Publications, 1988.

Leopold, Aldo. *A Sand County Almanac.* New York: Oxford University Press, 1949. Also, *The River of the Mother of God and Other Essays,* Edited by Susan L. Flader and J. Baird Callicott. Madison, Wis.: The University of Wisconsin Press, 1991.

Martin, Lawrence. *The Physical Geography of Wisconsin.* Madison, Wis.: The University of Wisconsin Press, 1965.

Roe, Lawrence A. *A History of Wisconsin Mining.* Madison, Wis.: Roeco, 1991.

Teale, Edwin Way. *The Wilderness World of John Muir.* Boston: Houghton Mifflin Company, 1954.

# ■ GREEN BAY PACKERS

Kramer, Jerry. *Instant Replay: The Green Bay Diary of Jerry Kramer.* New York, New American Library, 1968.

Lombardi, Vincent T. *Run to Daylight.* New York: Grosset & Dunlap, 1963.

Torinus, John B. *The Packer Legend: An Inside Look.* Neshkoro, Wis.: Laranmark Press, 1982.

# ■ GUIDEBOOKS

DeLorme Mapping. *Wisconsin Atlas and Gazetteer.* Freeport. Me.: DeLorme Mapping, 1992. The best atlas available!

Hall, Ginny. *Meandering Around Walworth County: An Auto Tour Guide.* Vols I-IV. Lake Geneva, Wis.: The Lake Geneva Public Library, 1992.

Kulibert, Gary. *Wisconsin Outdoor Recreation & Camping Guide.* Rhinelander, Wis.: Explorer's Guide Publishing, 1988.

Small, Dan. *Fishing Wisconsin.* Iola, Wis.: Krause Publications, 1993.

State Historical Society of Wisconsin. *Travel Historic Wisconsin: A Guide to Wisconsin's Historic Markers.* Madison, Wis.: Guide Book Press, 1989.

Stuttgen, Joanne Raetz. *Cafe Wisconsin: A Guide to Wisconsin's Down-Home Cafes.* Minocqua: Heartland Press, 1993

Umhoffer, Jim. *Guide to Wisconsin Outdoors.* Minocqua, Wis.: Northword Press, Inc., 1990.

Wisconsin Library Association. *Wisconsin: A Guide to the Badger State.* Compiled by Workers of the Writer's Program of the Work Projects Administration. New York: Duell, Sloan and Pierce, 1941

# ■ NATIVE AMERICANS

Lapham, Increase A. *The Antiquities of Wisconsin.* Washington, D.C.: Government Printing Office, 1982. 92 p. 60 plates. (Smithsonian Institution Publications, no. 70.)

Mountain Wolf Woman. Ed. by Nancy Oestreich Lurie. *Mountain Wolf Woman, The Autobiography of a Winnebago Indian.* Ann Arbor, Wis.: Ann Arbor Paperbacks, The University of Michigan Press, 1961.

# ■ WISCONSIN HISTORIES

Aderman, Ralph M. *Trading Post to Metropolis: Milwaukee County's First 150 Years.* Milwaukee: Milwaukee County Historical Society, 1987.

Freeman, Samuel. *The Emigrant's Handbook and Guide to Wisconsin, Comprising Information Respecting. . . .* Milwaukee: Sentinel and Gazette Power Press Plant, 1851.

Glad, Paul W. *The History of Wisconsin, Volume V: War, a New Era, and Depression, 1914–1940.* Madison, Wis.: State Historical Society of Wisconsin, 1990.

Holmes, Fred L. *Badger Saints and Sinners.* Milwaukee: E. M. Hale and Company, 1939.

Johnson, Fred, ed. *Door County Almanack, Number 2: Orchards.* Sister Bay, Wis.: Door County Almanack, 1985.

Larsen, Lester. *Farm Tractors, 1950–1975.* St. Joseph, Mich.: American Society of Agricultural Engineers, 1981.

Matusow, Allen J., ed. *Great Lives Observed: Joseph R. McCarthy.* Englewood, N.J.: Prentice-Hall, Inc., 1970.

Nesbit, Robert C. *The History of Wisconsin, Volume III: Urbanization and Industrialization, 1873–1893.* Madison, Wis.: State Historical Society of Wisconsin, 1985. Also *Wisconsin: A History.* Madison, Wis.: The University of Wisconsin Press, 1989.

Nord, David Paul. *A Guide to Stonefield.* Madison, Wis.: State Historical Society of Wisconsin, 1977

Russell, John, and Lou Russell. *Wisconsin Lore and Legends: Vols I, II.* Menomonie, Wis.: Oak Point Press, 1989.

Smith, Alice E. *The History of Wisconsin: Volume I: From Exploration to Statehood.* Madison, Wis.: State Historical Society of Wisconsin, 1985.

# ■ PHOTOGRAPHIC ESSAYS

Gould, Whitney M., and Zane Williams. *Historic Places of Rural Dane County.* Madison, Wis.: Dane County Cultural Affairs Commission, 1981.

Lesy, Michael. *Wisconsin Death Trip.* New York: Doubleday, 1973

Mandell, David. *Settlers of Dane County: The Photographs of Andreas Larsen Dahl.* Madison, Wis.: Dane County Cultural Affairs Commission, 1985.

Mazomanie Historical Society. *Mazomanie Landmarks.* Mazomanie, Wis.: Mazomanie Historical Society, 1990.

Williams, Zane. *Wisconsin.* Portland, Oreg.: Graphics Arts Center Publishing Co., 1993.

# ■ BIOGRAPHY, FICTION

Cohn, Roy M. *McCarthy.* New York: New American Library, 1968.

Derleth, August W. *Still, Small Voice: The Biography of Zona Gale.* New York, London: D. Appleton-Century Company, Inc., 1940. Also, *Walden West.* New York: Van Rees Press, 1961.

Ferber, Edna. *Come and Get It.* Garden City, N.Y.: Doubleday, Doran & Company, 1935.

Gale, Zona. *Miss Lulu Bett.* New York, London: D. Appleton and Co., 1920. Also, *Portage, Wisconsin, and Other Essays.* New York: Alfred A. Knopf, 1943.

Garland, Hamlin. *Boy Life on the Prairie.* New York: The Macmillan Company, 1899. Also, *A Son of the Middle Border.* New York: The Macmillan Company, 1926.

Kinzie, John H., Mrs. *Wau-Bun, "Early Days" in the North-West.* New York, Cincinnati: Derby & Jackson, 1856.

Latimer, Margery. *Guardian Angel and Other Stories.* New York: H. Smith & R. Haas, 1932.

Matthias, Blanche C. *Letters to Blanche C. Matthias from Margery Latimer and Jean Toomer; and to Henry Chester Tracy from Margery Latimer, 1921–1934.* Madison: Memorial Library Special Collections.

Meine, Curt. *Aldo Leopold, His Life and Work.* Madison, Wis.: The University of Wisconsin Press, 1988.

North, Sterling. *Rascal: A Memoir of a Better Era.* New York: E. P. Dutton, 1963.

Reeves, Thomas C. *McCarthyism.* Ed. by Thomas C. Reeves. Hinsdale, Ill.: Dryden Press, 1973.

Stephens, Jim. *The Journey Home: The Literature of Wisconsin through Four Centuries.* Volumes 1–3. Madison, Wis.: North Country Press, 1989.

# I N D E X

# COMPASS AMERICAN GUIDES

Comprehensive, literate, and beautifully illustrated guides to the individual cities and states of the United States and Canada, Compass American Guides are unparalleled in their cultural, historical, and informational scope. They are to the 1990s what the WPA guidebook series was to the 1930s — insightful, resourceful, and entertaining.

*"Each [Compass American Guide] pairs an accomplished photographer with a writer native to the state. The resulting pictures and words have such an impact I constantly had to remind myself I was reading a travel guide."* — National Geographic Traveler

*"Entertaining and well-illustrated with maps and photographs, in color and vintage black and white...good to read ahead of time, then take along so you don't miss anything."* —San Diego Magazine

*"You can read [a Compass American Guide] for information and come away entertained. Or you can read it for entertainment and come away informed . . . an informational jackpot."* —Houston Chronicle

*"Wickedly stylish writing!"* —Chicago Sun-Times

Compass American Guides are available in general and travel bookstores, or may be ordered directly by calling 1-800-733-3000; or by sending a check or money order, including the cost of shipping and handling, payable to: Random House, Inc. 400 Hahn Road, Westminster, Maryland 21157. Books are shipped by USPS Book Rate (allow 30 days for delivery): $2.00 for the 1st book, $0.50 for each additional book. Applicable sales tax will be charged. All prices are subject to change. Or ask your bookseller to order for you.

*"Books can make thoughtful (and sometimes even thought-provoking) gifts for incentive travel winners or convention attendees. A new series of guidebooks published by Compass American Guides is right on the mark."* —Successful Meetings magazine

Consider Compass American Guides as gifts or incentives for VIP's, employees, clients, customers, convention and meeting attendees, friends and others. Compass American Guides are available at special discounts for bulk purchases (100 copies or more) for sales promotions or premiums. Special editions, including personalized covers, excerpts of existing guides, and corporate imprints, can be created in large quantities for special needs. For more information, write to Special Marketing, Fodor's Travel Publications, 201 E. 50th St., New York, NY 10022; or call 800/800-3246. Inquiries from the United Kingdom should be sent to Fodor's Travel Publications, 20 Vauxhall Bridge Rd., London, England SW1V 2SA.

**CHICAGO**
1st Edition
Author
Jack Schnedler
Photographer
Zbigniew Bzdak
1-878-86728-8

$16.95 Paper 288 pp.
($22.50 Canada)

Also available in a hardcover
edition:
1-878-86729-6
$24.95 ($31.50 Canada)

"Great to send to anyone coming to Chicago for the
first time, or anyone who left town before Wrigley
Field got lights." —*Chicago Sun-Times*

**LAS VEGAS**
3rd Edition
Author
Deke Castleman
Photographer
Michael Yamashita
1-878-86736-9

$16.95 Paper 304 pp.
($22.50 Canada)

"Visiting this neon oasis has been made much more
interesting thanks to Deke Castleman's *Las Vegas*."

—*Travel & Leisure*

**LOS ANGELES**
1st Edition
Author
Gil Reavill
Photographer
Mark S. Wexler
1-878-86717-2

$14.95 Paper 324 pp.
($19.95 Canada)

Also available in a hardcover
edition:
1-878-86725-3
$22.95 ($29.00 Canada)

"No cinephile should head out L.A. way without a
copy of *Los Angeles*." —*New York Daily News*

**NEW ORLEANS**
1st Edition
Author
Bethany Ewald Bultman
Photographer
Richard Sexton
1-878-86739-3

$16.95 Paper 304 pp.
($21.95 Canada)

Also available in a hardcover
edition:
1-878-86740-7
$24.95 ($31.50 Canada)

Vibrant photography and jaunty commentary guide
travelers through the heart and soul of sizzling New
Orleans.

**SAN FRANCISCO
& THE BAY AREA**
2nd Edition
Author
Barry Parr
Photographer
Michael Yamashita
1-878-86716-4

$14.95 Paper 396 pp.
($19.95 Canada)

"*San Francisco* tackles the 'why' of travel to that city as
well as the nitty gritty details." — *Travel Weekly*

**CANADA**
1st Edition
Author
Garry Marchant
Photographer
Ken Straiton
1-878-86712-1

$14.95 Paper 320 pp.
($19.95 Canada)

"*Canada* goes a long way in presenting this country
in all its complex, beautiful glory." —*Toronto Sun*

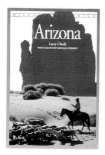

**A R I Z O N A**
2nd Edition
Author
Lawrence Cheek
Photographer
Michael Freeman
1-878-86732-6

$16.95  Paper  288 pp.
($22.50 Canada)

"This is my kind of guidebook."
—David Laird, *Books of the Southwest*

**C O L O R A D O**
2nd Edition
Author
Jon Klusmire
Photographer
Paul Chesley
1-878-86735-0

$16.95  Paper  320 pp.
($22.50 Canada)

"A literary, historical and near-sensory excursion across the state."  —*Denver Post*

**M O N T A N A**
1st Edition
Author
Norma Tirrell
Photographer
John Reddy
1-878-86710-5

$14.95  Paper  304 pp.
($19.95 Canada)

Also available in a hardcover edition:
1-878-86713-X
$22.95  ($29.00 Canada)

"The most comprehensive guide to the state...will have you ready and rarin' to go."  — *Travel & Leisure*

**N E W   M E X I C O**
1st Edition
Author
Nancy Harbert
Photographer
Michael Freeman
1-878-86706-7

$15.95  Paper  288 pp.
($19.95 Canada)

Also available in a hardcover edition:
1-878-86722-9  $22.95
($29.00 Canada)

"Bold yet artful in its photography. "

— *Albuquerque Journal*

**U T A H**
2nd Edition
Authors
Tom & Gayen Wharton
Photographer
Tom Till
1-878-86731-8

$16.95  Paper  352 pp.
($22.50 Canada)

"The jaunty text and eye-popping photos make this a keeper."  —*Deseret News*

Winner of the Rocky Mountain Book Publishers' Award for Best Guidebook

**V I R G I N I A**
1st Edition
Author
K.M. Kostyal
Photographer
Medford Taylor
1-878-86741-5

$16.95  Paper  320 pp.
($21.50 Canada)

Also available in a hardcover edition:
1-878-86742-3  $24.95
($31.50 Canada)

"History haunts Virginia like a lost lover," writes author Kostyal in this fascinating guide to the history and culture of Virginia.